AMERICAN EDUCATION

Its Men

Ideas

and

Institutions

The Academy System
of the
State of New York

George Frederick Miller

ARNO PRESS & THE NEW YORK TIMES
New York ∗ *1969*

Reprint edition 1969 by Arno Press, Inc.

*

Library of Congress Catalog Card No. 76-89205

*

Reprinted from a copy in Teachers College Library

*

Manufactured in the United States of America

Editorial Note

AMERICAN EDUCATION: *Its Men, Institutions and Ideas* presents selected works of thought and scholarship that have long been out of print or otherwise unavailable. Inevitably, such works will include particular ideas and doctrines that have been outmoded or superseded by more recent research. Nevertheless, all retain their place in the literature, having influenced educational thought and practice in their own time and having provided the basis for subsequent scholarship.

Lawrence A. Cremin
Teachers College

The Academy System
of the
State of New York

The Academy System of the State of New York

By

GEORGE FREDERICK MILLER

Submitted in Partial Fulfillment of the Requirements for the Degree of
Doctor of Philosophy in the Faculty of Philosophy,
Columbia University

———

ALBANY
J. B. LYON COMPANY, PRINTERS
1922

PREFACE

Of the several state systems of academies established in the United States during the early national period, the one evolved by the State of New York is usually considered to have been the most judicious and successful. It is the aim of this monograph to present the most important facts, collected from available sources, concerning the academy system of the State of New York from its origin in 1787 to the close of the nineteenth century; and to organize those facts in a way that will make evident their significance.

There seems to have been no very close connection between the secondary schools of colonial New York and the system of academies organized by the State. The schools of the colony, with rare exceptions, were not supported by the government, and so far as the administrative aspect was concerned the State had to organize its system *de novo*. However, in order to show some relation in curriculum and aim between the schools of the colonial period and those that developed later, an introductory chapter on the educational situation prior to the organization of the State, based upon the investigations of Brown, Clews, Kemp, and Kilpatrick and others as indicated by the references, has been included. This chapter differs from the rest of the monograph in not having been written from the sources, and in not dealing directly with the academy system. It has been inserted to make the whole more intelligible to readers who may not be familiar with the writings upon which it is based and who do not have convenient access to them.

The close of the nineteenth century has been chosen as a limit of the treatment of the subject, because by that time the typical old time academies had nearly all disappeared, and even those that were operating under charters of former periods had changed in their plans and purposes. A new type of academy had developed to meet the many and various demands of a more complex society. Public high schools, which had become very numerous and which were giving instruction to nearly eighty-five percent of the secondary pupils in the State had supplanted the academy system. The latter, although not formally abolished, was really extinct by the beginning of the twentieth century.

A work by Dr. Walter John Gifford entitled "History of the New York High School System" to be published in the near future deals with the academy system from another point of view, and contains information on phases of the history of secondary education in the State not included in this monograph.

This publication was written in 1915, and was to have been printed as a part of the annual report of the University of the State of New York. But due to the disturbed conditions brought about by the World War the printing of this monograph has been delayed, and it is now published as a reprint of the 132nd annual report of that institution.

It is a pleasure to acknowledge the valuable advice of Professors Paul Monroe and William H. Kilpatrick; the kind encouragement of Dr. John H. Findley, Dr. Frank P. Graves, Dr. Thomas E. Finegan, and Dr. Henry L. Taylor; the helpful cooperation of Dr. Walter John Gifford; and the friendly suggestions of Mr. Tien Toh Liu.

CONTENTS

CHAPTER I

The Academy System of the State of New York

CHAPTER I

Educational Conditions in New York Before the Revolution

With the growth of democracy and the rise of a middle class of people after the Revolutionary War, came a type of secondary school, which was better adapted than the Latin grammar school of the colonial period to the new political and economic conditions. Throughout the Nation until after the Civil War, the academy was the chief institution for preparing pupils for college, and for furnishing the means of a general cultural education beyond the elementary branches. But in no state of the Union were academies established in such great numbers and supported so well, in no state did they reach such a high degree of development and continue to dominate the field of secondary education so long as in New York.

An explanation of the factors that contributed to this result in New York will be attempted in the following chapters. A brief sketch of the educational situation in New Netherland and colonial New York is, however, first required to furnish an adequate understanding of later developments.

The commercial character of the first Dutch control of New Netherland, the activity and influence of the official church, the change to English rule and the resulting division of languages, institutions, and religions were all closely connected with the schools and the educational interests of the times.

Political and Economic Status of the Province

A charter, which conferred upon the company complete civil power in New Netherland except the right to negotiate international agreements, was granted to the Dutch West India Company in 1621. The States-General of the United Netherlands, which granted the privilege, had the power to amend the charter in any way, but this right was seldom exercised, and the company enjoyed almost unlimited control until the advent of the English in 1664.

The company acted through its lord directors, who in turn chose

[7]

a director general and a council as their representatives and local authorities. The latter were given extensive but indefinite political power in the colony. They used their own judgment in all matters not especially determined by their superiors, and became the chief factor in the government of the province.

During the Dutch régime, nine villages were incorporated in what is now the State of New York. Their administration and general local control were placed in the hands of the burgomasters and schepens; but the powers of these village officials were extremely limited. They were chosen by the director general, who reserved the right to annul almost any measure adopted by them. It is evident that the Dutch government in New Netherland was in no respect democratic, for neither the municipal nor colonial officers were elected by popular vote.[1]

Under English rule, New York was a royal province; the governor was appointed by the king of England, a legislature was chosen by the citizens of the province, and the villages were given more freedom. Although no law was valid unless sanctioned by the king or his representative, the English system of government contained some elements of a democracy, especially in local matters.

The economic status of New Netherland and the character of the inhabitants are indicated by the fact that the Dutch West India Company was a commercial enterprise, and was not interested primarily in colonization and education. The settlers, however, established permanent homes, and sought a normal domestic life such as they had been accustomed to in Holland. Since the total number of them, until after the English occupation, was small and they were divided into several communities, there could not have been very many in any one place. In 1623 a number of settlements, each consisting of a few families, were made. Seven years later New Netherland had about 500 inhabitants, and in 1660 the population was estimated at 6000.[2] At the close of the century, the number had increased to 25,000, and in 1714 the population was probably about 45,000.[3] According to the first census of the United States (1790), the inhabitants of New York numbered 340,121.

---

[1] Kilpatrick, The Dutch Schools of New Netherland and Colonial New York, chap. 1; chap. 5, p. 78, 79, 80. Clews, Educational Legislation and Administration of the Colonial Governments, p. 198 ff.
[2] Kilpatrick, op. cit., p. 13.
[3] Kemp, The Support of Schools in Colonial New York by the Society for the Propagation of the Gospel in Foreign Parts, p. 64.

Schools and Education

The charter of the West India Company did not require that schools should be established, but the States-General later probably insisted that schools be maintained. It is certain that after 1638 the company contributed to the support of schools in the province, and thus recognized its obligations. The influence of the Reformed Dutch Church was a prominent factor in promoting education in New Netherland; in fact, the church and the state were so closely connected in educational affairs that the duties of the two were never clearly differentiated.

Except for New Amsterdam and the outlying villages, it was a common practice for the company through its officials to elect the masters of the schools, and to pay a part of their salaries. The church passed upon the religious qualifications of the prospective teachers, and supervised that part of the instruction pertaining to religion. The local civil authorities generally provided the school building as well as a house for the teacher, fuel and other supplies. All patrons except the poorest paid a small fee, which the master received as part of his compensation.[4]

Under English rule government support of Dutch elementary schools was confined to municipal initiative. In most of the Dutch villages public support continued, and took various forms. In Bergen, now in New Jersey, and probably in Kingston, a tax for the support of the schools was assessed. Rents from school lands, public subscriptions, and other means were common. The practice of charging rate bills was continued practically without exception throughout the colonial period. Although the English provided no state support for elementary schools, and only limited aid to secondary schools, yet governors enforced certain certification requirements. During the first few years of English rule, licenses to teach were granted by the governor. After 1686, teachers coming from England were required to be licensed by the Archbishop of Canterbury, or later by the Bishop of London. Governor Cornbury, during the six years of his administration (1702–8), would permit no Dutch schoolmaster to teach without a license from him. His successors, however, were more lenient in this respect.

The transition from Dutch to English rule, 1664, had a far-reaching effect upon educational interests. The Dutch system of schools was adapted to a close coöperation between church and state, and

[4] Kilpatrick, op. cit., p. 228.

when the change in government took place the schools were left with only the church, except in villages that had been granted special charters, and were not readily modified to meet the new situation. Neither the Dutch church nor school received support from the English government. Furthermore, a conflict in languages and religions arose when the English settlers came. In many cases, the support of a community that had previously been concentrated upon one school and church came, sooner or later, to be divided. In sparsely settled villages this tended toward weakness and inefficiency. The Dutch conservatives could not foresee the inevitable predominance of the English language, and so hampered progress by clinging to a waning tongue and decadent customs.[5] Evidence of such a condition in New York is to be found in the following:

> The presence of two languages in New York City must have operated to the injury of the cause of education within the city. . . . Had the system of municipal schools been retained after 1674, giving instruction, however, in both languages, the transition from the Dutch to the English language could have been made with greater ease and with far less hurt to the Dutch church; and New York City would have gained a full hundred years in the development of its school system.[6]

It seems that some Dutch schools used English as early as 1708, while others clung to their own language until 1780; so the struggle to perpetuate the Dutch language lasted the greater part of the century.[7] This change was slow and gradual, and it was not until after the middle of the eighteenth century that English was used extensively in these schools.

In some instances, however, the conflict in beliefs, customs, and languages may have evoked a greater effort in educational affairs. In 1755 the school of the Reformed Dutch Church in New York City secured a teacher from Holland who was, presumably, a more able man for the position than any teacher in the colony, and was paid a much higher salary than was then customary. This effort to improve the school represented an attempt to check the tendency toward the English language. But it was an improvement that was in opposition to the trend of events, and hence soon dwindled and disappeared.[8] It seems that the rivalry of religious sects aroused increased activity and interest in at least one school in Albany, in which the representative of the Society for the Propagation of the Gospel made a special effort to increase the attendance of his school.[9]

---

[5] Kemp, op. cit., p. 67.
[6] Kilpatrick, op. cit., p. 159.
[7] Ibid., p. 204, 208.
[8] Ibid., p. 154, 155.
[9] Ibid., p. 203. Kemp, op. cit., p. 198, 199.

The Dutch probably had no official public school in New Netherland before 1638. Before that time at least some of the children
were very likely taught privately or in a private school. Considering the antecedents of the colonists, it is reasonable to suppose that
not all the children were allowed to grow up for fifteen years without any instruction in reading and religion.[10] During the next
twenty-six years of Dutch supremacy, practically every village was
supplied with an elementary school, which was under joint control
of church and state. The masters were usually also employed by
the church as choristers and visitors of the sick. Other occupations
through which the teachers often undertook to supplement their
meager salaries, were clerk, bell ringer, janitor for the church,
sexton, court secretary and messenger. The teacher of the school
of the Dutch Reformed Church in New York City in 1755 was paid
$350 a year, which was considered a very high salary and which was
later reduced.[11] In addition to their regular salaries, house rent and
fuel were furnished to the masters.

For the most part, what English elementary schools there were in
the colony during the eighteenth century were private enterprises,
or were maintained by religious organizations. The Society for
the Propagation of the Gospel in Foreign Parts, an organization
within the Church of England, was especially active in supporting
schools in New York. Ministers and missionaries of the society
supervised the schools, and sometimes taught in them as a means of
additional support. The charity school in the city of New York,
afterward Trinity School, was the first supported by the society,
and was typical of all such schools. The pay of the teachers, always
low, was provided in part by the society and partly by the community benefited by the school.[12] The curriculum of these schools,
with some rare exceptions, was confined to the three R's and the
church catechism. Great emphasis was placed upon religious instruction.[13] In regard to subject matter, the same thing might be said
of the Dutch schools; the three R's and religion were practically all
that was taught. It seems that both English and Dutch schools
offered ample opportunity for the elementary education of girls as
well as boys.[14]

---

[10] Kilpatrick, op. cit., chap. 3.
[11] Kilpatrick, op. cit., p. 155, 156.
[12] Kemp, op. cit., p. 124, 125, 129.
[13] Ibid., chap. 12.
[14] Ibid., p. 265, 266. Kilpatrick, op. cit., p. 228.

The number of elementary schools in New York City in 1741 was eight, in 1745, twelve; and by 1762 the number had increased to fifteen. Among the last mentioned there were one Hebrew and two French schools; the maximum number of Dutch schools was three, and in 1761 the English had thirteen.[15] There are no statistics showing the number of schools in the whole colony, but Kemp gives the following opinion: "There is a basis for believing that between 1740 and 1775 both the city and the province enjoyed school facilities probably comparable with the other provinces, except those of New England."

Other schools, both English and Dutch, were conducted by private teachers. Before the advent of the English these were, of course, all Dutch; but the Dutch gradually disappeared, and at the time of the Revolution most of them were English. These private institutions differed in several significant respects from those fostered by the churches. They were free from sectarian limitations and the necessity of teaching a catechism. They were at liberty to modify their curriculums so as to include any subject for which there was a demand. Some of them extended their courses beyond the elementary branches, but as a rule not in a way that made them Latin grammar schools. Needle-work and many other accomplishments were taught the girls; while courses in navigation, surveying and languages were offered for young men. It was the purpose of the sectarian schools to serve the church by training able leaders and faithful followers; whereas the private schools were interested in meeting any popular demand for vain or useful learning. The two classes of schools differed in clientele as well as in curriculums. The sectarian schools could teach only those who would tolerate a certain religious doctrine, while the others appealed to people of all creeds and also to those of no particular belief. But the private institutions were not supported by charity, and for this reason were probably more expensive and more select. They were often so small and irregular that they resembled a system of tutoring rather than schools. An advertisement in a newspaper in 1755 indicates a school of the latter kind. It reads:

"Writing, Arithmetick, Merchants Accounts, Navigation, Surveying, Mensuration, Guaging, Dialing, and Astronomy, etc. regularly taught by James Bragg, at the foot of Pot-Baker's Hill, in one of Mr. Peck's new houses; where there is a commodious Room for Young Gentlemen, to be

---

[15] Kemp, op. cit., p. 78.

instructed in any of the Branches of Mathematics, retired from those that are only taught, Reading, Writing, and Arithmetick.   Due attention will be given to Young Gentlemen and Ladies at their Houses if required, Gentlemen Sailors and others, are taught Navigation in a short time and reasonable." [16]

Secondary schools in colonial New York were few and poorly attended, and for the most part depended upon private enterprise. Until the middle of the eighteenth century the Latin grammar school was practically the only kind of secondary school.   However, this kind of institution was never established in all parts of the colony by a general law; for this reason the transition to academies was easy.   The change was made by gradually broadening the curriculum of the grammar school, and by including in its purpose an education of immediate value as well as a preparation for college entrance.

From 1652 to the time of the English occupation, a period of about twelve years, the Dutch maintained an official Latin school; but it was interrupted for five years, 1654 to 1659, and also from 1661 to 1662.   The West India Company exercised about the same degree of control over this school as it did over the schools of elementary grade in New Amsterdam.   The master's salary was paid partly by the company, partly by the city, and partly by parents whose children attended it.   Three different masters, each serving about two years, were employed for the few years that the school was continued.   It seemed to have been in a flourishing condition and to have given promise of developing into a college when the overthrow of the Dutch government brought it to a close.   In every respect, it was doubtless a typical Latin grammar school.[17]

From 1664 until the establishment of the colonial Latin grammar school by a law passed in 1702, there was no school supported by the government.   Meanwhile a number of private Latin schools appeared; and after a few years passed out of existence.   Some of these were sectarian institutions; all of them were small and weak, and the last one was closed probably in 1688.[18]   The province may have been without a Latin school from that time until the one provided for in 1702 was opened in 1704.

Under the leadership of Cornbury, who was governor of New York Colony from 1702 to 1708, an act was passed (1702) providing for a Latin grammar school in the city of New York.   The dominant influence of the Church of England is indicated by the act repeating

[16] New York Weekly Post Boy, March 31, 1755.   Quoted by Kemp, op. cit., p. 264.
[17] Kilpatrick, op. cit., chap. 6.
[18] Brown, The Making of Our Middle Schools, p. 53.   Boone, Education in the United States, p. 53.

the general requirements for teachers in specifying that the master must obtain a license from " the Bishop of London or the Governor or Commander in Chief of this Province." [19] The school was opened in 1704, and continued for five years or longer. The master received 50 pounds a year from the government and fees from his students, which were about thirty-three in number.[20]

Incomplete records show the existence of a private grammar school in New York City from 1716 to 1722; some teaching of Latin in New Rochelle for an indefinite period; and a private grammar school in New York City in 1731. Details concerning the curriculums and the pupils of these schools are lacking.[21]

In 1732 a school for instruction in Latin, Greek and mathematics was established in New York City by the colonial government, and was made free to twenty boys selected from the various political divisions of the province. It was not continued after 1738, and was the last attempt of the colonial government to support a secondary school.[22] It seems that this was the first instance in the province of pupils being admitted to a secondary school free of all tuition charges.

It is stated that from 1741 to 1762 from one to two private grammar schools were in operation in the city of New York.[23] Since King's College opened a preparatory school in 1763 to fit students for entrance to the college, evidently the city of New York was supplied with a secondary school of some kind practically all of the eighteenth century. After 1740 Latin schools and other types of secondary schools were opened in a number of villages, and a few of them were continued into the nineteenth century. Some of these places were: Hempstead, where a grammar school was kept from 1742 to 1779; Rye; New Rochelle; Schenectady, where a Latin school, begun in 1771, was later expanded into an academy; Claverack; Salem; Goshen; and Kingston, where an academy was founded in 1774.[24]

No evidence is found to indicate that previous to the middle of the eighteenth century any of the secondary schools were very much like an academy. The principal subject matter was Latin, with occasionally Greek and mathematics; which means that they were generally Latin grammar schools. However, before the Revolution,

[19] Clews, op. cit., p. 235.
[20] Kemp, op. cit., p. 72, 73.
[21] Ibid., p. 73, 74, 161.
[22] Brown, op. cit., p. 94; Kemp, op. cit., p. 73.
[23] Kemp, op. cit., p. 75.
[24] References to these are found on pages 17 and 18.

the conception of a secondary school, giving instruction in a wide range of subjects of immediate practical value, began to find expression.

One writer, probably William Livingston, suggested that two grammar schools be maintained in each county; not only to prepare pupils for college entrance, but to instruct those who could not hope for a college education.[25] The significant part of that suggestion is that secondary schools should have a broader function than preparation for college, a characteristic of the nineteenth century academies. Another tendency toward the academy is seen in the private and tutorial institutions that extended their curriculums freely to supply all popular demands.[26] Later a number of institutions began as grammar or classical schools, and by a change in curriculum and aim were transformed into the academy type. For example, the Latin school at Schenectady opened by the Rev. William Andrews in 1771, and continued by the Rev. John Doty until 1777 was one of the first places where such a change was contemplated. Mr Andrews outlined his plan as follows:

I lately took the Liberty of acquainting You, that I had opened a Grammar School in this Town, and since that, I have determined on forming it into an Academy, and propose giving Instruction in Reading, Writing, Arithmetic, Geography and History to those who may be designed to fill the Stations of active Life, exclusive of those who may be taught the Learned Languages — Bookkeeping, and Merchants accounts to fit them for Business, and the Mechanic Arts.[27]

We do not know to what extent this plan was carried out. The Rev. J. G. Gebhard's classical school at Claverack, begun in 1776, developed into Washington Seminary 3 years later. Washington Academy at Salem, one of the most prominent secondary schools in the State during the nineteenth century, was the outgrowth of a classical school that dates from 1780. Another important academy of the following century, Farmers' Hall, grew out of Noah Webster's classical school at Goshen, which was opened in 1784.

It is notable that the earliest academies were an extension and enlargement of the Latin grammar schools in both purpose and curriculum, and not a substitute for them. The academies under-

---

[25] The Independent Reflector, November 8, 1753. Quoted by Pratt, Annals of Public School Education in the State of New York.
[26] Cf. p. 12 and 13.
[27] Correspondence of the Rev. William Andrews to Sir William Johnson, Documentary History of New York, v. 4, p. 470. Quoted by Kemp, op. cit., p. 203.

took all the work of the grammar schools and, in addition, gave instruction in many subjects without any reference to college requirements. There was no conflict resulting in the extermination of the old and the rise of the new, but simply an absorption of the old by the new.

A number of factors contributed to the rise of academies, but it is impossible to say which one was the most important. It seems that the laws of 1704 and 1732 could have had no considerable influence in bringing about the change, because the schools created by them were not similar to academies either in support, organization, curriculum or aim. But private institutions, free to experiment and to broaden their curriculums to meet popular demands, seem, on the basis of similarity, to have been the forerunners of academies. They were independent; their existence was determined by their popularity; they sought pupils of all grades; and they undertook to give instruction in any subject for which there was a demand. Certain economic conditions, such as the increase in wealth, population and general prosperity of the country, and the consequent rise of a middle class in society, were fundamental in calling forth a new kind of school.

The following résumé contains an incomplete list of secondary schools that prevailed during the colonial period, with a few data concerning them. A chronological order is followed as indicated by the dates on the left of the page.

1652   A Latin grammar school was established in New Amsterdam. It was continued not longer than two years.[28]

1659   A Latin school was reopened in New Amsterdam with A. C. Curtius as master. He left the school in 1661.[29]

1662   The last-named school was continued by the Rev. Mr Luyck, who returned to Holland in 1665, when the school probably stopped.[30]

1668   A private Latin school was conducted in New York City by Mr David Jamison.[31]

1677   A Latin school was opened in New York City.[32]

1688   The Latin school of Fathers Harvey and Harrison in New York City was closed in 1688.[33]

---

[28] Kilpatrick, op. cit., p. 95–99.
[29] Ibid., p. 104.
[30] Ibid., p. 107. But the statement is made in Brown, op. cit., p. 52, that this school was closed about 1672.
[31] Brown, op. cit., p. 53.
[32] Boone, op. cit., p. 53.
[33] Brown, op. cit., p. 53.

1700 New York seems to have been without a grammar school.[34]

1702 Legal and financial provisions were made for a grammar schoolmaster.[35]

1704 The school provided for in 1702 was opened.[36]

1709 The last-named school ended about 1709.[37]

1716 The Rev. Robert Jenny kept a private grammar school in New York City, which probably ended in 1722.[38]

1720 Foster at New Rochelle had " some Latin scholars besides his elementary pupils." [39]

1731 Alexander Malcom kept a private grammar school in New York City.[40]

1732 A grammar school was established by the Legislature. This school was the supposed germ of King's College.[41]

1738 The last-named school was ended in 1738.[42]

1741 From one to two private grammar schools were operated in New York City from 1741 to 1762.[43]

1742 The Rev. Samuel Seabury kept a grammar school in Hempstead, which was closed in 1764.[44]

1747 From 1747 to 1749, T. B. Chandler, a Harvard student, kept a Latin school in Rye.[45]

1763 The grammar school of King's College was opened.[46]

1764 From 1764 to 1767, Timothy Wetmore conducted a Latin school at Rye.[47]

1771 The Rev. William Andrews kept a Latin school at Schenectady, which was continued until 1777 by the Rev. John Doty.[48]

1774 Kingston Academy, Ulster county, was begun.[49]

---

[34] Ibid., p. 93.
[35] Ibid., loc. cit.; Kemp, op. cit., p. 70.
[36] Kemp, op. cit., p. 68, 71.
[37] Ibid., p. 73.
[38] Ibid., p. 74.
[39] Ibid., p. 161.
[40] Ibid., p. 73.
[41] Brown, op. cit., p. 94.
[42] Kemp, op. cit., p. 73.
[43] Ibid., p. 75.
[44] Ibid., p. 182.
[45] Ibid., p. 144.
[46] Brown, op. cit., p. 95.
[47] Kemp, op. cit., p. 144.
[48] Ibid., p. 202, 203.
[49] University of the State of New York, Convocation Proceedings, 1884, p. 63.

1776   The Rev. Samuel Seabury set up a grammar school at New Rochelle, which was closed about 1777.[50]

1776   The Rev. J. G. Gebhard opened a classical school at Claverack, which was reorganized 3 years later as Washington Seminary.[51]

1779   The Rev. Leonard Cutting continued the school established by Seabury at Hempstead in 1742, from 1766 to 1779.[52]

1780   Washington Academy, Salem, was begun by the Rev. John Watson in a log house as a classical school.[53]

1784   A classical school was opened by Noah Webster at Goshen, which became Farmer's Hall in 1784.[54]

1787   With the incorporation this year by the Regents, of Erasmus Hall at Flatbush and Clinton Academy at West Hampton, began a new period of secondary education in the State, the period of academies.

Summary

A number of conspicuous changes mark the development of the educational situation in New York during the colonial period. The influences of the churches in directing and governing schools continually grew weaker. Teachers were no longer required to secure their licenses from church officials, nor did the church continue to control curriculums. The schools gradually became secularized.[55] The Dutch language was finally reduced to a minimum, and English came to be used in nearly all the schools. Curriculums were broadened, and the religious element was given less time and attention. The Latin grammar schools were nearly extinct by the close of the Revolution, and academies were springing up. The democratic spirit of the age was being felt in educational affairs.

[50] Kemp, op. cit., p. 161.
[51] University of the State of New York, op. cit., p. 64.
[52] Kemp, op. cit., p. 182, 183.
[53] University of the State of New York, op. cit., p. 64.
[54] Ibid., loc. cit.
[55] Kilpatrick, op. cit., p. 215.

CHAPTER II

Legal Status of the Academies of the State of New York

The academies of the State of New York received legal recognition at the first session of the State Legislature in 1784, when provisions were made for their establishment as quasi-public institutions. Governor George Clinton in his message on January 21st of that year had called the attention of the Legislature to the need of education in these words:

Neglect of the Education of Youth, is among the Evils consequent on War. Perhaps there is scarce any Thing more worthy your Attention, than the Revival and Encouragement of Seminaries of Learning; and nothing by which we can more satisfactorily express our Gratitude to the supreme Being, for his past Favours; since Piety and Virtue are generally the Offspring of an enlightened Understanding.[1]

The Legislature exercised its control over academies in two ways: directly, by means of general and special enactments, and indirectly through the Regents of the University of the State of New York. On account of its peculiar organization and vital connection with the academies, a knowledge of the latter institution is required for an intelligent conception of these secondary schools.

Establishment of the Regents of the University of the State of New York

A definite, comprehensive plan for the establishment and operation of colleges and academies was provided by the two separate acts of 1784 and 1787. These provisions, with some minor modifications noted below, remained in force throughout the nineteenth century, and determined the type of secondary school, the academy, that was predominant in the State until about 1875.

The Act of 1784

The law passed May 1, 1784, entitled "An Act for granting certain Privileges to the College heretofore called King's College, for altering the Name and Charter thereof, and erecting an University within this State," was the culmination of a number of events [2] of

---

[1] Senate Jour., 1784, p. 6.
[2] Some of these were: The Governor's message calling attention to the need of education, January 21, 1784; reports of various committees in the Senate and Assembly, and resolutions of these two bodies favoring the establishment of "seminaries of learning," January 23–28; the Senate gave Mr Duane leave to bring in a bill, "for establishing a University within this State, February 19; petition of the Governors of King's College asking for a revision of their charter, March 24; revisions, amendments, and readings

educational significance. This act marks the beginning of legislative provisions for schools in the State of New York. The chief features of the law so far as academies are concerned were: (1) The creation of a corporation, called the Regents of the University of the State of New York,[3] whose principal function was to establish and control schools and colleges. (2) Eight ex-officio members (Regents) of the corporation and twenty-four designated by name were provided for. In addition to these the churches were given permission to elect a Regent (or perhaps each church was allowed to appoint one Regent, the law not being clear), and any school or college whose endowment produced an annual income of the value of a thousand bushels of wheat was allowed to elect one Regent. (3) " Provided, That nothing in this Act contained, shall be construed to deprive any Person or Persons, of the Right to erect such Schools or Colleges as to him or them may seem proper, independent of the said University." [4]

An amendment to this law, passed November 26, 1784, increased the number of Regents, reduced the quorum, provided for an annual meeting, made it clear that each religious denomination might elect a Regent, and made some other minor changes,[5] which did not affect the interests of secondary schools.

It is evident that the university thus created was not an institution for instructing students directly, but an administrative body for supervising the schools and colleges of the State. In this respect it was like our modern state departments of education. But it was given a more direct control over the management of schools than is exercised by state officials in our country. The Regents were given the power to perform the functions usually delegated to trustees, curators, or similar bodies, such as administering the finances and electing members of the faculty. No school under the authority of the University needed a charter, because the latter was a corporation that included all schools of the State recognized by the law.

During the three years that the Regents were organized under this act they received no academies into the University. That this neglect was not due to a failure of the Regents to recognize the supervision of these schools as a part of their duty, is shown by the

of the bill in the Legislature, March 25 to April 30; the Council of Revision reported favorably and the bill became a law, May 1, 1784. (Proceedings of the University Convocation, 1875, p. 197–203.)

[3] This title was later changed to " University of the State of New York," and is often referred to under the name of Regents, or University.
[4] Proceedings of the University Convocation, 1875, p. 208.
[5] Ibid., p. 221.

minutes of that body, February 28, 1786 when a committee was appointed to consider "Ways and Means of promoting literature throughout the State." [6] Under the date of February 8, 1787, is this entry: "A Petition of Samuel Buell, Nathaniel Gardiner, and David Mulford, in behalf of themselves and others, Founders of an Academy at East Hampton, in Suffolk county, was read, and committed to Mr L'Hommedieu, Mr Tredwell, Mr Stoutenburgh, and Mr Vanderbilt." [7] However, it was not until the University was reorganized by the act of 1787 that it became effective in developing the academies.

The Act of 1787

Since the law of 1787, reorganizing the University, served as a basis upon which the academies were built, its principal features, and especially those pertaining to academies, will be sketched here.

One of the important changes brought about by the revised act was the incorporation of colleges and academies under boards of trustees. According to the first plan, the Regents were to act as trustees of all the institutions subject to their authority. The law of 1787 provided that a board of trustees should be selected for each college or academy incorporated, and forbade any such trustee to be at the same time a Regent. The Regents were thus relieved of the task of managing directly all the business affairs of the various incorporated schools. The complete separation of the personnel of Regents and trustees prevented any school from attempting to secure special favors through its trustees on the board of Regents. There was a similar clause governing the relation of faculties and trustees. No one was allowed to be at the same time a teacher and a trustee of the same institution. The Regents were, by this part of the law, made an imperial rather than a federative body. It has ever since been a fundamental principle of educational institutions in our country that the teaching staff shall have no voice in the board of trustees. Sectarian and denominational influence were guarded against by forbidding any incorporated school to require a religious test or oath of its teachers.

This law of 1787 was the Magna Charta of academies. It specified in detail the conditions under which academies might be incorporated; also the powers and duties of their trustees. The chief requirements of an academy applying for incorporation were: (1) The petition presented to the Regents should be signed by those

---

[6] Minutes of the Regents of the University, February 28, 1786.
[7] Ibid., February 8, 1787.

who had contributed more than a half of the funds for the support of the school; (2) the trustees, not more than twenty-four or not fewer than twelve, were to be named; (3) the name of the intended corporation should be specified; (4) its annual revenue should not exceed 4000 bushels of wheat. When the Regents were satisfied that all legal requirements had been met, they could incorporate the academy "if they conceived such Academy calculated for the Promotion of Literature."

The duties and powers of the trustees of an incorporated academy are fully described. Some of the most important were: (1) The trustees shall constitute a corporate body; (2) they shall be in charge of the property and revenues of the institution; (3) they shall have power to appoint and discharge teachers, officers and servants; to fix the tuition rate of pupils; to fill vacancies in their own body. All subsequent legislation concerning trustees of incorporated academies was in harmony with these principles.

Article 17 of this act declared that a student from an academy should, upon examination, be entitled to admission to any college under the visitation of the Regents. Article 19 stated that when "the State of Literature in any Academy is so far advanced, and the funds will permit thereof" the academy might be reorganized into a college.

The functions of visitation, examination and reports, which developed so extensively during the nineteenth century and served to systematize the work of the academies, were assigned to the Regents in the following articles:

3 And it is further Enacted by the Authority aforesaid, That it shall and may be lawful to and for the said Regents, and they are hereby authorised and required to visit and inspect all the Colleges, Academies and Schools, which are or may be established in this State; examine into the State and System of Education and Discipline therein, and make a yearly Report thereof to the Legislature; . . . and to make such Bye-Laws and Ordinances, not inconsistent with the Constitution and laws of the State, as they may judge most expedient for the Accomplishment of the Trust hereby reposed in them.[8]

18 . . . That to entitle the Scholars of any such Academy to the Privileges aforesaid, the Trustees thereof shall lay before the Regents of the said University, from Time to Time, the Plan or System proposed to be adopted, for the Education of the Students in each of the said Academies respectively, in order that the same may be revised and examined by the said Regents, and by them be altered or amended, or approved and confirmed, as they shall judge proper.[9]

---

[8] Session Acts, chap. 82, art. 3, passed April 13, 1787.
[9] Ibid., art. 18.

well-regulated colleges." [20] The next year they adopted the rule that " four-fifths of the sum annually distributed among the Academies of the State, be distributed in proportion to the number of students studying in the classics," [21] which was the same class of students mentioned the previous year, because college preparatory subjects and the classics were then practically identical. After 1864, the apportionment was determined by the number of pupils who had passed the " preliminary examination" of the Regents.[22] This was the rule until 1882, when " a part of the income of the Literature fund not to exceed one-fourth" was distributed in proportion to the number of pupils who had passed the advanced examination of the Regents.[23] The method of payment by results, adopted in 1882, was abandoned at the close of the century. The ordinance making this change, passed December 12, 1900, reads: "Academic students counted for grants shall include only those who have passed all preliminary or ' preacademic' subjects and are enrolled in or are enjoying the facilities of a secondary school in the University." [24]

So long as there were only a few academies, and the Regents by committees could visit each one every year, there was no need for annual reports by trustees. Until 1804 only brief and informal reports had been made. That year the Regents required the reports to be written on printed forms. Four years later this system was discontinued, and until 1818 but little more than the number of pupils attending was reported. That year the Regents instructed the trustees and principals to distinguish between elementary pupils and those pursuing classical studies, and to report the number of pupils in each group.

An ordinance of the Regents passed March 18, 1828 instructed academies to report on the following particulars: [25] " Value of academy lot and building; value of its other real estate; value of its library and philosophical apparatus; value of its other personal estate; its tuition money received or accrued, for the year ending on the date of the report; interest or income of its permanent funds, received or accrued during said year; amount of its debts remaining unpaid; amount of money received by it from the Regents of

[20] Minutes of Regents, April 7, 1817. (Hough).
[21] Ibid., March 24, 1818. (Hough).
[22] Regents Ordinance, passed July 27, 1864.
[23] Regents Instructions, 1882, p. 133, 134. This examination was equivalent to a college entrance examination.
[24] Regents Rep't, 1900, Administrative Dep't, p. r48, r49.
[25] Regents Instructions, 1834, p. 24.

the University since its last annual report, and how the same has been expended; number and names of its teachers, and the annual salary or compensation allowed to each; whole number of students, including classical and all others, belonging to the academy on the date of its report; number of students belonging to the academy on the date of its report, or who belonged to it during part of the year ending on the date of its report, and who are claimed by the trustees to have pursued for four months of said year, or upwards, classical studies, or the higher branches of English education, or both, according to the true intent and meaning of the foregoing ordinance " ; the age, name and studies of each of the last mentioned students; the time devoted to each study and the textbook used; a statement that all classical students had passed an elementary examination, and that composition and declamation were taught; meteorological reports. Every report was required to be " verified by the oath of the principal, or one of the trustees of the academy."

The Regents instructions of 1834, 1845 and 1849 contain the same ordinance, except a few minor changes. An ordinance passed October 20, 1853,[26] revised and codified all previous instructions concerning annual reports of academies. This new ordinance enumerated twenty-five items, many of which were included in the ordinance of 1828, on which academies were required to report. The instructions for 1864 [27] and 1870 [28] contain the twenty-five items with but little change, but in increasing detail. In 1882 [29] academies were instructed to report on nineteen subjects including the affidavit, but each of these subjects included a number of topics, so the reports were more complete and detailed than in previous years. At the close of the century, an academy report was composed of no less than one hundred four entries,[30] which were grouped into seven divisions.

Legislation Directly Affecting Academies

The Legislature not only governed academies indirectly through the Regents, but reserved the right to pass any special or general act directly affecting these schools. Such laws were often wholly independent of any intermediation on the part of the Regents.

[26] Ibid., 1853, p. 66ff.
[27] Ibid., 1864, p. 82ff.
[28] Ibid., 1870, p. 104ff.
[29] Ibid., 1882, p. 161ff.
[30] Regents Rep't, 1900, High School Department, v. 2, table 1.

However, there was no conflict between laws of the State and the ordinances of the Regents. The harmonious operation of this system of dual control is illustrated in the granting of charters of corporation. Before the year 1817, the Regents had incorporated forty academies. The Legislature that year incorporated one academy [31] and one special institution,[32] which were probably the first to be incorporated by special acts. By 1854 the Legislature had incorporated 177 institutions classed as academies, while the total number of the same kind of schools incorporated by the Regents up to that time was 137.[33] By 1874 the Legislature had incorporated 201, and the Regents 233.[34] In some of these acts incorporating academies, the Legislature specified that the school was not to be subject to the visitation of the Regents.

These acts of incorporation usually contained a clause, stating that the academy should be received under visitation by the Regents when it had met the conditions required of other schools incorporated by them. In a few cases of a special kind, the act allowed the Regents no choice in the matter, but required them to receive the school into their system.[35] Although the Regents were not given the exclusive power to incorporate academies, they did, except in a few instances, control the admission of such schools into the University. It evidently was the intention of the Legislature to supplement, not to parallel or oppose the work of the Regents.

By numerous special and general grants of land and money to academies, the Legislature established the important principle that public funds might be used for the support of secondary education, a principle not expressed in the fundamental law of 1787. The policy of financial support began with the reservation of lands for churches and schools in 1782. In an act relating to public lands the following occurs: " Provided always that in every such township there shall be laid out one lott containing four hundred acres for the support of the gospel, and two other lotts containing each two hundred acres for the use of schools; and if any number of acres less than the least right shall remain they shall in like manner be appro-

---

[31] Clinton Grammar School; Session Acts, 1817, chap. 119.
[32] New York Institute for the Deaf and Dumb; Session Acts, 1817, chap. 264.
[33] Regents Instructions, 1853, p. 139ff.
[34] Ibid., p. 143, 150.
[35] New York Institution for Deaf and Dumb (Session Acts, 1830, chap. 170) and Genesee and Wesleyan Seminary (Session Acts, 1836, chap. 44) are types of this kind.

priated to the use of schools." [36]   This was supplemented by further acts, 1786,[37] 1790,[38] 1801,[39] and in 1813 [40] which resulted in the establishment of a permanent fund, the literature fund, the proceeds of which have since been used for the benefit of secondary schools. In 1838 a part of the income from the United States deposit fund was granted to the support of academies.[41]

Special grants of lands and donations were also common during the early part of the academy period.   The Legislature in 1796 granted lot 36 in the village of Johnstown to the Johnstown Academy.[42]   A large number of appropriations to individual academies followed during the next fifty years.[43]

The Legislature in establishing permanent funds or in making general appropriations, specified, in some cases, under what conditions academies were to be allowed to share in the revenue.   The funds appropriated in 1792,[44] 1801,[39] 1813,[40] 1814,[45] and 1816 [46] were distributed at the direction of the Regents.   The Legislature in 1827 specified how the annual appropriation to academies should be apportioned.[47]   This act merely defined terms and indorsed practices that the Regents had been following for a decade except that pupils studying higher English branches as well as classical students were counted in apportioning state aid.   In 1838, an act [48] relating to the United States deposit fund fixed the conditions upon which academies would be granted a part of the proceeds.

Legislation relating to academies was less frequent during the second half of the century.   The union free school law of 1853,[49]

---

[36] "An act for raising troops to complete the line of this State in the service of the United States, and the two regiments to be raised on bounties of unappropriated lands and for the further defence of the frontiers of this State."   Session Acts, 1782, chap. 22, art. 7.

[37] Session Acts, 1786, chap. 67.

[38] Ibid., 1790, chap. 38.

[39] Ibid., 1801, chap. 126.

[40] Ibid., 1813, chap. 187.

[41] Ibid., 1838. chap. 237, § 8.

[42] Session Acts, 1796, chap. 50.

[43] Pratt: Annals of Public Education, Convocation Proceedings, 1872, p. 207ff.

[44] Session Acts, 1792, chap. 69.

[45] Session Acts, 1814, chap. 83.

[46] Session Acts, 1816, chap. 90.

[47] Session Acts, 1827, chap. 228.

[48] Session Acts, 1838, chap. 237.

[49] Session Acts, 1853, chap. 433.

the stock corporation laws of 1851 [50]–1857,[51] and the mill tax law of 1872 [52] will serve as illustrations.

The union free school law was primarily a measure to provide for local option in the matter of tax-supported common schools. But the boards of education of union schools were permitted to organize departments for secondary education and to adopt academies existing in their districts. This relation between the union schools and academies is made clear by the following section of the law: " Whenever an union school shall be established under the provisions of this act, and there shall exist within its district an academy, the trustees thereof may, by an unanimous vote, to be attested by their signatures and filed in the office of the clerk of the county, declare their offices vacant; and thereafter the trustees of such union school, shall become the trustees of the said academy, and be charged with all the duties of the former trustees, and the said academy shall be regarded as the academical department of such union school." [49] This law marks an important step in the shifting of secondary education from academies to modern high schools. However, the transition was at first slow. During the second decade after the law was passed, academies more frequently were merged in union schools, and by 1874 there were 64 academies that had been changed into academic departments of union schools.[53]

The law of 1851 permitted stock companies that were operating academies to declare dividends. Very little was paid in dividends during the operation of the law. The act of 1857 put an end to the payment of dividends by any company organized and incorporated for the purpose of instruction.

An act passed in 1872 provided a tax upon all taxable property for the support of secondary schools. So much opposition to this measure arose that it was repealed two years later.

Constitutional Provisions

The constitution adopted in 1777, amended in 1801, and the constitution of 1821 contain no reference to secondary schools. The constitution adopted in 1846 provides that " the revenues of the said literature-fund shall be applied to the support of academies." [54] The constitution of 1894 repeats the same clause, and contains the following new paragraph:

---

[49] Session Acts, 1853, chap. 433.
[50] Ibid., 1851, chap. 544.
[51] Ibid., 1857, chap. 527.
[52] Ibid., 1872, chap. 736.
[53] Cf. table 5.
[54] Constitution, 1846, art. 9, sec. 1.

Neither the state nor any subdivision thereof, shall use its property or credit or any public money, or authorize or permit either to be used, directly or indirectly, in aid or maintenance, other than for examination or inspection, for any school or institution of learning wholly or in part under the control or direction of any religious denomination, or in which any denominational tenet or doctrine is taught.[55]

Summary

The laws of the State at no time required communities to support academies. All such institutions were established by local initiative. The legislation concerning them had for its purpose the protection of endowments, financial support, and the maintenance of high standards of scholarship in them.

The academies were governed by the Legislature acting under the constitution of the State. The Legislature delegated to the Regents the direct management of the incorporated academies, except in some few instances. The board of trustees of each academy was permitted to adopt rules for its school. The Superintendent of Public Instruction, later called Commissioner of Education, exercised a limited legislative power over academies in connection with academic classes for the instruction of common school teachers.

---

[55] Constitution, 1894, art. 9, par. 4.

CHAPTER III

Relation of Academies to Other Schools

The policy of the State of New York, leaving the establishment of schools largely to local and private initiative, and resorting to numerous special acts to aid and control such institutions, produced many kinds and an indefinite variety of schools. It is the purpose of this chapter to explain the reciprocal influence of the more important of those schools, including the Latin grammar schools which preceded them, and the incorporated academies. The types of schools discussed in this connection are: (1) Latin grammar schools, (2) private, unincorporated, and select schools, (3) monitorial high schools, (4) " manual labor seminaries," (5) high schools in the modern sense, or " academical departments of union schools," [1] and (6) colleges.

The incorporated academies of the nineteenth century formed a distinct type; but they had characteristics in common with all other schools of the State, both of lower and higher grade. During the second half of the century they were so fused with public high schools that it is difficult during that period to differentiate in every instance, between the two. Academies may be defined in terms of such factors as legal status, source of support, local board of control, curriculum, and rank; the latter measured by the ability to meet Regents' requirements.

The first of these factors, legal status, has already been explained and was determined chiefly in the act of incorporation. The typical academy derived its support largely from tuition fees, and was aided by state appropriations and voluntary donations, or endowments; but no statement can be made in regard to support, or concerning the other factors of control, legal status, curriculum, and rank, that will apply strictly to all academies. There were only occasional instances of tax support.[2] The typical academy was administered by a board of trustees, named in the charter and made self-perpetuating, or elected by stockholders, appointed by civil officials, or chosen in some similar manner; but not elected by popular vote. Its curriculum included subjects of a more advanced grade than those taught in elementary schools, but did not exclude elementary

---

[1] For the purposes of this discussion, the term " academical department of union school," which was used in official reports during the last half of the nineteenth century, will be considered synonymous with the term " high school."

[2] Session Acts, 1814, chap. 79; 1835, chap. 169; 1872, chap. 736.

subjects.   Nearly all subjects offered in colleges were taught in academies.   A building and grounds were owned by the corporation in charge of the school, which tended to make it permanent.

The relation of academies to the Latin grammar schools which preceded them has been mentioned above.   The former were under state supervision and supported in part by the State.   These provisions were not generally true of the latter.   Both depended upon local or private initiative for their establishment.   A comparison of the curriculums of the grammar school maintained by the colonial Legislature from 1732 to 1739, and Erasmus Hall (academy) in 1787, will show that the aims and course of instruction in the latter were broader than those of the former.

Curriculum of Latin grammar school of 1732–39[3]	Curriculum of Erasmus Hall (academy), 1787[4]	
Latin	Latin	English
Greek	Greek	language
Mathematics	Arithmetic	Reading
Bookkeeping(?)	Bookkeeping	Writing
	Geography	Elocution
	History (General)	French

Private, Select and Unincorporated Schools

The law of 1787, establishing the policy of the State in regard to secondary and higher education, provided that nothing in the act should be so construed as to " deprive any person or persons of the right to erect such schools or colleges as to him or them may seem proper, independent of the University." Probably at all times during the nineteenth century, and certainly after 1840, there was a large number of such institutions, which received no legal recognition, were not required to meet the standards set by state officials, and were regulated only by the law of supply and demand.   Unincorporated academies, select schools,[5] and private schools were terms applied to schools of this class, but they were never differentiated nor their curriculums determined.   However, it is certain that the higher grade of them ranked between regular academies and public common schools.[6]

---

[3] Colonial Documents Relating to the History of New York, v. 4, p. 118; New York Historical Society, Collections, ser. I, v. 5, p. 2.

[4] Cf. chapter V, on Curriculum, p. 101.

[5] The Revised Statutes of 1829 provided for the incorporation of select schools, but with practically no results. The two or three that were incorporated soon were dissolved. Session Acts, 1829, chap. 267.

[6] Evidence that school officials considered them of this grade is found in the State Superintendent's reports as follows: 1843, p. 146, 147, 213, 234, 274; 1844, p. 241, 331; 1848, p. 6.

Judging by their numbers and the large attendance in them, it seems that they would have been rivals of the incorporated academies, especially for pupils in elementary subjects. But they came into conflict most directly with common schools. By those most interested in developing the public elementary schools, select and private schools were looked upon as pernicious and injurious to educational interests. Two charges were brought against them: (1) By attracting pupils who would have otherwise attended common schools and paid rate bills, they deprived those schools of support; (2) they fostered an aristocratic spirit, by appealing to the wealthier class of people, and reduced the common schools to the appearance of charity institutions.[7]

The numerical relation of private, unincorporated and select schools to academies, from 1844 to the close of the century, is indicated by table 1. The statistics on these schools, recorded in the State Superintendent's annual reports, were prepared from data furnished by county superintendents, and are not accurate.[8]

The figures of table 1 indicate: (1) That the number of private schools remained about the same after 1855 (except for the inconsistent number given for 1900); (2) that the number of pupils attending those schools continued to increase rapidly until 1895, when it was about five times what it was in 1844; (3) both the number of private schools and the attendance in them far exceeded the same numbers for academies at all times.

---

[7] State Superintendent of Schools, Annual Rep'ts, 1843, p. 146, 147, 274, 292; 1844, p. 393, 481, 519; 1848, p. 8.

[8] The State Superintendent in 1848, said that but little confidence could be placed in the reports on private schools, and gives the following figures to show the inconsistencies in the data furnished him:

"Name of county	Number of private schools	Number of pupils attending private schools
Allegany	3	1 172
Cattaraugus	12	18
Cortland	8	88
Herkimer	22	24
Montgomery	0	2
Schoharie	8	38
Seneca	25	21
Warren	7	78
Yates	21	68

None are reported from New York or Albany while there must be a large number in each." The figures show that in some counties the number of pupils in each school was less than one on the average, and two pupils were reported from Montgomery county where there were no such schools. State Superintendent of Schools, Annual Rep't, 1848, p. 8.

TABLE I

Year	PRIVATE, SELECT, AND UNINCORPORATED SCHOOLS			Year	ACADEMIES	
	Number of schools	Number of pupils attending	References to Superintendents' reports		Number of academies	Number of pupils attending
1844	954	34 105	1844, table A	1844	146	22 782
1846	1 981	56 058	1846, table A	1846	155	22 077
1850	2 277	45 840	1852, p. 5	1850	163	27 653
1855	1 505	43 096	1857, p. 7	1855	155	36 585
1860	1 275	29 603	1861, p. 44	1860	170	29 061
1865	1 481	54 345	1866, p. 12	1865–6	190	32 008
1870	1 514	127 061	1871, p. 78	1870–1	132	21 015
1875	1 437	134 644	1876, p. 72	1875–6	113	15 124
1880	1 176	108 567	1881, p. 72	1880–1	79	10 371
1885	1 116	124 816	1886, p. 84	1885–6	74	11 868
1890	1 988	160 996	1891, p. 18	1890	99	15 271
1895	1 118	165 860	1896, p. 11	1895	131	11 220
1900	238	11 982	1901, p. 92	1900	[9] 140	[10] 12 722

Note: The figures "for private, select and unincorporated schools" include unincorporated academies, which were not reported separately, except in the census of the State of New York for 1865, from which the following figures were obtained.[11]

Number of non-incorporated boarding academies for 1864   110
Average attendance in them the same year, males 3 693
        females 4 066   7 759
Number owned by stock companies   10
  " " " churches and religious bodies   15
  " " " individuals   85

The years of establishment for some of them were as follows:

1821	one	1838	two	1851	three	1858	four
1832	one	1839	one	1852	four	1859	four
1834	one	1840	one	1853	three	1860	four
1835	one	1845	one	1854	one	1861	six
1836	one	1849	two	1855	seven	1862	two
1837	one	1850	five	1856	three	1863	nine

The Development of a Free Secondary School

The growth of democratic sentiment in the first part of the nineteenth century contained the idea of equal opportunities for all. Philanthropic schemes for elevating the poorer classes were characteristic of the times.[12] Many realized that the mass of children could not command the means of attending academies, and had no opportunity to learn any more than the three R's which were taught in the elementary schools.[13]

A report of the literature committee of the Assembly in 1831 said: "Our beloved country ought not to be behind in the pleasing employment of giving facilities to the poor and industrious young men of our State, thereby enabling them to obtain situations in life which they otherwise could not do." Assembly Document, 1831, no. 262.

[9] Three of these were "special schools."
[10] Including 2519 pupils in three "special schools."
[11] Census for the State of New York for 1865, p. cxxv.
[12] Assembly Document, 1831, no. 262. Messages from the Governors, vol. 5, p. 381.
[13] Messages from the Governors, v. 2, p. 350.

John B. Yates, petitioning the Legislature for a loan for a secondary school, said: " The diffusion of instruction in all its branches, among every class of our citizens, is evidently too intimately connected with the duration of our government, the religious and political safety of our institutions" to need any expression of approval. Senate Document, 1830, no. 39, p. 3.

With a view to making the poor more prosperous and promoting the welfare of the State, elementary instruction had been provided by the State and by charity organizations. A logical result of that policy, a step further in the same direction, was the notion of bringing a better, more complete, and more advanced education within the reach of the masses so as to make them efficient members of society. The academies were not a sufficient means for the realization of such an aim. Something, in addition to them or in the place of them, was necessary.

Between 1825 and 1850 three wholly unsuccessful attempts were made to bring secondary education within the reach of all; in each instance the two elements that finally effected the solution of that problem were not discovered. In 1853 another plan for the accomplishment of the same purpose, a plan that contained one of the necessary elements, public control, was put into operation; but this was not entirely successful until the other element, public support, was adopted by the laws of 1864 and 1867.

The monitorial high school was one of the first attempts to provide a more democratic secondary school than academies were. The plan of the few monitorial high schools, which were confined to the decade following 1825, was to apply the Lancasterian method of instruction to advanced studies. The best type of this kind of institution was the New York (City) High School, established by a stock company in 1825. John Griscom, who had observed similar institutions in Europe, was one of the leaders in the movement. The curriculum [14] was composed of the same subjects usually taught in other secondary schools of that period. The primary and elementary departments were not unlike the elementary departments of academies.[15] Governor De Witt Clinton was one of the most ardent supporters of the scheme that promised a high school education at low cost,[16] and in his last message to the Legislature recommended

---

[14] Cf. table 2.

[15] An Address at the Opening of the New York High School, by John Griscom, 1825.

[16] The tuition rates of the New York High School were: Introductory department, $3; junior department, $5; and senior department $7 a quarter respectively, with a few cents of incidental fees for the last two. Ibid., p. 213.

a law providing a tax for the erection of such a school in every county seat.[17] About ten of these schools were organized in various parts of the State; but this attempt at the solution to the problem of secondary education was abandoned almost entirely before 1835.

Another attempt to improve the opportunities for advanced education was in progress during the same decade. The idea of a "manual labor school," which has since been realized in successful industrial schools, notably Hampton and Tuskegee, was tried in connection with secondary education. The curriculum of academies, with the addition of a little instruction in trades and skilled labor, was adopted by those institutions.[18] The labor involved in the scheme was usually considered as simply a means of self-support for the students, the educative value of it was not recognized, and it was not well correlated with the intellectual phase of the school. Agriculture, carpenter work, coopering, printing, bookkeeping, and other forms of industry were employed in the labor institutes. The plan was enthusiastically recommended by legislators,[19] and indorsed by Governor Throop.[20] But the "labor institutions" never developed far enough to menace the dominance of academies in the field of secondary education. The few that were established in the decade following 1825 soon passed out of existence, leaving the problem of popular secondary education still unsolved.

Elementary Schools

Until 1814, incorporated academies were the only institutions, officially recognized by the State, that were giving instruction in elementary subjects; that is except during the five years after the act of 1795 when state aid was given to common schools. During the period before common schools were established by the State, as well as later, the academies instructed a large number of pupils of elementary grade. The academies were never simply "secondary schools" in the sense that that term is usually used in this country; but they were much like the secondary schools of European coun-

---

[17] Messages from the Governors, 1828, v. 3, p. 212.
[18] Cf. table 2.
[19] The literature committee of the Senate in 1830, recommending a loan to one of these schools said: "The plan of the Polytechny, is more peculiarly fitted to the condition of our country, and the nature of its political institutions, than that of any other establishment which has come under their observation. . . . In what better way can it [the diffusion of information to the utmost limits of society] be done, than to foster institutions in which the scientific pursuits of the rich, and the laborious operations of the poor are united." Senate Document, 1830, no. 124, p. 5, 6.
[20] Messages from the Governors, 1832, v. 5, p. 381.

tries. They taught pupils of all grades from the age of 6 to about 18 or 20. In 1787, 12 out of the 53 pupils in Clinton Academy were studying advanced subjects, the others elementary subjects.[21] In 1807, about two-thirds of the 1490 pupils in the 19 academies were pursuing elementary studies;[22] and in 1818, the proportion in subjects was again about two-thirds. Until late in the century, from one-half to three-fourths of the pupils in academies were enrolled in elementary grades.[23] The curriculum and instruction of academies were extended downward to include all the work generally done in elementary schools, so that the functions of these two schools overlapped to this extent.

But a still greater similarity in the curriculums of the two appeared for a decade or more after 1835, when elementary schools began to extend their curriculum upward to include advanced subjects.

After the unsuccessful attempts to bring advanced instruction within the reach of all by the monitorial high schools and the " manual labor institutes," the public common schools were looked upon as a means of effecting that object. School officials and legislators encouraged the practice of offering advanced instruction in elementary schools, which could be done freely since the law had not prescribed a course of study and textbooks for them.[24] The arguments that the county superintendents gave for the advantages of offering advanced instruction in common schools were: (1) That nine-tenths of the pupils do not go beyond the common school;[25] (2) that good citizens need a knowledge of such subjects as agriculture, physiology, business forms and civics;[26] (3) that pupils spend enough time in the lower schools to learn many advanced subjects;[27] (4) that common and poorer people should be given the opportunities for education which were enjoyed by the rich.[28] The State Superintendent also emphasized the importance of extending the

---

[21] Senate Jour., 1788, February 26th.
[22] Assembly Jour., 1808, p. 400.
[23] Regents Rep'ts.
[24] Governor De Witt Clinton advanced this idea in 1826. He said that ten years of the child's life are spent in the common school, and that " In two years the elements of instruction may be acquired, and the remaining eight years must either be spent in repetition or in idleness, unless the teachers of common schools are competent to instruct in higher branches of knowledge. The outlines of geography, algebra, mineralogy, agricultural chemistry, mechanical philosophy, surveying, geometry, astronomy, political economy, and ethics might be communicated in that period of time by able preceptors." Messages from the Governors, v. 3, p. 116.
[25] State Sup't Rep't, 1844, p. 167.
[26] Ibid., p. 301, 302.
[27] Ibid., p. 169.
[28] Loc. cit.

course of study in those schools.[29]   This movement began early, but was especially stressed between 1835 and 1850.   In 1846 the literature committee of the Assembly reported that a large number of districts were teaching algebra, chemistry, astronomy, vocal music, natural philosophy; some were offering instruction in physiology, surveying, bookkeeping and higher branches of mathematics; and that no doubt a sound English education could be obtained in common schools.[30]

Table 2 furnishes quantitative information on the extent of advanced studies in elementary schools, from the time the movement gained importance until near its close.   Until 1844, the data of the table are based upon the number of towns reporting textbooks in the various subjects, but the number of pupils studying each subject is not specified, which makes the data indefinite.   For example, one town in 1833 reported a textbook was used in algebra; this might have been used in only one district and by one pupil, or in ten or twelve districts and by several hundred pupils.   The table shows all advanced subjects reported, except history, philosophy and rhetoric, all of which appear in less than 1 per cent of the towns.   The proportion of pupils enrolled in each study was probably much smaller. The figures indicate that the number of elementary pupils studying history was about 1 per cent of the total enrolment, and the number studying all other higher subjects was much smaller.[31]   The data reported in 1844 and 1846 are more definite and contain more information.   Six subjects, counting chemistry and astronomy as one, that might be called advanced, were studied by 1 per cent or more of the whole number of pupils enrolled.

One conclusion that the table justifies is that a large number of common schools were attempting to give much of the instruction that had been previously left to academies.   It is equally evident that this attempt was not extensive enough to deprive the latter of much support, nor to reach any considerable number who were unable to attend academies.   However, it did serve to define the issue between academies and free secondary schools and led to a beginning of the solution of the question of providing equal opportunities for all who desired an education higher than could be obtained in the public common schools.

---

[29] State Sup't Rep't, 1851, p. 125.
[30] Assembly Document, 1846, no. 133.
[31] This estimate is based upon the numbers given for the years 1844 and 1846.

TABLE 2

The extent of advanced studies in the common schools. The per cent of the number of towns, or for 1844 and 1846 of the number of pupils, when it exceeds 1 per cent is given in parentheses, in the nearest whole number.

	NUMBER OF TOWNS REPORTING TEXTBOOKS USED IN THE VARIOUS SUBJECTS					NUMBER OF PUPILS REPORTED ENROLLED IN THE VARIOUS SUBJECTS		
	1833	1836	1837	1838	1839	1844 Winter session	1846 Winter session	1846 Summer session
Algebra..............	1	......	3	5	7	2 316	3 620	1 706
Astronomy...........	......	1	.....	......	3	217	[32]4 532	4 372
							(1%)	
Blair's lectures........	......	......	1	1	1	......	......	......
Bookkeeping..........	1	3	[33]6	4	2	903	922	631
Botany..............	......	......	......	1	1	......	......	......
Chemistry............	......	2	2	7	8	189	Reported with Astronomy in 1846	
Chronology...........	1	......	......	......	......	......	......	
Civics................	......	1	......	7	7	6 000	20 601	14 357
Composition..........	......	......	......	......	......		(4%)	
Elocution.............	......	1	1	1	4	......	......	......
Evidence of Christianity	1	1	2	2	1	......	......	......
Geometry.............	......	1	2	1	1	......	......	......
Geometry, surveying, and higher mathematics............						644	906	646
Globes and scientific apparatus..........						2 342	14 298	14 406
							(4%)	
Greek................	......	......	2	......	2	11 139	14 161	9 094
History, New York....	......	......	2	1	3			
History, United States.	83 (10%)	174 (20%)	......	220 (25%)	244 (28%)	(3%)	(3%)	
History, other kinds...	8	24 (3%)	27 (3%)	40 (5%)	7	......	......	......
Latin................	......	......	4	3	8	......	......	......
Mental or moral philosophy...............	......	......	1	1	......	558	537	478
Mensuration..........	1	1	1	......	......	......	......	......
Natural philosophy....	1	4	1	4	......	4 712	7 106	5 015
						1%	(2%)	
Navigation...........	1	......	1	1	2	......	......	......
Philosophy...........	1	17 (1%)	17 (1%)	34 (2%)	16 (1%)	......	......	......
Physiology...........	......	......	......	1	......	76	1 395	2 172
Political economy.....	......	......	......	......	3	......	......	......
Rhetoric[34]...........	......	4	8	12 (1%)	13 (1%)	......	......	......
Surveying............	7	4	7	6	7	10 220	71 890	77 921
Vocal music..........	......	......	......	......	......	(3%)	(20%)	
Number of towns reporting.............	811	842	853	864	870	......	......	......
Number of pupils enrolled..............	494 595	541 404	532 167	524 188	528 913	[35]657 782	......	736 045

NOTES: [32] Includes chemistry.
[33] One " book of commerce " was counted as bookkeeping.
[34] Textbooks called " expositors " were counted as rhetoric.
[35] This number is the attendance for the year.

As a result of the extension of the curriculum of academies downward to include all elementary subjects, and the attempt to make elementary schools assume the task of secondary schools, these two classes of schools conflicted. Each accused the other of neglecting its proper duties and encroaching upon a field foreign to its function. The case of the academies as presented by the friends of those schools was: (1) The common schools in trying to teach the advanced subjects neglected elementary studies; (2) as a result, academies were compelled to enrol many pupils in elementary studies, and so failed to receive the state aid that they would have obtained had they been able to enrol those pupils in higher English or classical studies; (3) a further injury to academies resulted from pupils attending common schools for the study of higher subjects, because tuition in the latter was lower. This drew the patronage from the academies.[36] The advocates of advanced instruction in common schools claimed that academies were aristocratic; that their benefits were confined to a chosen few;[37] and that they should not injure common schools by drawing elementary pupils from them.[38]

With the coming of union free schools and their academical departments in the next decade, 1850–60, the burden of popular and inexpensive secondary education was transferred from the common schools, which had proved wholly inadequate for that purpose, to the academical departments of union schools, which in turn became the rivals of academies. The reconciliation of academies and common schools was expressed by the Superintendent of Public Instruction in 1861. He said no antagonism could exist between the two when they were correctly organized and administered, and continued, " Each is an indispensable agency in promoting sound and true education; the common school in the elementary, and the academy in the higher departments of instruction. It is a mark of progress that the jealousy once existing between them has disappeared." [39]

High Schools in Conflict with Academies

Incorporated academies in the State of New York, at their inception and for many years after, were considered the correct solution to the problem of secondary education, and the best means of fur-

---

[36] Regents Rep't, 1845, p. 149.
[37] Regents Rep't, 1844, p. 503; 1845, p. 144, 145, 149.
[38] State Sup't Rep't, 1843, p. 275. Regents Rep't, 1845, p. 54.
[39] Rep't of Sup't of Public Instruction, 1861, p. 35, 36.

nishing the rising generation an education that would fit them for citizenship and the preservation of a republican form of government. The policy of the State was to contribute support to academies established by voluntary contributions. It was thought best that pupils, who were directly benefited by these schools, should pay a tuition fee; just as pupils in common schools were required to pay tuition. The idea of free schools supported by public taxation had not yet developed.

The incorporated academies were looked upon as an integral and essential part of the state system of education, and not as private establishments. Evidence of this attitude is seen in the way they were founded, organized and maintained: (1) The State specified how they should be governed, the powers and limitations of their boards of trustees, and also required certain conditions to be met before incorporation; (2) a system of supervision and administration was provided for academies by the State; (3) the State appropriated large sums of money to academies, not as donations to private individuals, but as an aid to institutions that were rendering an important service to the State; a policy that placed these institutions on the same basis as the common schools which received support in the same way; (4) an academy, as a rule, was regarded as the common property of the community where it was located. This is apparent from the way communities established and supported them. (a) They were often established by voluntary contributions from local citizens. The subscription list for the establishment of Erasmus Hall contains forty names of persons who gave from 5 to 10 pounds each.[40] Clinton Academy was established in a similar way by contributions amounting to £1000.[41] Canton Academy was begun in 1831 after the sum of $1250 had been subscribed by twenty-five citizens of the town.[42] (b) The community in some instances was willing to levy a tax for the support of the academy.[43] (5) By special acts, a number of academies were assigned duties supplementing the work of common schools. Erasmus Hall was given the money appropriated to " Old Town," a part of Flat Bush; and was required to teach a number of poor pupils of the town free

---

[40] Strong, Thomas H., History of Flat Bush in King's County, p. 123, 124. Quoted by Boughton, Chronicles of Erasmus Hall, p. 30, 31. It is a matter of passing interest to note that this list contains the names of Alexander Hamilton and Aaron Burr, each of whom donated £10.
[41] Gardiner L. Lyon, East Hampton. Quoted in New York Historical Society, Collections, Publication Fund Series, v. 2, p. 206.
[42] Hough, F. B., History of St Lawrence and Franklin Counties, p. 545.
[43] Assembly Document, 1831, no. 262, p. 1. Session Acts, 1835, chap. 169.

of charge.[44] This was virtually establishing a common school within
the academy. No sharp distinction was made during the early period.
The trustees of Farmers' Hall Academy were made by law, upon
consent of the voters of the village, the directors of the school district in the village.[45] The trustees of Oyster Bay Academy were
delegated similar powers in their village.[46] The trustees of Montgomery Academy and their successors were made trustees of school
district 7 of the town of Montgomery.[47] The Schenectady Lyceum
and Academy was required to instruct free of charge one pupil,
chosen yearly by the county school superintendent from each town
in the county.[48] (6) Academies were officially distinguished from
private schools.[49] The Regents from the beginning of the University considered academies " under the auspices of the public."[50] The
literature committees of the Senate and Assembly took the same
view. It was stated that academies have an intimate connection
with common schools, " as a part of the same system of public and
popular education." [51]

With the further development of democracy, however, academies,
which were more expensive than common schools, were looked upon
as exclusive and aristocratic. The fact that they were not accessible
to all was recognized by Governor George Clinton. In a message to
the Legislature he said : " While it is evident that the general establishment and liberal endowment of academies are highly to be com-
mended, and are attended with the most beneficial consequences,
yet it can not be denied that they are principally confined to the
children of the opulent, and that a great proportion of the community
is excluded from their immediate advantages." [52] But this sentiment gained no prominence until the first quarter of the nineteenth
century had passed, and attempts were begun to diffuse education
that was not limited to the three R's. It was then seen that as
academies were free to fix their tuition rates, the expense of attending them was a barrier to many; and at the same time no way was
seen to control the tuition rates charged. The privilege of deciding

---

[44] Session Acts, 1814, chap. 79.
[45] Session Acts, 1822, chap. 197.
[46] Session Acts, 1823, chap. 150.
[47] Laws of 1815, p. 93.
[48] Session Acts, 1837, chap. 95.
[49] Cf. table 1.
[50] Assembly Jour., Dec. 27, 1788; Senate Jour., 1825, p. 580.
[51] Report of the committee on colleges, academies and common schools,
Assembly Document, 1838, no. 236, p. 4.
[52] Messages from the Governors, v. 2, p. 350, 1795.

upon tuition fees was considered indispensable to the officials of academies. Public-spirited individuals then felt that these institutions were in the way of progress, and called them obsolete and unadapted to the times.[53]

Since monitorial high schools, industrial schools and elementary schools had all proved unsuccessful as a means of advancing the cause of secondary education, the idea of establishing " free academies " supported by public funds was entertained. The issue that arose then was, Is the State or community justified in supporting by a tax upon all a school that only advanced pupils may attend? The negative argument was: (1) It is unjust to grant a superior education free to a favored few. (2) The weak, unfortunate and destitute members of the community have a stronger claim upon the public funds than the intelligent and prosperous, who would be benefited by such a school.[54] (3) The State is justified only in providing education as a police measure, and as a means of educating intelligent voters; both of which are accomplished by the common schools. The State has no right to provide training which will enable an individual to excel his fellows.[55] (4) A state-supported school would be at a disadvantage in not being able to offer religious instruction, for in it " pupils of all sects and creeds must have equal rights." (5) The State has no right to tax one person in order to educate another, who is able to educate himself.[56]

On the affirmative side it was argued: (1) The principle upon which our government is founded requires a higher education for the voter than was afforded in the common schools. (2) Free secondary schools do not discriminate in favor of the wealthy, because they are open to all who are qualified academically to attend. All do not reach the high school, for the same reason that all men do not reach high offices of honor in the state government.[57] (3) Tuition fees in academies make instruction in them inaccessible to a large number of deserving students, so the public money the schools receive is used for the benefit of the few.[58]

This discussion near the middle of the century accompanied a movement to make secondary education attainable to all deserving

---

[53] Regents Rep't, 1845, p. 150.
[54] Horace Greely, in Rep't of State Sup't of Schools, 1851, p. 63, 64.
[55] Regents Rep't, 1877, p. 628, 629.
[56] Benedict, E. C., An Address Delivered at the First Anniversary of the Free Academy of the City of New York, June 24, 1850.
[57] Ibid.
[58] Report of State Sup't of Schools, 1853, p. 14.

pupils, by radically modifying academies or substituting a different kind of school for them; but it was not until nearly twenty years later that academies began to disappear rapidly and to be replaced by high schools.[59]

The transition from academies to high schools is marked by three laws of the dates 1853, 1864 and 1867, which represent stages in the development of public opinion in favor of high schools.

The law of 1853, which permitted a number of adjacent rural districts to combine and establish a high school, and urban communities to maintain similar schools, was preceded by much discussion, many recommendations and suggestions, and a number of special acts granting the privileges provided by that law to certain schools and villages. The Assembly committee on colleges, academies and common schools in 1838 advised that districts be authorized to unite "to form a high school district and to establish a district high school," a plan which they claimed had been tried with success by "some towns in the interior of the State."[60] A few years later a number of county superintendents suggested similar plans of consolidation and gradation; the higher grades to form a high school.[61]

One of the early special acts to unite districts to afford opportunities for advanced instruction was that of 1834, permitting two districts in the town of Galen, Wayne county, "to form a permanent school district to be known by the name of The Clyde High School." The trustees of this school were permitted to grant gratuitous tuition to the poor.[62] The act did not determine the curriculum. The New York Free Academy, Lockport Union School, and the village of Salem, were some of the places where, by special acts prior to the general law of 1853, schools of secondary rank similar to those contemplated by the law passed that year, were permitted.[63] The first two of these were made free, but Salem was permitted to charge tuition for pupils over 16 years of age, or for those "who shall pursue studies which said board shall deem should not be tuition free." [64]

---

[59] Cf. table 4.

[60] Assembly Document, 1838, no. 236, p. 13, 14.

[61] Sup't Rep't, 1843, p. 113; 1844, p. 307, 117, 118.

[62] Session Acts, 1834, chap. 175.

[63] Session Acts, 1847, chap. 206; 1850, chap. 77; 1851, chap. 206.

[64] Session Acts, 1851, chap. 206, par. 112.

The union free school act contained three provisions, among many others not relevant to the present discussion, which were the beginning of general local tax support and public control of secondary education, the two factors that ultimately led to the displacement of academies by high schools. These provisions were: (1) The power of the board of education of any union free school to "establish in the same an academical department"; (2) when such department was established, it was by this law placed under the visitation of the Regents, with the rank and privileges of an academy; (3) an academy in the district of a union school was permitted to unite with it and become the academical department of the union school.[65] But until 1867, there were only 22 academical departments of union schools and free academies, and a number of those had been organized under special acts.[66] Only 11 of the 22 had been formed by adopting an academy as their advanced department.[67] Tuition fees were generally charged in academical departments, until they were legally abolished by the act of 1864.[68]

Some reasons for the slow development of high schools under the law of 1853 were given by the Superintendent of Public Instruction, who said: "The act needs revision. Its provisions are in many respects ambiguous, in some contradictory, in others odiously unequal." [69] He explained further that a two-thirds vote was required to establish a union district, and a vote of the same majority was necessary annually to raise the teachers' salaries and other expenses; that is, where the district in question was not coextensive with a city or village. In cities and villages, the tax fixed by the school board was required to be assessed without a vote of the citizens. The word "free" in the law was a misnomer, because rate bills were common in schools established under the act.[70]

The law of 1864 was an improvement upon the preceding act. It represented an attempt to facilitate the establishment of high schools by abolishing rate bills. It declared: "Any moneys required to pay

---

[65] An act to provide for the establishment of union free schools, Session Acts, 1853, chap. 433, par. 11, 16, 17.
[66] Cf. table 4.
[67] Cf. table 5.
[68] Consolidated School Act, 1864, chap. 555, title IX, sec. 11.
[69] Sup't Rep't, 1861, p. 15.
[70] Ibid., p. 15, 16.

teachers' wages, in a union free school, or in the academical department thereof, after the due application of the school moneys thereto,
shall be raised by tax, and not by rate bill." [71]   But partly on
account of many special acts permitting tuition fees contrary to the
general law, this provision had but little effect.   Even after the free
school law of 1867 was in operation, at least one district was
exempted from its provisions in regard to tuition in high schools.[72]
In 1874, eight secondary schools supposed to be free were receiving
25 per cent or more of their revenue from tuition fees.[73] They were
certainly charging tuition, at least for nonresidents.

During the five years from 1866 to 1871 the number of high
schools increased from 22 to 59, and the academies decreased at the
same time from 190 to 132.   It is significant that during the last four
of these five years the general free school law of 1867 was opera-
tive.   The slow growth of high schools and the continued increase
in the number of academies until rate bills in public schools were
abolished, point clearly to this one conclusion: so long as rate bills
were assessed the high schools were poor competitors of academies,
because the former under those conditions possessed no financial
advantage.   But when tuition fees were abolished in the first and
retained in the second, academies, rapidly gave way to high schools.[74]
The comment of the Regents on this situation was "There is a
natural unwillingness to contribute to the support of one school by
the payment of tuition, when, at the same time, the law imposes a
tax for the support of another." [75]

In curriculums, and probably in the grade of work done, academies
and high schools did not differ materially; but when high schools

---

[71] Consolidated School Act, 1864, chap. 555, title IX, sec. 11.
[72] "The board of education of the union school in district number two of
the town of Warsaw is hereby authorized to establish rates of tuition in the
academical department of said union school, and to collect the same in the
same manner as the trustees of other academies in the State." Session
Acts, 1868, chap. 222.
  Similar special acts allowing tuition contrary to the law of 1864 were:
Phoenix Union Free School, academical department, Session acts, 1865, chap.
458, sec. 1, par. 14; Jordan Academy, Session Acts, 1867, chap. 43, sec. 1,
par. 4.
[73] Cf. table 3.
[74] Cf. table 4.
[75] Regents Rep't, 1878, p. xi.

began rapidly to replace academies, the Regents considered the former inferior in rank, and suggested that they should be schools for giving practical instruction in sciences, bookkeeping, and all subjects related to business, trades and minor professions; and that they should be made practical to attract pupils who wanted an education for immediate use.[76] Academies, it was claimed, should be used for preparing students for college, as they " stood higher in the educational scale than academical departments which were difficult to hold up to the Regents requirements.[77]

[76] " The experiment of free education in subjects above the grade of common school studies is now being made in this State," but attendance in high schools is too low as shown by the following figures, which represent the conditions in 1865:

Name of High School	Number of persons in the high school district between 12 and 21 years of age	Attendance in the high school for the year
Auburn High School...............................	1 855	132
Buffalo Central School.............................	13 000	154
Elmira Free Academy..............................	2 240	185
Lockport Union School.............................	1 991	324
Oswego High School...............................	4 034	114
Rochester Free Academy...........................	11 255	228
Syracuse High School..............................	7 133	138
Troy High School.................................	7 935	130
Utica Academy...................................	4 178	143
Totals..	53 621	1 548

Per cent of high school population attending, 2.88. This per cent for the whole State was 5.84 Regents Rep't, 1869, p. xvii, xviii.

[77] Regents Rep't, 1878, p. xii; 1882, p. xiv.

TABLE 3

(Compiled from the Regents Report of 1875, for the year 1874)

Note: This table shows: (1) What per cent of the total revenue of academies and high schools was derived from tuition fees; (2) an estimate of the average tuition fee of each pupil for the year, found by dividing the total amount each school received from tuition during the year by the annual enrolment. The following will explain the abbreviations used:

A, Academy
Ac, Academic
F, Female
H. S., High School
I, Institute
S, Seminary
U. A. D., University Academic Department
U. S. A. D., Union School, Academic Department

ACADEMIES	HIGH SCHOOLS	PER CENT OF TOTAL REVENUE RAISED BY TUITION		AVERAGE ANNUAL TUITION RATE PER PUPIL, IN DOLLARS	
		A.	H. S.	A.	H. S.
	Addison U. S. A. D.		7		2
Adelphi A.		97		71	
	Afton U. S. A. D.		27		11
Albany A.		84		50	
Albany F. A.		97		50	
	Albany H. S.		0		0
Albion A.		73		13	
	Alfred U. S. A. D.		29		6
Amenia S.		38		40	
	Arcade U. S. A. D.		7		3
Argyle A.		57		8	
	Attica U. S. A. D.		15		4
	Auburn Ac. H. S.		10		2
Augusta A.		74		8	
Aurora A.		42		6	
	Bainbridge U. S. A. D.		19		5
	Baldwinsville Free A.		11		3
	Batavia U. S. A. D.		3		2
	Binghamton Central H. S.		7		5
Brookfield A.		78		7	
Brooklyn Collegiate and Polytechnic I.		94		102	
	Buffalo Central School		0		0
Buffalo F. A.		93		50	
Canandaigua A.		55		19	
	Canastota U. S. A. D.		3		1
	Candor Free A.		6		1
Canisteo A.		83		10	
	Canton U. S. A. D.		9		1
	Carthage U. S. A. D.		10		3
Cary Collegiate S.		41		9	
	Castile U. S. A. D.		4		1
	Catskill Free A.		9		3
Cayuga Lake A.		33		18	
Cazenovia A.		24		13	
Chamberlain I.		25		12	
	Champlain U. S. A. D.		16		18
	Chester U. S. A. D.		7		2
Chili S.		48		7	
Cincinnatus A.		40		6	
	Clarence Classical Union School		17		3
Claverack A. and Hudson River I.		43		38	
Clinton Grammar School F. Dep't		94		46	
Clinton Liberal I.		21		21	
	Cobleskill U. S. A. D.		8		3
Colgate A.		40		19	
Cook A.		62		55	
	Corning Free A.		4		1
Coxsackie A.		82		12	
Danville A.		62		10	
Delaware A.		59		10	
Delaware Literary I.		50		12	
Deposit A.		57		8	
	Dryden U. S. A. D.		14		8
	Dunkirk U. S. A. D.		0		0

ACADEMIES	HIGH SCHOOLS	PER CENT OF TOTAL REVENUE RAISED BY TUITION		AVERAGE ANNUAL TUITION RATE PER PUPIL IN DOLLARS	
		A.	H. S.	A.	H. S.
East Bloomfield A...	....	71	......	13	....
East Hamburgh Friend's I......		54	......	16	....
	Egberts H. S............	......	12	......	1
	Elizabethtown U. S. A. D....	......	12	......	2
	Ellington U. S. A. D........	......	10	......	3
	Elmira Free A............	......	4	......	2
Erasmus Hall A....	....	69	......	33	....
Evans A............	....	23	......	8	....
Fairfield A.........	....	34	......	27	....
	Fairport U. S. A. D.........	......	5	......	2
Falley S............	....	46	......	18	....
	Forestville Free A..........	......	23	......	3
Fort Covington A....	....	21	......	4	....
Fort Edward Collegiate I............	....	79	......	17	....
	Fort Edward U. S. A. D.....	......	2	......	(less than 1)
Fort Plain S. and F. Collegiate I......	....	45	......	32	....
	Franklin A. (Malone).......	......	27	......	15
	Franklin A. (Prattsburg).....	......	17	......	2
Friend's A.........	....	27	......	24	....
Friendship A.......	....	56	......	9	....
Genesee and Wyoming A........	....	62	......	11	....
Genesee Valley S....	....	44	......	6	....
Genesee Wesleyan S..	....	30	......	11	....
Geneseo A.........	Geneva Classical and Union School................	23	......	28	....
Gilbertsville A......		51	0	9	0
Glens Falls A......		80	......	12	....
	Gloversville U. S. A. D.......	......	2	......	3
Gouverneur Wesleyan S............	....	37	......	6	....
Greenville A........	....	39	......	?	....
	Greenwich U. S. A. D........	......	6	......	4
Griffith I...........	....	36	......	8	...........,
	Groton U. S. A. D...........	......	6	......	3
Halfmoon A........	....	45	......	11	....
	Hamburgh U. S. A. D......	......	9	......	3
Hartwick S........	....	48	......	11	....
	Haverling U. S. A. D.......	......	7	......	2
	Holland Patent U. S. A. D...	......	16	......	4
	Holley U. S. A. D.........	......	5	......	2
	Homer U. S. A. D.........	......	10	......	3
	Hoosic Falls U. S. A. D......	......	6	......	1
	Hornell Free A.............	......	0	......	0
Hudson A.........	....	81	......	34	....
Hungerford Collegiate I................	....	34	......	19	....
	Huntington U. S. A. D......	......	21	......	7
	Ilion U. S. A. D.	......	3	......	3
Ithaca A...........	....	56	......	13	....
Ives S..............	....	46	......	8	....
	Jamestown U. S. A. D......	......	42	......	10
	Johnston U. S. A. D..........	......	10	......	3
	Jordan A.................	......	24	......	6
	Keeseville U. S. A. D........	......	16	......	4
	Kingston A................	......	?	......	?
Lansingburgh A.....	....	49	......	13	....
Lawrenceville A....	....	49	......	6	....
Leavenworth I.....	....	3	......	1	....
Le Roy Ac. I........	....	79	......	26	....
Liberty Normal I....	....	58	......	7	....
	Little Falls U. S. A. D.......	......	8	......	2
	Lockport U. S. A. D.........	......	18	......	6
Lowville A.........	....	43	......	11	....
	Lyons U. S. A. D............	......	4	......	7
Macedon A........	....	60	......	13	....
	McGrawville U. S. A. D......	......	9	......	1

ACADEMIES	HIGH SCHOOLS	PER CENT OF TOTAL REVENUE RAISED BY TUITION		AVERAGE ANNUAL TUITION RATE PER PUPIL IN DOLLARS	
		A.	H. S.	A.	H. S.
Marion Collegiate I..	....	78	......	6	....
Marshall S. of Easton	....	?	......	?	....
	Massena U. S. A. D.........	......	24	......	3
	Mayville U. S. A. D.........	......	5	......	3
Mechanicville A....	....	75	......	17	....
	Medina Free A..............	......	25	......	4
Mexico A..........	....	57	......	9	....
Middlebury A......	....	48	......	7	....
Montgomery A.....	....	72	......	10	....
Monticello A.......	....	93	......	18	....
	Moravia U. S. A. D........	......	29	......	5
	Mount Morris U. S. A. D...	......	0	......	0
Munro Collegiate I...	....	23	......	6	....
Naples A...........	....	72	......	8	....
Nassau A...........	....	55	......	21	....
	Newark Union School and A..	......	10	......	4
New Berlin A.......	....	44	......	6	....
New Paltz A.......	....	70	......	27	....
New York Conference S.................		?	......	?	....
	Nichols U. S. A. D........	......	?	......	?
	Norwich U. S. A. D..........	......	40	......	12
Nunda A...........	....	77	......	13	....
	Olean U. S. A. D...........	......	20	......	8
	Onondaga A................	......	35	......	10
Ontario F. S.......	....	91	......	49	....
	Oswego H. S...............	......	2	......	(less than 1)
	Ovid U. S. A. D...........	......	6	......	3
	Owego Free A..............	......	10	......	2
Oxford A..........	....	44	......	16	....
Packer Collegiate I..	....	87	......	67	....
	Palatine Bridge U. S. A. D...	......	10	......	3
	Palmyra Classical Union School....................	......	2	......	(less than 1)
Peekskill A........	....	26	......	30	....
Penn Yan A........	....	50	......	19	....
Perry A...........	....	11	......	3	....
	Phelps Union and Classical School....................	......	2	......	1
Phipps Union School.	....	100	......	16	....
Pike S.............	....	20	......	5	....
	Plattsburg H. S............	......	14	......	8
Pompey A..........	....	69	......	8	....
	Port Byron Free School and A.	......	8	......	5
	Port Jervis U. S. A. D.......	......	?	......	?
Pulaski A..........	....	33	......	8	....
Red Creek Union S...	....	48	......	11	....
Rensselaerville A...	....	51	......	?	....
Rochester F. A.....	....	94	......	37	....
	Rochester Free A...........	......	2	......	2
Rogersville Union S..	....	60	......	9	....
	Rome U. S. A. D...........	......	4	......	1
Rural S...........	....	37	......	5	....
	Rushville U. S. A. D........	......	18	......	2
	Sandy Creek U. S. A. D.....	......	30	......	7
	Sandy Hill U. S. A. D......	......	6	......	5
	Saratoga Springs U. S. A. D..	......	2	......	1
Sauquoit A........	....	76	......	8	....
	Schenectady U. S. A. D.....	......	28	......	7
	Schoharie U. S. A. D.......	......	6	......	5
	Seneca Falls A.............	......	?	......	?
	Sherburne U. S. A. D.......	......	12	......	3
Sherman A.........	....	19	......	3	....
	Sherman U. S. A. D........	......	?	......	?
	Skaneateles U. S. A. D......	......	7	......	2
Sodus A...........	....	27	......	3	....
S. S. Seward I......	....	34	......	8	....
Starkey S..........	....	65	......	19	....
	Syracuse H. S..............	......	3	......	2
	Ten Broeck Free A..........	......	14	......	4

ACADEMIES	HIGH SCHOOLS	PER CENT OF TOTAL REVENUE RAISED BY TUITION		AVERAGE ANNUAL TUITION RATE PER PUPIL IN DOLLARS	
		A.	H. S.	A.	H. S.
Troy A.............		96	......	37	....
	Troy H. S...................	......	4	......	2
Trumansburgh A....		65	......	53	....
Unadilla A.........		73	......	10	....
Union A of Belleville		64	......	9	....
	Utica (Free) A...............	......	2	......	1
	Vernon A...................	......	?	......	?
	Wallkill A..................	......	3	......	1
	Walton U. S. A. D..........	......	17	......	8
Warrensburgh A.....		31	......	5	....
	Warsaw U. S. A. D..........	......	3	......	2
	Warwick I..................	......	23	......	8
	Washington A...............	......	34	......	5
	Waterford U. S. A. D.......	......	?	......	?
	Waterloo U. S. A. D........	......	4	......	3
	Watertown H. S.............	......	10	......	4
	Waterville U. S. A. D.......	......	9	......	8
	Watkins Ac. Union School....	......	10	......	2
	Waverly U. S. A. D.........	......	4	......	4
	Weedsport U. S. A. D.......	......	?	......	?
	West Winfield U. S. A. D....	......	5	......	4
	West Hebron U. S. A. D....	......	18	......	3
	Westport U. S. A. D........	......	15	......	2
West Winfield A.....		33	......	8	....
	Whitehall U. S. A. D.......	......	?	......	?
Whitestown S.......		35	......	18	....
	Whitney's Point U. S. A. D...	......	15	......	8
	Wilson U. S. A. D..........	......	9	......	2
	Windsor U. S. A. D........	......	5	......	1
Woodhull A.........		67	......	6	....
Yates A............		41	......	7	....
	Yates U. S. A. D..........	......	6	......	28

The typical academy, supported chiefly by tuition, incorporated by the Legislature or the Regents, and controlled by a board of trustees who were not elected by the people, was distinct from the typical high school, which was supported chiefly by taxation, and controlled by a board of education elected by popular vote; but many institutions did not conform strictly to either of these types, thus making it difficult to decide in some instances whether a particular school should be called an academy or a high school. There was a lack of discrimination in the following respects:

1 The name applied to a school was not characteristic of its type. (a) The New York High School of 1825 was an incorporated monitorial school, controlled by a stock company offering instruction in all branches, and was not free. (b) The New York Free Academy was in nearly every respect a high school. High schools under the name of academy were not always called " free."

2 The source of support did not differentiate the two kinds of schools. In 1874, eleven high schools were receiving 25 per cent or

more of their support from tuition; while ten academies were receiving less than 25 per cent of their support from tuition.[78]

3 The nature of the local board of control would, as a rule, decide to what class a school belonged; but there was confusion even in this respect. The board in charge of the Franklin (Free) Academy at Malone in 1867 was composed of five elected trustees, and five trustees of Franklin Academy, but it was not made free to all residents of the school district until 1880.[79]

It is evident that at the time of transition in the state system of secondary education, there were a number of schools that were neither exactly academies nor high schools. The Regents mentioned this situation in 1875. In case of high schools, " there is much confusion in names, produced mainly by many having been organized under special laws," and some academies " though connected with public schools which in other departments are free, are supported by the payment of tuition." [80]

Nearly every combination of support and control was tried. Warsaw High School was under a board elected by popular vote, but was supported by tuition. Ten Broeck Free Academy was supported chiefly by endowment, but controlled by a board of trustees who were appointed by the county judge and surrogate, and the supervisors of the towns of Farmersville, Machias, and Franklinville, and who served indefinitely.[81] The Regents classified this school as an academy.

Table 4, compiled from Regents Reports, shows the numerical relation between academies and high schools during the second half of the nineteenth century.[82]

---

[78] Cf. table 3.
[79] Regents Rep't, 1890, p. 1823.
[80] Regents Rep't, 1875, p. xii.
[81] Session Acts, 1862, chap. 353. Catalog of Ten Broeck Free Academy, 1891, last page.
[82] A number of contradictions and evident inaccuracies occur in some of the Regents Reports used in compiling this table. The data have been checked in various ways to obtain the most reliable information. For example, the Regents Report of 1882, p. xiii, gives the number of high schools that were in operation in 1870–71, as 45. The Regents Report of 1869, p. xvi, xvii, contains the names of 23 academies that had been transformed into high schools, and the names of 30 additional and separate schools that were classed as high schools. On page xxi of the same report the name of another high school not included in the other lists is given. This makes a total of 54 high schools that were established before 1869. The Regents Reports of 1870, p. xii; 1871, p. xiii; and 1872, p. viii, contain the names of four high schools admitted as Regents schools by the year 1870–71. With the 54 given in 1869, this makes a total of 58 for the year 1870–71, not including Ten Broeck Free Academy.

TABLE 4

The relation between academies and high schools in number of each reporting to the Regents and in number of pupils enrolled in each for the year is shown in this table. Cf. tables 1 and 2.

(Based upon Regents Reports for the corresponding years)

YEAR	NUMBER REPORTING TO THE REGENTS		WHOLE NUMBER OF PUPILS ENROLLED FOR THE YEAR		POPULATION OF THE STATE OF NEW YORK
	Academies	High schools	Academies	High schools	
1850	163	3	27 653	1 184	3 097 394
1855	155	9	36 585	2 149	3 466 212
1860	170	22	29 061	7 072	3 880 735
1865	167	35	29 423	6 710	3 831 777
1870	115	67	19 717	10 596	4 382 759
1875	97	119	15 932	14 222	4 698 958
1880	82	155	12 116	18 983	5 082 871
1885	71	190	12 265	24 778	?
1890	99	236	15 271	34 243	5 997 853
1895	131	373	11 220	38 717	?
1900	149	565	12 722	66 929	7 268 894

Table 4 shows that: (1) Academies were the principal secondary schools in the State, judged by the number of institutions and the number of pupils in attendance, until about 1875. In 1875–76, the number of high schools for the first time exceeded the number of academies, and the number of pupils attending the academies at that time was greater than the number attending high schools. (2) The high schools had made nearly all their progress and academies had declined most rapidly during the ten years preceding 1875, which was a period of rapid transition from academies to high schools. (3) The process of transition continued until 1885–86, when the readjustment was apparently complete, and each kind of school had found its place.

The rapidity of transition from academies to high schools after conditions were made favorable is explained in part by the merging of academies with union schools in the same district, as authorized by the law of 1853.[83] In communities where the academy was looked upon as one of the public institutions of the locality, which was probably the case in most communities, the reorganization meant only a change in form, a different method of support, and a readjustment. It was neither depriving the community of any privileges, nor entirely abolishing a cherished institution, and not imposing a

---

[83] Session Acts, 1853, chap. 433, par. 17.

new burden. The board of trustees of the passing academy and the board of education placed in charge of the new high school were no doubt composed of the same individuals in many instances, so the personnel of the governing body was not changed.[84]

The teachers of the academy going out of existence were often taken over by the new organization. Out of 64 academies that had merged in high schools before 1874, 15 had retained the principal of the former academy as principal of the high school.[85] Tables 5 and 7 show that by the year 1874, 112 academies had disappeared, and high schools had taken their places. Of this number, 64 had been merged in high schools. The other 48 had gone out of existence entirely, but high schools had been organized in the same districts or villages to take their places. Ten other academies had become extinct by that time, 4 of which had been reorganized into normal schools and 6 had expanded into colleges. In addition to the 122 extinct academies accounted for above, a number of others had disappeared before 1874, and had not yet been superseded by any other kind of secondary school.

Colleges

The framers of the fundamental educational law of the State contemplated establishing a close relation between academies and colleges. They considered the former preparatory to the latter, and provided that students from academies should upon examination be admitted to any college under the visitation of the Regents. But it is evident that they intended academies to be more than preparatory schools, because it was specified that when " the state of Literature in any academy is so far advanced, and the funds will permit thereof " the academy might be reorganized into a college.[86]

---

[84] Regents Rep't, 1890, p. 1823.
[85] Cf. table 5.
[86] Session Acts, 1787, chap. 82, art. XIX.

TABLE 5

(Compiled from Regents Reports)

This table contains a list of academies that, previous to 1874, were transformed into high schools, according to the law of 1853, the law of 1864, or special acts, and the names of the high schools thus formed.

The column on the left of the page contains the names of the academies, and the date following each is when it was incorporated or recognized by the Regents. The column on the right contains the names of the high schools, and the date preceding each represents the year the transformation was effected. The abbreviations used are the same as those for table 3.

ACADEMIES		SAME PRINCIPAL RETAINED		HIGH SCHOOLS
Academy at Little Falls	1844	Yes	1873	Little Falls U. S. A. D.
Addison A	1849	Yes	1869	Addison U. S. A. D.
Ames Academy	1839	Yes	1872	Ames U. S. A. D.
Arcade A	1862	Yes	1867	Arcade U. S. A. D. (Laws '67, ch. 944)
Auburn A	1815	No	1866	Auburn Ac. H. S.
Ball S	1843	No	1863	Hoosick Falls U. S. A. D.
Binghampton A	1842	No	1861	Binghampton Central H. S., U. S. A. D.
Cambridge Washington A	1815	?	1873	Cambridge Washington A, U. S. A. D.
Canton A	1840	No	1869	Canton A, U. S. A. D.
Champlain A	1842	No	1873	Champlain U. S. A. D.
Chester A	1844	No	1869	Chester U. S. A. D.
Clarence A	1854	No	1869	Parker Union Free School
Cortland A	1819	No	1873	Homer U. S. A. D.
East Genesee Conference S	1864	No	1873	Ovid U. S. A. D.
Ellington A	1853	No	1872	Ellington U. S. A. D.
Elmira A	1840	Yes	1859	Elmira Free A
Fort Covington A	1831	Yes	1853	Fort Covington A, U. S. A. D.
Franklin A (at Malone)	1831	No	1867	Franklin (Free) A, U. S. A. D.
Franklin A (at Prattsburg)	1824	Yes	1870	Franklin Free A, U. S. A. D.
Gloversville Union S	1855	No	1868	Gloversville U. S. A. D.
Groton A	1839	No	1872	Groton U. S. A. D.
Hamilton A	1824	?	1869	Hamilton U. S. A. D.
Holley A	1850	No	1868	Holley U. S. A. D.
Jamestown A	1839	No	1866	Jamestown Union School and Collegiate I
Jefferson County I	1846	No	1865	Watertown H. S.
Johnstown A	1794	No	1870	Johnstown U. S. A. D.
Jordan A	1842	No	1867	Jordan (Free) A
Keeseville A	1839	Yes	1873	Keeseville U. S. A. D.
Kingston A	1795	Yes	1864	Kingston (Free) A
Manlius A	1839	?	1870	Manlius U. S. A. D.
Mayville A	1839	No	1868	Mayville U. S. A. D.
Monroe A	1843	No	1871	East Henrietta U. S. A. D.
Moravia I	1840	?	1868	Moravia U. S. A. D.
Newburgh A	1806	?	1853	Newburgh Free School. (at first a common school)
New York Central A	1864	No	1868	McGrawville U. S. A. D.
Norwich A	1843	Yes	1873	Norwich U. S. A. D.
Ogdensburg A	1839	Yes	1857	Ogdensburg (Free) Educational I
Olean A	1853	No	1868	Olean U. S. A. D.
Onondaga A	1813	No	1866	Onondaga (Free) A
Owego A	1828	No	1869	Owego (Free) A
Plattsburg A	1829	No	1867	Plattsburg H. S., U. S. A. D.
Richburg A	1850	No	1873?	Richburg A, U. S. A. D.
Rushford A	1852	No	1867	Rushford A, U. S. A. D.
Sag Harbor I	1848	No	1862	Sag Harbor U. S. A. D.
Schoharie A	1839	No	1873	Schoharie U. S. A. D.
Seneca Falls A	1839	Yes	1867	Seneca Falls (Free) A, U. S. A. D.
Sherburne Union A	1840	?	1867	Sherburne U. S. A. D.
Spencertown A	1847	Yes	1870	Spencertown (Free) A, U. S. A. D.
Union Village A	1840	Yes	1868	Greenwich U. S. A. D.
Utica A	1814	No	1853	Utica Free A (first a common school)
Vernon A	1839	No	1865	Vernon U. S. A. D.
Wallkill A	1842	No	1868	Middletown U. S. A. D.
Walton A	1854	No	1868	Walton U. S. A. D.
Warwick I	1854	Yes	1868	Warwick I, U. S. A. D.
Washington A (at Salem)	1791	No	1853	Salem U. S. A. D. (also Laws '51, ch. 206)
Waterford A	1839	No	1871?	Waterford U. S. A. D.
Waterloo A	1842	?	1855	Waterloo U. S. A. D.
Watkins A	1860	Yes	1863	Watkins U. S. A. D.
Waverly I	1858	No	1872	Waverly U. S. A. D.
Westfield A	1839	No	1868	Westfield U. S. A. D.
West Hebron Classical School	1855	?	1858	West Hebron U. S. A. D.
Wilson Collegiate I	1846	No	1869	Wilson U. S. A. D.
Windsor A	1849	No	1871	Windsor U. S. A. D.
Yates Polytechnic I	1853	No	1868	Yates U. S. A. D.

TABLE 6

(Compiled from Regents Reports)

This table contains a list of academies that, previous to 1874, had been reorganized into normal schools or colleges. The arrangement of dates and names is the same as for table 5.

ACADEMIES			NORMAL SCHOOLS
Brockport Collegiate I.........	1842	1867	Brockport Normal School
Cortlandville A...............	1843	1868	Cortland Normal School
Fredonia A..................	1830	1866	Fredonia Normal School
St Lawrence A...............	1816	1868	Potsdam Normal School

			COLLEGES
Geneva A...................	1813	1824	Geneva College
Hamilton Oneida A...........	1793	1812	Hamilton College
Ingham Collegiate I..........	1853	1857	Ingham University
Rutgers F. I................	1840	1867	Rutgers Female College
Schenectady A...............	1793	1795	Union College
Wells S. a..................	1868	1870	Wells College

a Did not report to Regents

TABLE 7

(Compiled from Regents Reports)

This table contains a list of academies that had become extinct before 1874, and which had been replaced by public high schools, which were organized independently either before the academy had passed out of existence or afterward.

The dates following the names of the academies show when the institution was incorporated or recognized by the Regents. In case the school was incorporated by the Legislature and never recognized by the Regents, the date of its incorporation is preceded by the letter L.

The column on the right contains a list of academic departments of public schools, or high schools, and the date preceding each shows when it was recognized by the Regents.

Those academies and high schools that were in the same place, village or city, appear in the columns opposite each other.

The abbreviations of names are the same as those used in table 3.

ACADEMIES		HIGH SCHOOLS	
Albany Female Seminary........	1828 ⎱		
Albany Pearl Street A..........	L1836 ⎰	1873	Albany High School
Auburn Female Seminary........	1840	1866	Auburn Academic High School
Batavia Female A..............	1839 ⎱		
Catskill A....................	1804 ⎰	1861	Batavia U. S. A. D.
Catskill Classical School........	L1832 ⎱		
Catskill Female Seminary.......	L1820 ⎰	1868	Catskill Free A
Clarkson A...................	1835	L1859	Clarkson H. S. (Extinct in 1874)
Coopertown Female A..........	L1822 ⎱		
Coopertown S. and F. Collgte. I..	1854 ⎰	1873	Coopertown U. S. A. D.
Cortland Female Seminary......	1828	1843	Cortlandville A
Dunkirk A...................	L1837	1871	Dunkirk U. S. A. D.
Eastern Collegiate I. of New York City.......................	L1844	1849	New York Free A
Elmira Collegiate S.............	1853	1863	Elmira Free A
Essex County A...............	1838	1863	Westport U. S. A. D.
Genesee Seminary.............	L1835	1861	Batavia U. S. A. D.
Grammar School of New York Central College	1858	1860	McGrawville U. S. A. D.
Hobart Hall..................	1840	1871	Holland Patent U. S. A. D.
Lockport A...................	L1841	1850	Lockport U. S. A. D.
Lyons A.....................	L1837 ⎱		
Lyons A.....................	L1840 ⎰	1857	Lyons U. S. A. D.
Monroe A....................	L1827	1871	East Henrietta U. S. A. D.
New York High School..........	1825	1849	New York Free A
Norwich Union Seminary........	L1837	1873	Norwich U. S. A. D.
Otsega A....................	1796	1873	Coopertown U. S. A. D.
Palmyra A...................	L1842 ⎱		
Palmyra High School..........	1833 ⎰	1858	Palmyra Classical Union School
Penn Yan Female A (General Law)	1853	1860	Penn Yan U. S. A. D.
Rhinebeck A..................	1841	1874	Rhinebeck U. S. A. D.
Rochester I of General Education.	L1828 ⎱		
Rochester I of Practical Education	L1832 ⎰	1862	Rochester Free A
Sandy Hill A.................	L1836	1871	Sandy Hill U. S. A. D.
Saratoga A and Scientific I......	L1835	1868	Saratoga Springs U. S. A. D.
Schenectady Lyceum and A......	1839 ⎱		
Schenectady Young Ladies' S....	1839 ⎰	1854	Schenectady U. S. A. D.
Seward F. S. of Rochester.......	1840	1862	Rochester Free A

ACADEMIES			HIGH SCHOOLS
Skaneateles Seminary	L1829	1868	Skaneateles U. S. A. D.
Susquehanna Seminary	1854	1861	Binghamton Central H. S.
Syracuse A	1839	1862	Syracuse H. S.
Troy Episcopal I	L1839	1863	Troy High School
Washington A (at Warwick)	1811	1854	Warwick Institute, U. S. A. D.
Waterford Female A[87]	L1819	1871	Waterford U. S. A. D.
Watertown A	L1835	1866	Watertown High School
Wayne and Ontario Collegiate I.	1855	1863	Newark Union School and S.
Weedsport A	L1838	1873	Weedsport U. S. A. D.
Whitehall A	L1839 }	1871	Whitehall U. S. A. D.
Whitehall A	1848 }		
Yates County A and F. S.	1830	1860	Penn Yan U. S. A. D.

[87]Moved to Troy, and continued as Troy Female Seminary.

Preparation of pupils for college entrance was not the most important function of academies at any time before 1875. Evidence of this is seen in the following facts: (1) The curriculums of academies far exceeded college entrance requirements, which were principally Latin, Greek and mathematics until about 1875.[88] (2) The number of pupils attending academies was far in excess of the number entering or attending colleges of the State.[89] The number of students entering colleges in the State until the middle of the nineteenth century is indicated in table 8. The number of graduates, those receiving the B. A. degree, for the years when the number of freshmen was not reported, represents approximately the number entering. The per cent of those attending academies who entered college, assuming that all who entered came from academies, is very low. If the number entering college is compared with one-fourth of the attendance in academies, the number that might be supposed to have completed the preparatory course each year, the per cent is some higher.[90] The large number of elementary pupils attending academies would tend to make the average number of years spent by a pupil in an academy high, and if this fact were considered, the per cent of pupils completing the academy course of study each year who could possibly have entered colleges in the State would be increased. But there are no available data to determine such facts. However, the data of table 7 afford evidence that during the time specified the academies were not primarily preparatory schools. (3) A number of the more important colleges maintained a preparatory

[88] Cf. table 2.
[89] Of course, some students from academies in the State of New York entered colleges in other states, but this factor would be counterbalanced by the number entering colleges in New York who were prepared in other states.
[90] Cf. table 8.

school of their own, or were affiliated with one in the same city, until late in the nineteenth century. Columbia College maintained a grammar school as a preparatory institution from 1763 to 1864.[91] Union College used Schenectady Academy for the same purpose.[92] The University of the City of New York maintained a grammar school for a few years after 1837. It was incorporated by the Regents in 1838 as the Grammar School of the University of the City of New York. Colgate Academy was associated with Madison University as a preparatory school after 1853.

Table 8 indicates that the number of pupils whom incorporated academies prepared for college was small in proportion to the whole number attending academies. The data reported before 1805 are so meager and irregular that they are scarcely significant. The proportion prepared for college decreased after 1805, but slowly and to a small extent. Considering the large number of elementary pupils enrolled in academies, it is not surprising that such a small proportion of the whole number attending can be counted among those that probably entered college. When only those students in advanced studies in academies are considered, the per cent of the maximum possible number entering college is much higher.

In the second half of the century, some who were conducting academies felt that the few pupils preparing for college received too much attention, and that so much time should not be spent in teaching the Latin and Greek demanded for college entrance. They considered the most important work of academies to consist "not in preparing a few hundred for college, but in educating many thousands who never think of college." [93] It is evident that academies prepared many for college, but that many more, who never intended to attend college, were educated in academies. The large number of girls in academies were for the most part in the latter class.

A comparison of the curriculums of colleges and academies for the first part of the nineteenth century, shows that academies were offering nearly all the subjects found in college curriculums. It is also apparent that new subjects, such as those in science, history, and

---

[91] Regents Rep't, 1890, p. 543, 544.
[92] Session Acts, 1818, chap. 192; 1831, chap. 273.
[93] Regents Rep't, 1867, p. 665, 666, 671.

literature, which appeared in colleges then were readily taken up by the secondary schools.

The tendency of academies to aspire to the work of colleges is seen in the fact that by 1870 six institutions that had been organized as academies had been expanded into colleges.

TABLE 8

Relation between the number of students entering or graduating from colleges of the State and the number of pupils enrolled in academies at the date of report, probably about the average number for the year.

NUMBER OF FRESHMEN OR SENIORS IN COLLEGES

YEAR	Columbia	Union	Hamilton	Hobart	Univ. of City of N.Y.	St John's	Madison	Genesee	TOTAL FOR STATE	NUMBER OF PUPILS IN ACADEMIES	PER CENT THE "TOTAL FOR STATE" IS OF "NUMBER IN ACADEMIES"
1790	7s	....	....	....	....	....	....	....	7s	150a	4.66
1795	26s	....	....	....	....	....	....	....	26s	451	5.76
1800	16s	7s	....	....	....	....	....	....	23s	191	12.04
1805	19s	13s	....	....	....	....	....	....	32s	653	4.90
1810	29s	27s	....	....	....	....	....	....	56s	1 819b	3.07
1815	19s	39s	....	....	....	....	....	....	58s	2 887c	2.00
1820	13s	16	....	....	....	....	....	....	29	2 230	1.30
1825	21s	62s	....	....	....	....	....	....	83s	2 446	3.39
1830	19s	96s	....	....	....	....	....	....	115s	4 303	2.67
1835	24s	88s	....	....	....	....	....	....	112s	5 548	2.00
1840	30	31	18	38	27	....	....	....	144	11 477	1.25
1845	32	32	37	30	33	....	....	....	164	12 608	1.30
1850	28	9	13	12	22	22	12	17	135	15 477	.87

s Seniors, where the number in the freshman class is not given. The other numbers refer to freshmen.
a For 1788.
b For 1812.
c For 1816.

TABLE 9

Curriculums of six typical institutions, college, academy, monitorial high school, manual labor institute, public high school, and elementary school, between 1825 and 1850 (References are given at the foot of the table)

COLLEGE	ACADEMY	MONITORIAL HIGH SCHOOL	LABOR INSTITUTE	PUBLIC HIGH SCHOOL	COMMON SCHOOLS
Union College 1831	*Erasmus Hall 1831*	*New York (City) High School 1825*	*Oneida Institute of Industry and Science 1829*	*Lockport Union School 1850*	*All considered but subjects not taught in all 1835*
Algebra	Algebra		Algebra	Algebra	
Anatomy				Anatomy	
Antiquities, Roman	Antiquities, Roman	Antiquities			
Arithmetic	Arithmetic	Arithmetic, advanced	Arithmetic	Arithmetic	Arithmetic
Astronomy		Astronomy		Astronomy	Astronomy
		Belles letters			
	Bookkeeping			Bookkeeping	Bookkeeping
Blackstone					
Botany, lectures on				Botany	
Calculus, differential and integral					
Chemistry, lectures on and Kames		Chemistry		Chemistry	Chemistry Civics
Composition		Composition		Composition	
Conic sections					
Declamation				Declamation	
Electricity, magnetism, and optics, lectures on					
Elements of criticism		Elocution			Elocution
Evidence of Christianity					
French		French		French	
	Geography	Geography	Geography	Geography	Geography
		Geology			
Geometry, analytical	Geometry	Geometry	Geometry	Geometry	Geometry
Geometry, descriptive					
Geometry, plane					
Geometry, solid					
	Grammar (English)	Grammar	Grammar (English)	Grammar (English)	
Greek	Greek	Greek	Greek	Greek	
		Gymnastics			
Hebrew					
History, Titler's	History	History		History (general)	History (New York)
Intellectual philosophy					History United States, History, other kinds
Kent					
Latin	Latin	Latin	Latin	Latin	
Literature, biblical, lectures on					
Logic		Mapping	Logic		
Mechanics				Mensuration	Mensuration
Mineralogy		Mineralogy			
Moral philosophy			Moral philosophy		
Natural history		Natural history			
Natural philosophy	Natural philosophy	Natural philosophy		Natural philosophy	Natural philosophy
Natural theology					
	Navigation			Orthography Penmanship	
Oratory, lectures on		Physical geography (climate seasons)			Philosophy
Physiology				Physiology Pronunciation Reading	
Political economy					
Rhetoric	Rhetoric	Rhetoric	Rhetoric	Rhetoric	Rhetoric
Trigonometry, plane	Surveying	Trigonometry	Surveying	Surveying Trigonometry	Surveying
Trigonometry, spherical					

References

Union College: Assembly Documents, 1832, v. 3, no. 271, table opposite p. 4.

Erasmus Hall: Assembly Document, 1832, v. 2, no. 72, table opposite p. 14.

New York (City) High School: John Griscom, Address at the Opening of the New York (City) High School, p. 51, 52, 53, 54.

Oneida Institute of Industry and Science: Legislative Documents, 1830, no. 216, table opposite p. 8.

Lockport Union School: Regents Report, 1851, p. 172-83.

Common schools: Superintendent of Common Schools, Report of 1836, p. 115, 116, 119.

Note: The New York (City) High School and the common schools taught all the common elementary subjects in addition to those mentioned in the above table. The extent to which the latter offered advanced subjects is shown in table 2.

More definite information concerning the number of pupils enrolled in academies preparing for college and who actually entered college is furnished by the Regents Report after 1885. These data corroborate some of the earlier and less definite information, although they were not reported systematically and ceased entirely before the close of the century.

TABLE 10

Number of pupils enrolled in high schools and academies who were preparing for college, and the number of such who entered college in 1894, 1895, 1896.

(Compiled from Regents Reports)

YEAR	WHOLE NUMBER ENROLLED FOR THE YEAR	NUMBER WHO WERE PREPARING FOR COLLEGE	PER CENT OF TOTAL NUMBER ENROLLED PREPARING FOR COLLEGE
1885	37 043	2418	6.53
1887	39 523	2964	7.50
1890	49 514	4142	8.37
1895	49 937	2300[b]	4.61[d]
1896	10 273[a]	850[c]	8.27[e]

Table 10 shows that during the decade following 1885 the number preparing for college increased about 2 per cent. One would expect the number entering college in one year to be about one-fourth the whole number preparing for college, or the number entering college in two years to be one-half the number preparing. Upon this basis, the number entering college in the two years preceding 1896 would be about 2071 (one-half of 4142), which is very near the actual number, 2300. The difference in these two numbers corresponds to the slight increase in the total number enrolled for 1896 over the year 1890. By this means of comparing the numbers pre-

a This number is for academies only.

b This is the number for academies and high schools that actually entered college in 1894 and 1895 (two years).

c The number attending academies only who *entered* college in the two years 1895 and 1896.

d The per cent of the total enrolment that *entered* college in the two years 1894 and 1895.

e Per cent of total enrolment in academies alone that *entered* college in the two years 1895 and 1896.

paring with those entering college, it is probable that about 33 per cent of the pupils enrolled in academies in 1896 were preparing for college entrance. The conclusion drawn from this somewhat meager evidence is that academies toward the close of the nineteenth century were becoming " feeders for colleges," which could not be said of old-time academies.

A list of all the subjects in the various curriculums of academies in 1812, and the curriculum of Columbia College two years before that date, with the dates when the subjects of the latter were first reported taught in any academy, will show how the majority of new subjects first appeared in the college curriculum.

TABLE II

A comparison of college and academy curriculums

		All subjects taught in academies in 1812 [96]	
Curriculum of Columbia College in 1810 [94]	Dates when the subjects in Columbia's curriculum of 1810 or equivalent subjects first appeared in the curriculum of an academy [95]	Name of subject	Number of academies offering it
Algebra..............	Algebra, 1825..........	....	......
Analysis of intellectual powers	Intellectual philosophy, 1826.................	....	......
Antiquities, Grecian........	Grecian antiquities, 1828..	....	......
Antiquities, Roman........	Roman antiquities, 1827...	....	......
Astronomy...............	Astronomy, 1797.........	Astronomy..............	1
Belles letters..............	Belles letters, 1817........	Bookkeeping.............	21
Chronology...............	Chronology, 1826.........	....	......
Composition..............	Composition, 1804........	....	......
Conic sections.............	Conic sections, 1827......	....	......
Criticism................	Criticism, 1826..........	....	......
Declamation..............	Declamation, 1787........	....	....
Ethics..................	Ethics, 1827.............	....	......
Fluctions................	Fluctions, 1827..........	....	......
Geography...............	Geography, 1787........	French.................	2
Geometry................	Geometry, 1825..........	Geography...............	3
Grammar (English)........	Grammar (English), 1787 .	Elementary English (Grammar).................	21
Greek...................	Greek, 1787.............	Greek...................	20
History..................	History, 1787............	....	......
Latin...................	Latin, 1787.............	Latin...................	20
Law of nature.............	?...................	Logic...................	5
Mathematics.............	Mathematics, 1787.......	Mathematics.............	21
		Moral philosophy........	1
Natural philosophy........	Natural philosophy, 1787..	Natural philosophy.......	4
		Penmanship.............	21
Reading.................	Reading, 1787...........	Reading.................	21
Rhetoric.................	Rhetoric, 1799...........	Rhetoric................	5
Science of mind, &c........	Intellectual philosophy, 1826.................	....	......
Trigonometry.............	Trigonometry, 1826......	....	......
Trigonometry, spherical.....	Trigonometry, spherical, 1831.................	....	......

Of the twenty-seven subjects offered by Columbia in 1810, only twelve had appeared in the curriculums of academies; and most of the twelve were ordinary subjects such as Latin, Greek and mathematics that had been in the curriculums of colleges for centuries.

[94] History of Columbia University 1754–1904, p. 90, 91.
[95] Cf. tables 3 and 4.
[96] Assembly Jour., 1813, p. 496. The number of academies reporting in 1812 was 21.

Five subjects were taught in academies in 1812 that did not appear in the curriculum of Columbia in 1810.

New subjects offered by colleges were soon adopted by academies which, during the second and third quarters of the nineteenth century, were offering nearly all the subjects in college curriculums of the period.[97]

Conclusions

1 Many types and varieties of schools were in operation in New York during the nineteenth century. Complexity of the educational situation was due chiefly to two conditions: (a) Local option in the establishment, support, and control of schools was the rule; (b) special legislation granted local privileges and in some instances immunity from general laws.

2 Seven fairly well-defined types may be marked out from the various schools that prevailed: (a) Latin grammar schools, which are confined to the eighteenth century, and which are mentioned in this connection merely because they were the schools out of which the academies grew. (b) Public elementary tax-supported schools, which were called common schools. (c) Private, select and unincorporated schools designate a large group of poorly defined institutions that occupied an intermediate place between academies and common schools. They were patronized by people who were too aristocratic for the common schools and who could not be accommodated by an academy. These schools were about ten times as numerous as academies. (d) Monitorial high schools, an attempt to apply the monitorial system of instruction to secondary schools, were transitory and a factor in the development of a free secondary school. Manual labor seminaries, representing an attempt to bring advanced education within the reach of all, differed from the monitorial high schools only in plan; the aim of the two was the same. (e) Modern high schools developed in the second half of the century, after 1850, as the true solution of the problem of secondary education for all, at least so far as it was solved at all, and replaced the academies as the principal secondary schools. (f) Academies as a rule were not supported by a tax nor controlled by a school board elected by the people. These were the two factors that differentiated them most clearly from the high schools. Academies

---

[97] Cf. table 21.

dominated the field of secondary education until about 1875. (g) Colleges were at all times very distinct from the other types of schools. The curriculums and the methods of academies show the influence of the colleges.

3 Academies were not strictly secondary schools in the sense in which the term secondary school is now used in this country. Until after 1875 from one-half to three-fourths of all the pupils enrolled in academies were studying elementary subjects.

4 Until about 1850, academies were considered an integrant part of the public educational system of the State. Later they were looked upon as private institutions and not a necessary part of the educational system.

5 The relation of academies to other schools of the State is revealed most clearly in connection with the development of the modern high school. After elementary schools were established in accordance with the principles of democracy, the notion of secondary schools within the reach of all began to grow. Since academies did not meet that demand, other kinds of schools were advocated and tried. The first of these were the monitorial high school and the manual labor seminary, neither of which was successful. Another unsuccessful attempt to solve the problem was made when common elementary schools were encouraged to offer instruction in advanced subjects. This brought the common schools into a mild conflict with academies. It was not until high schools were established as separate departments of union free schools that the issue of free secondary schools was brought clearly before the public. During the third quarter of the nineteenth century that issue was worked out, and decided in favor of high schools. While the transition was going on, many academies were changed gradually into free secondary schools. But it was only after the acts of 1864 and 1867 made instruction in high schools free that they began to develop rapidly and to replace academies.

6 After high schools replaced the old-time academies a readjustment ensued. Popular secondary education was provided for by high schools, and a new type of academy which catered to the wealthy and prepared boys for college arose. By 1885 each type of school had found its field and the conflict between academies and high schools ceased.

CHAPTER IV

Development and Support of Incorporated Academies

Establishment and maintenance of incorporated academies in the University of the State of New York, until the latter part of the nineteenth century, was closely related to the state aid granted them. The appropriations made by the State to academies had two important effects. They encouraged the establishment of those schools in parts of the State that could not have otherwise maintained them, and gave the Regents a means of control over them that was provided in no other way. This last effect was of special significance.

The policy of the State in leaving secondary education to local and private initiative precluded direct requirements for the regulation of academies. Any community or individual could open a school, and conduct it independently, irrespective of established standards. But if an institution wished to secure the advantages and privileges offered by the State through the Regents, it had to observe the laws and ordinances relating to Regents schools. One of the principal advantages of being a Regents school was the opportunity of sharing in the funds appropriated by the State; and the chief penalty that the Regents could impose upon an academy for negligence of ordinances and laws was to deprive it of its share of state aid. The funds that the State contributed toward the support of academies formed the basis of the authority of the Regents, and provided a means for the growth and development of those schools into a well-defined system under the supervision of the Regents.

The most important sources of revenue for academies were state aid and tuition fees, although a considerable part of their support came from voluntary contributions which included endowment funds. Before 1875, about three and one-half million dollars worth of property had been contributed to academies.[1] A number of academies received local tax support, and a general state tax was levied one year only for the benefit of all secondary schools.[2]

---

[1] Proceedings of the University Convocation, 1872, p. 120.
[2] Session Acts, 1872, chap. 736, 541.

3

State Aid to Academies

The obligation of the State to support education was recognized before the close of the Revolutionary War. In his message to the Legislature in 1782, Governor George Clinton said:

"In the present respite from the more severe distresses and calamities of the war, I can not forbear suggesting to you a work which I conceive ought not to be deferred, as the business of peace, the promotion and encouragement of learning. Besides the general advantages arising to society from liberal science, as restraining those rude passions which lead to vice and disorder, it is the peculiar duty of the government of a free state, where the highest employments are open to citizens of every rank, to endeavor by the establishment of schools and seminaries, to diffuse that degree of literature which is necessary to the due discharge of public trusts. You must be sensible that the war has occasioned a chasm in education, extremely injurious to the rising generation; and this affords an additional consideration for extending our earliest care to their instruction." [3]

In the same year, and probably in response to the Governor's suggestion, the Legislature passed an act containing a clause which reserved parts of public lands for "gospel and school lots." [4]

Following this precedent, the State provided by both special and general acts grants to academies, principally in the form of appropriations and lands. Special legislation for the relief and support of particular academies was more often resorted to in the early period before generous permanent funds had been provided for the benefit of all. After the literature fund and the United States deposit fund had been established, special grants were not so numerous.

The Legislature early committed itself to the policy of responding to appeals from academies for temporary aid, loans, cancellation of financial obligations, local tax support, and similar assistance, by passing the desired acts. Some of the land grants, which will serve to illustrate the nature of the many similar ones passed, were: In 1796, a half acre which had been previously set aside for a school in the village of Johnstown was vested in the trustees of the Johns-

---

[3] Messages from the Governors, v. 2, p. 183.
[4] Session Acts, 1782, chap. 22, art. VII. Cf: Cubberley, in Cyclopedia of Education, art., New York.

town Academy to be used by them in any way they saw fit for the benefit of their academy.[5]   In 1800, the trustees of Oxford Academy were authorized to select one of the lots that had been reserved for the promotion of literature in the State, to aid them in rebuilding after a fire, and the commissioners of the land office were directed to grant the trustees a title to the lot they would select.[6]   A lot of 275 acres of land in the township of Scipio was granted to the trustees of Cayuga Academy in 1806, in fee simple, provided the trustees would pay the occupants of the land for the improvements on it.[7]   Lot no. 56 in the town of Potsdam was granted to the trustees of St. Lawrence Academy in 1816, but with the restrictions that they should not lease the lot for a term of more than 31 years, and that the proceeds from it should be used only for the payment of teachers' salaries.[8]   In 1818, a lot of 640 acres was granted to the trustees of Lowville Academy, who were instructed to use only the income of the property, and to apply it to the maintenance of instruction.[9]

Examples of the appropriation of money to particular institutions are: Lowville Academy in 1836 was given $2000 by the Legislature to be used in rebuilding, after the academy building had been destroyed by fire.   It was provided that this amount should be collected by taxation on the county of Lewis, and returned to the State at 6 per cent interest.[10]   A simple donation of $3000, without any obligation on the part of the academy to repay the State, was made by the Legislature to Washington Academy in 1819, for the purpose of rebuilding after a fire.[11]

Many other similar special acts granting aid in some form to individual academies were passed, but after the middle of the nineteenth century such measures more often took the form of permissive local taxation, and showed a tendency toward free secondary schools, or high schools.   An instance of this practice is afforded in the case of Gouverneur Wesleyan Seminary.   The town of Gouverneur was permitted in 1869 to raise by taxation $20,000 for an academy building.[12]

---

[5] Session Acts, 1796, chap. 50.
[6] Session Acts, 1800, chap. 112.
[7] Session Acts, 1806, chap. 73.
[8] Session Acts, 1816, chap. 148.
[9] Session Acts, 1818, chap. 134.
[10] Session Acts, 1836, chap. 63.
[11] Session Acts, 1819, chap. 55.
[12] Session Acts, 1869, chap. 291.

However, the most substantial and consistent state aid resulted from general legislation and the establishment of permanent funds. The first general act, relating to the support of schools, mentioned above, to the extent that it based school support upon public lands, was typical of many provisions that followed. The second act of the kind appropriated 690 acres of each township of public lands to the support of schools.[13] The act of 1786 was similar to the previous two, and reserved one lot in each township of unappropriated land for the promotion of literature and one for schools and the gospel.[14] Four years later, the Regents were authorized to rent certain public lands and tenements and to apply the proceeds to the support of academies,[15] but no immediate funds were provided until the appropriation bill of 1792 was passed. By that act, £1500 was appropriated each year for a period of five years, and was ordered to be distributed by the Regents to the academies subject to their visitation according to any plan they might adopt.[16] The first distribution was made the following year to the ten academies then incorporated.

The next general appropriation to academies was from a sum of $12,500 which was raised by lotteries and distributed without restrictions by the Regents.[17] Previous to 1813, all sums granted to academies were appropriated or raised directly and temporarily, but in that year a permanent fund was set aside, the revenue from which was apportioned annually to academies. The law in accordance with which this fund was established directed that, except certain lots, the unappropriated lands in the military tract and in the counties of Broome and Chenango, be sold, the proceeds to be invested by the Regents, and the income to be apportioned to incorporated academies in any way the Regents might think best.[18] The money made available in this way formed the beginning of the literature fund, which was one of the principal sources of state aid to academies the rest of the century. The amount and condition of this fund was reported by the Regents six years after its establish-

---

[13] Session Acts, 1784, chap. 60.

[14] Session Acts, 1786, chap. 67. It is evident that there is a distinction made here between the terms literature and education in general. The former is used to designate some advanced form of instruction and learning. This distinction was preserved in the expression " literature fund," a fund which was established for the benefit of secondary schools. The term literature is further used with this significance in Assembly Journal, 1819, p. 865.

[15] Session Acts, 1790, chap. 38.

[16] Session Acts, 1792, chap. 69.

[17] Session Acts, 1801, chap. 126.

[18] Session Acts, 1813, chap. 187, 199.

ment, 1819, in compliance with a resolution of the Legislature.   An excerpt from the Regents Minutes of March 24, 1818 showed the literature fund to consist of the following:

Bonds for the consideration of lands sold.....................	$21 925 81
Bonds and mortgages taken to secure payment of loans........	7 750 00
Balance of principal in treasury	59 28
Total	$29 735 09

And 4759 acres of land reserved for the promotion of literature.[19]
Exclusive of the literature fund, there was in charge of the Regents:

579 shares in the N. Y. State Bank, at $100 each..............		$20 625[20]
100 do in the Albany Insurance Company, $100 each.......		10 000
Loans to E. C. Genet...............................	$6 350	
Loans to Gillaspie	500	6 850
Cash in the hands of the Treasurer..........................		8 000
Total amount		$45 115[20]

The revenue derived from the above funds was:

State Bank stock, at 8 per cent...............................		$1 621 20
Albany Insurance Stock, 8 per cent..........................		800 00
Interest on loans made by the Regents.......................		479 50
Interest on loans of the Literature Fund...........	$512 50	
Interest on Bonds on account of do................	1 315 54	1 828 74[20]
Estimate of interest on $8000, to be loaned or funded.........		560 00
		$5 288 74[20]

Resolved that $4000 be distributed the present year amongst the several academies.

The literature fund was further increased by an act of 1819 directing that one-half of the quit rents received into the treasury be added to the literature fund and the income apportioned by the Regents to the academies as before.[21]

The greatest increase in the literature fund was made in 1827, when $150,000 in the form of mortgages and bonds taken on the sale of lands belonging to the canal fund, was added to it.[22]

---

[19] Assembly Jour., 1819, p. 865.
[20] So printed, but evidently a mistake.
[21] Session Acts, 1819, chap. 298.
[22] Session Acts, 1827, chap. 228.

A clause in the constitution adopted in 1846 declared that the literature fund should be preserved inviolate, and the revenue from it should be applied to the support of academies.[23]

The revenue derived from this fund varied somewhat at different periods, but was close to $18,000 annually for the greater part of the century.

In 1838 another fund, composed of the excess revenue apportioned to the State of New York by the United States Congress, was made available for educational purposes; and the income from a part of it was contributed by the State to the support of academies. An act passed in 1838 granted the Regents $28,000 annually from the revenue of this fund, which was known as the United States deposit fund, to be apportioned to the incorporated academies subject to their visitation.[24]

No further state aid to academies was provided by general law, except for one year by the ill-fated tax measure of 1872, until the increase in annual appropriations in 1887, which raised the whole amount distributed by the Regents to secondary schools on the basis of attendance and examinations to $100,000; two-fifths of which was produced by the literature and the United States deposit funds. The act making the increase contained a provision that the incorporated academies should not receive more than $40,000 of the whole amount distributed in any one year.[25] This provision was useless, because according to the ordinances that governed the distribution of funds, the academies were at that time receiving a relatively small part of the money appropriated, and in 1890 their share of the $100,000 was only $17,802.[26]

The laws governing permanent funds and appropriations made no distinction between incorporated academies and high schools, except the ineffective clause mentioned above; so that all appropriations provided were shared by high schools, which developed after the middle of the nineteenth century.

Incorporations, Admissions, and Growth of Academies

The number of academies incorporated or received under visitation by the Regents increased slowly until the third decade of the nineteenth century. Prior to 1800, only 19 academies had been

---

[23] Constitution of 1846, art. IX.
[24] Session Acts, 1838, chap. 237.
[25] Session Acts, 1887, chap. 709.
[26] Cf. table 14.

incorporated. In 1813, the year in which the literature fund was established, more academies were incorporated than in any previous year; but there was no marked change in the number admitted to the University until 1828, the year after the literature fund had been increased by $150,000. Then within three years, 27 academies were received or incorporated by the Regents, as many as had been admitted during the twenty preceding years.[27] In the absence of evidence to the contrary, it appears that the increased appropriations provided in 1813 and 1827, and the more liberal rules in regard to its distribution in the latter year, were the immediate causes for the rapid development at those particular times. Another period

[27] Cf. table 13.

TABLE 12

General legislation granting state aid to academies

A summary of the more important general legislation providing state aid for academies is made in this table. No reference is made here to the laws governin appropriations to academies for the teacher-training classes conducted in them.

Year and reference to laws	Source and form of aid	Amount granted	How apportioned	Comments
Session Acts, 1782, chap. 22, art. 7	Public lands	Two lots (400 acres) in each township appropriated to volunteers $?	Not stated	Reserved for schools in general
Session Acts, 1784, chap. 60, sec. 13	All unappropriated lands of the State	600 acres in each township 6 miles square $?	Not stated	Reserved for schools in general
Session Acts, 1786, chap. 67	Sale of unappropriated lands of the State	One lot in each township, except in counties of New York, Kings, Queens, Suffolk, Westchester $?	By the Legislature for promoting literature	One lot in each township was also granted for schools and the gospel
Session Acts, 1790, chap. 38	Rent of lands and tenements of the State	$?	By the Regents to Columbia and incorporated academies. No restrictions	£1000 was appropriated to Columbia by the same act
Session Acts, 1792, chap. 69	Money from state treasury	£1500 annually for five years.	By Regents, according to the needs of the academies	To incorporated academies only
Session Acts, 1801, chap. 126	Money raised by lotteries	$12,500.	By Regents as in preceding act	To incorporated academies as preceding act
Session Acts, 1813, chap. 187, 199	Sale of unappropriated lands in military tract, counties of Broome and Chenango, certain lots excepted	Interest on sums so raised. $1828 by 1818. (See p. 138)	By Regents. No restrictions	The sums so realized were the first of the literature fund
Session Acts, 1814, chap. 83	Money from the sale of public lands in towns of Maryland and Milford in Otsego county	One-half of proceeds to academies $?	By Regents as before	The other half of the money so obtained was to be given to the common schools
Session Acts, 1816, chap. 90	This law contained practically the same provisions as the act of 1814 cited above. It seems to have been a reenactment of the latter			
Session Acts, 1819, chap. 222	Quit rents received into the treasury	One-half of the amount so received $?	Added to the literature fund and income distributed as before	
Session Acts, 1827, chap. 228	Bonds and mortgages taken on sale of lands belonging to canal fund	$150,000. $?	By Regents to academies. All pupils in higher English as well as classical studies should be counted in making the distribution	Regents had since 1818 made apportionments on basis of pupils enrolled in classical studies
Session Acts, 1831, chap. 281	This act made a change in the form of funds without affecting their amount or distribution			
Session Acts, 1832, chap. 8	Transferred the funds from the custody of the Regents to the Comptroller, without further changes			

Session Acts, 1834, chap. 140.....	From income of literature fund	$250 or less to each academy..	By Regents. Academies were required to raise a sum before Regents contributed an equal sum, not to exceed $250 in any one year	The amounts so raised and granted by Regents were to be used for the purchase of books and apparatus
Session Acts, 1838, chap. 237.....	Revenue from the United States deposit fund	$28,000 annually to incorporated academies in the University	By Regents as in 1827.......	Academies entering the University after 1838 required to have building and apparatus worth not less than $2500
Session Acts, 1872, chap. 736....	General state tax of one-sixteenth of a mill on a dollar	$125,000 annually	By Regents as the literature fund	Was appropriated one year only. For all secondary schools
Session Acts, 1873, chap. 642.....	Directed in greater detail how the $125,000 appropriated the previous year should be apportioned. $3000 or more should be used for the purchase of books and apparatus under the law of 1834; $12,000 for the education of teachers, and the remainder, $110,000, to be apportioned as the literature fund, except none was to be granted to any school under the control of a religious organization.			
Session Acts, 1887, chap. 709.....	Appropriated by Legislature from general revenue of the State	$60,000 annually..........	By Regents. Not more than $40,000 in any one year to incorporated academies, including their share of other funds	For all secondary schools

of remarkable activity in admissions to the University followed the law of 1838, which appropriated $28,000 annually to incorporated academies from the revenue of the United States deposit fund. In the following year (1839) 34 academies were admitted by the Regents, in spite of the fact that the qualifications for admission had been raised, requiring a building and apparatus valued at not less than $2500; and in the next three years, 15, 10, and 13 academies respectively were admitted.

The relatively large number entering during the three years beginning with 1853 is partly accounted for by the fact that the Regents began to issue " provisional charters " allowing institutions that could not meet the requirements for full incorporation to enter for a limited number of years, at the expiration of which they were given full charters if they had developed sufficiently in the meanwhile.[28]

After the effect of this change was spent, the number admitted from year to year was smaller, and by 1870 or 1871 practically no more academies were entering the Regents system of schools. The rapid transition from academies to high schools and the increase in the number of the latter accounts for this condition. In 1871, no academies were incorporated or admitted, but in that year 9 high schools were recognized by the Regents and in 1873, 19 high schools were admitted, but not one academy.[29] The general taxation law of 1872 was probably the cause of 5 academies being incorporated that year. After the failure of that measure, the number of academies admitted to the University was less than one a year until after the increased funds provided in 1887 were available.[30] The increased activity in organizing academies in the last decade of the nineteenth century was due in a large measure to the development of a new type of academy.

TABLE 13

The number of academies incorporated or admitted by the Regents each year, excluding high schools and academies incorporated by the Legislature but not recognized by the Regents. Compiled from Regents Reports, especially those of 1874, 1886, and 1900, and Regents Instructions, 1853, p. 139–50. Cf. table 17.

---

[28] Regents Instructions, 1853, p. 46, 143.
[29] Regents Rep't, 1886, schedule 15, p. 691–709.
[30] Cf. table 13.

YEAR	NO. ACADEMIES ADMITTED	YEAR	NO. ACADEMIES ADMITTED	YEAR	NO. ACADEMIES ADMITTED	YEAR	NO. ACADEMIES ADMITTED
1787	2	1816	3	1845	6	1874	1
1788	..	1817	..	1846	6	1875	1
1789	..	1818	1	1847	4	1876	..
1790	2	1819	2	1848	4	1877	..
1791	2	1820	1	1849	7	1878	1
1792	2	1821	..	1850	7	1879	..
1793	2	1822	..	1851	6	1880	2
1794	2	1823	..	1852	4	1881	1
1795	3	1824	2	1853	12	1882	1
1796	3	1825	..	1854	15	1883	1
1797	1	1826	1	1855	10	1884	..
1798	..	1827	2	1856	5	1885	2
1799	..	1828	11	1857	7	1886	2
1800	..	1829	6	1858	4	1887	..
1801	1	1830	9	1859	4	1888	3
1802	..	1831	4	1860	3	1889	6
1803	2	1832	..	1861	4	1890	16
1804	1	1833	3	1862	3	1891	9
1805	..	1834	..	1863	2	1892	8
1806	1	1835	1	1864	4	1893	4
1807	1	1836	4	1865	2	1894	13
1808	2	1837	1	1866	2	1895	13
1809	..	1838	6	1867	3	1896	6
1810	..	1839	35	1868	5	1897	4
1811	3	1840	15	1869	4	1898	11
1812	..	1841	10	1870	1	1899	3
1813	4	1842	14	1871	..	1900	8
1814	1	1843	7	1872	5		
1815	2	1844	4	1873	..		434

The following conclusions may be drawn from table 13:

1 Academies were established in greatest numbers during the period of twenty-seven years beginning with 1828.

2 The last decade of the eighteenth century was a period of substantial progress, and in proportion to the population of the State and economic conditions, a large number of academies were admitted.

3 The first quarter of the nineteenth century was a time of but little progress in the establishment of academies.

4 For a period of twenty years following 1869, the establishment of academies under the Regents had nearly ceased.

5 The last decade of the nineteenth century was marked by a new growth of academies, but these were a new kind in many important respects.

6 From a comparison of tables 12 and 13, it is evident that the old-time academies were established under the Regents in largest numbers in response to state aid. With each increase in appropriations, in 1813, 1827, 1838, 1872, there is a corresponding increase in the number of academies entering the University. A close relation between support and development is here shown.

A comparison of the amount of revenue the academies reporting received from year to year from the Regents with the support derived from other sources affords a basis for determining the extent to which they depended upon the State for support. Such a comparison is made in tables 14 and 15. Before 1850 all state aid appropriated to secondary schools was given to academies, because there were then no high schools. Beginning with 1850, high schools shared in the funds that were originally intended for academies, which resulted in a reduction of state aid to the latter.

TABLE 14

Revenue of incorporated academies

This table shows the amount of revenue academies reporting to the Regents received from the State, the amount received from tuition, and the total amount for the year, including that received from all other sources than the two mentioned. The amounts received by high schools and academies not recognized by the Regents are not included in this table. The data are found chiefly in Regents Reports.

YEAR	REVENUE RECEIVED FROM REGENTS [1]	REVENUE RECEIVED FROM TUITION FEES	TOTAL REVENUE RECEIVED DURING THE YEAR
1793	$3 750	?	?
1795	3 650	?	?
1804	2 400	?	?
1810	2 200	?	?
1815	4 010	?	?
1820	2 577	?	?
1825	6 220	$23 558	c$29 778
1830	10 000	50 733	c60 733
1835	12 000	74 121	95 652
1840	a35 651	181 776	236 643
1845	a38 199	200 766	261 177
1850	a38 723	237 051	306 253
1860	34 486	341 207	465 587
1870	24 785	b416 314	b600 499
1880	9 382	319 043	489 146
1890	17 802	557 955	1 157 869
1900	12·849	726 899	2 056 368

[1] Does not include that apportioned for the education of teachers, and for the purchase of books and apparatus.

a The whole amount apportioned these years was $40,000; the difference is due to some academies not reporting their share.

b For the year 1871 by 105 academies reporting.

c From state aid and tuition fees only.

It will be noticed that the amount of revenue provided by the State increased until after 1850, then decreased until the law of 1887 provided additional support for secondary schools.

The extent to which academies of the early period depended upon state aid, and the gradual falling off of that means of support, leaving the academies almost entirely dependent upon their own means at the close of the nineteenth century, are seen more clearly by the data of table 15.

TABLE 15

Proportion of revenue derived from state aid and from tuition, and the rates per pupil for the two. Prepared from the data presented in tables 14 and 16.

YEAR	PER CENT OF TOTAL REVENUE RECEIVED FROM THE REGENTS	RATE PER PUPIL ENROLLED	PER CENT OF TOTAL REVENUE RECEIVED FROM TUITION	ESTIMATED AVERAGE ANNUAL TUITION RATE
1825	20.9	$2.54	79	$9.63
1830	16.4	2.32	84	11.79
1835	12.5	2.16	77	13.36
1840	15.0	3.10	76	15.84
1845	14.6	1.52	77	7.97
1850	12.6	1.40	77	8.57
1860	7.4	1.18	73	11.74
1870	a24.1	1.25	69	21.11
1880	1.9	0.77	65	26.33
1890	1.5	1.16	48	36.52
1900	0.6	1.00	35	57.13

Notes: The rate per pupil enrolled is found by dividing the amount apportioned by the Regents on the basis of attendance, or beginning with 1880 on the basis of attendance and the number who passed the advanced examinations, by the total number enrolled for the year.

The average annual tuition rate is found by dividing the amount received from tuition by the total annual enrolment.

The Regents did not apportion the funds on the basis of total attendance after 1818, but on the number enrolled for four or more months of the year in advanced studies, and after 1878, partly on the basis of the number who had passed advanced examinations. The rate per pupil enrolled in advanced studies is more irregular, and does not show the relation between state aid and attendance, because the standards were at times abruptly raised, which decreased the number of advanced pupils and raised the rate without a change in the amount of money distributed. For this reason the rate as shown in table 15 gives a more accurate view of the relative amount of state aid.

The figures in the table expressing per cents for 1825 and 1830 are not accurate, because the tuition receipts and state aid are considered the total revenue for those years. This difference, for the early period, however, is small. The revenue from other sources than these two, was in 1835 only 10 per cent and in 1840, 9 per cent of the total.

The estimated average annual tuition rate before 1845 is based upon the number of pupils attending at the date of report, and afterward upon the whole number enrolled for the year. This accounts for the apparent decrease in tuition rates in 1845.

The data show that the per cent of total revenue derived from the State declined from about 21 to less than 1. Two factors contributed to this result: (1) The increase in the number of secondary schools and pupils by the development of high schools; (2) the increase in the total revenue of academies in proportion to the number of them and the number of pupils attending them.

If the average amount granted by the State for each pupil enrolled is considered, the decrease in state aid is not so marked as a comparison between the amount appropriated by the State and the total revenue indicates. The rate per pupil was highest in 1840, when it reached $3.10. It then decreased until in 1880 it was but 77 cents. At the close of the century, when academies were receiving only 0.6 per cent of their total revenue from the State, the rate per pupil enrolled was $1.

In addition to the amounts apportioned by the Regents upon the basis of attendance of advanced pupils and results as tested by

---

a The total revenue of 1871 compared with the amount of state aid received in 1870.

examinations, academies received appropriations for books and apparatus. By an act passed in 1834, the Regents were authorized to grant $250 or less to each academy for the purchase of books and apparatus, provided the trustees had raised an equal amount for the same purpose.[31] The Regents had made apportionments for the same purpose before the law of 1827 specified how the state aid should be apportioned, and did not make any provision for books and apparatus.[32] The amount apportioned in accordance with this law of 1834 varied in different years, but averaged about $3000 a year, including the amount paid to high schools.[33]

Appropriations to academies and high schools for conducting teacher-training classes, amounting to about $3500 a year to academies from 1835 to 1843, and about $15,000 from 1850 to 1886 to both academies and high schools, after which time it was increased, is shown in detail in tables 31 and 34. There is no doubt that the system of academies was much strengthened and increased in numbers by the several thousand dollars distributed every year for the education of teachers and by the attendance of a large number intending to teach.

The General Tax Law of 1872

Since academies were unable to meet the competition of free schools of the same grade, the plan of supporting them in part by a general tax was tried. Urged by the University Convocation,[34] composed of the Regents, college officials and principals of academies, the Legislature passed a law in 1872 which levied a general tax of one-sixteenth of a mill on a dollar valuation for the benefit of secondary schools under the Regents.[35] The amount appropriated by this act was $125,000, and with the income of $40,000 from permanent funds gave many academies new hopes for a continued existence. But the measure was vigorously opposed by many, including the Superintendent of Public Instruction, and was not renewed the following year.

---

[31] Session Acts, 1834, chap. 140.
[32] Assembly Jour., 1819, p. 865.
[33] The Annual Rep't of the Regents, 1871, contains a summary of all sums granted for books and apparatus after 1834.
[34] Proceedings of the University Convocation, 1872, p. 115–18.
[35] Session Acts, 1872, chap. 736.

The objections to this law, as voiced by the Superintendent of Public Instruction were: (1) Academies, except such as were academic departments of union schools, were private, organized by the voluntary action of their proprietors and operated on their account and at their pleasure. The State had no authority to regulate tuition charges in them, nor even to keep them in existence. A public tax for private interests was not justified. (2) The measure was unprecedented. It had not been the policy of the State to support secondary schools by a general tax, nor were such schools necessary in most localities. (3) The people did not want public secondary schools. This was proved by their failure to establish them under the permissive law of 1853; and tax support of such schools should not be forced upon an unwilling people. (4) The 300,000 children of the State who did not attend any school should first be " brought under instruction." (5) Academies were confined to certain districts, and could not benefit all. (6) Academies supported by public tax would be a duplication of the means for much of the instruction already provided in common schools. (7) Academies were managed for the profit of companies or religious bodies. Tax support would be merely an addition to this profit.[36]

The champions of the waning academies made a strong fight for their cause, and cited every possible argument to show that their institutions were an indispensable part of the state system of education. Their chief arguments were: (1) The constitution of the State recognized the academies as part of the educational system of the State, on the same basis as the common schools, by granting the income of the literature fund toward their support. (2) The laws of the State recognized academies as public institutions by providing for their incorporation, powers of their trustees, visitation and administration by the Regents, and by numerous special acts granting aid to them. (3) The State had been relieved of taxation to the extent of $3,500,000, by voluntary contributions and endowments to academies, which were given for the public good, and used under state control for public education. None of the contributors derived any financial benefit from this sum, except in a very few cases and then only for a short time. (4) The law providing for the incorporation of academies specified that they should

---

[36] Rep't of Sup't of Public Instruction, 1873, p. 61-66.

be open to teachers and students irrespective of their religious faith. There were only four academies whose boards of trustees were elected by religious organizations. (5) The principle of tax support was conceded in the case of high schools, and should apply also to academies since they had been considered public institutions. (6) It was the duty of the State to train leaders to direct its affairs, a work that could not be done in the high schools. (7) Academies afforded one of the best means of training teachers for the common schools. The annual cost to the State of training a teacher in a normal school was $122.12, in an academy it was $30. (8) High schools could never take the place of academies as boarding schools and as secondary schools in sparsely populated districts. (9) The State was supporting elementary education more generously than secondary. In 1870 the State paid $6.33 for every pupil in the common schools, but only $1.54 a pupil to secondary schools.[87]

But it proved to be the last stand of the old-time academy in the State of New York. The contention for tax support, the only hope of academies in competition with free schools, was lost. Academies were no longer to be considered an essential part of the state system of schools; the parting of the ways had come. The public had turned irrevocably to high schools. From that time, academies depended chiefly on tuition fees and endowment funds for support; while instruction in high schools was generally free to pupils, and supported by local taxation. This meant that academies were compelled to seek their patronage among people of means and among those desiring for their children some particular influence, condition or opportunity; whether social, religious or environmental; convenient sessions, segregation of sexes, definite preparation for college (perhaps some particular college), which high schools did not offer. A change in academies, in their relation to the public, in their means of support and their aims, resulted. When the crisis of 1872 had passed, many of the older kind of academies passed out of existence, or were merged in high schools, and many denominational and other special institutions sprang up. A new type of academy was ushered in.

---

[87] Most of these arguments are found in the University Convocation Proceedings, 1872, p. 118–23; 1873, p. 107–18. Some of them are also presented in Assembly Document, 1874, no. 78; Regents Rep'ts, 1874, p. xiii, xiv, 1882, p. xiv.

Support by Tuition

The most important effect of state aid was to bring academies into the University, and to encourage them to maintain the high standard of instruction demanded by the Regents. The principal source of revenue of academies was tuition fees. Until the third quarter of the nineteenth century, over three-fourths of the total revenue came from this source,[38] and until about 1890 tuition formed not less than 50 per cent of the total revenue. The relative decrease in the amount received from tuition in the last decade of that century was caused in part by the prevalence of the greater number of boarding schools that was characteristic of the new type of academies.

Table 15 shows that the tuition rate increased during the last three-fourths of the nineteenth century from $9.63 to $57.45.[39] Since the total annual enrolment was used in calculating the average annual tuition rates, the figures that express those rates are too low, but they indicate the relative increase in the expenses of pupils attending academies. This increase may be partly explained by a change in the monetary system of the country; but after making due allowance for that factor, it is evident that the new-type academy was far more expensive than the old. The fact that academies were not free differentiated them from high schools more than any other cause, and was the principal reason for the decline of the former when high schools were made free in 1864–67.

Number of Academies and Attendance in them at Various Periods

The extent to which academies served their purpose of providing opportunity for secondary education is indicated by the number of them in the State and the number of pupils enrolled compared with the whole number of pupils of school age in the State. The relation between the development of academies and their means of support is also made more evident by a consideration of the number in existence at various periods.

---

[38] Cf. table 15.
[39] The apparent decrease in 1845 is explained in the notes following table 15.

TABLE 16

Number of academies and the number of pupils attending them, exclusive of high schools. Based on the annual reports of the Regents and the State Superintendent of Schools.

YEAR	NO. ACADEMIES REPORTING TO REGENTS	INCREASE OR DECREASE	NO. PUPILS ATTENDING	INCREASE OR DECREASE	NO. PUPILS OF SCHOOL AGE IN THE STATE TO EACH ACADEMY
1737............	2	....	79	....	?
1788............	2	....	150	+71	?
1795............	8	+6	451	+301	?
1800............	3	—5	191	—260	?
1805............	11	+8	653	+462	?
1812............	21	+10	1 819	+1 166	?
1816............	25	+4	2 381	+562	8 758
1820............	31	+6	2 230	—151	10 944
1825............	34	+3	2 446	+216	12 096
1830............	57	+23	4 303	+1 857	8 947
1835............	66	+9	5 548	+1 245	8 158
1840............	126	+60	11 477	+5 929	4 614
1845............	153	+27	25 173 c	+13 696 c	4 597
1850............	163	+10	27 653	+2 480	4 620
1855............	155	—8	36 585	+8 932	7 833
1860............	170	+15	29 061	—7 524	7 741
1865............	167	—3	29 423	+362	8 376
1870............	115	—52	19 717	—9 706	12 876
1875............	97	—18	15 932	—3 785	16 321
1880............	82	—15	12 116	—3 816	20 014
1885............	71	—11	12 265	+149	24 241
1890............	99	+28	15 271	+3 006	18 632
1895............	131	+32	11 220	—4 051	14 857
1900............	140a	+9	12 722 b	+1 502	11 212

Notes: Only the number of academies reporting for the years named are included in the above table. Practically every year a few schools subject to the visitation of the Regents and in operation would fail to report; and some would make partial reports, that is, report the financial condition but not attendance.

The number of pupils in attendance in the year 1787 was those attending at the time the committee of the Regents visited the schools. They stated that the attendance was usually larger. The significance of the number reported attending after that time until 1820 is not certain, and seems to have varied. For the years 1820, 1825, 1830, 1835 and 1840, the attendance numbers show how many pupils were in attendance at the date of support. Beginning with 1845, the numbers in this column indicate the whole number of pupils enrolled during the year. This explains the unusual increase in 1845.

The whole number of pupils in the State of school age were those " between the ages of 5 and 15 " until 1830, when the number between 5 and 16 years of age was reported until and including the year 1850. After 1850, the number of school age was all those in the State between the ages of 4 and 21. This change tended to increase the number of children of school age to each academy.

The significant points shown by table 16 are:

1 Academies under the Regents reached their highest development, measured by the number of schools and the number of pupils attending them, in the decade following 1855.

2 The period of most rapid growth was from 1835 to 1845.

3 The number of academies increased faster than the school population of the State until the middle of the nineteenth century. About 1845, the number of academies in proportion to the school population was highest.

4 Academies reporting to the Regents were most numerous about 1860, and fewest about 1885.

---

a Three of these were " special schools."
b Including 2519 pupils in three " special schools."
c A part of this increase is only apparent, caused by a change in the method of reporting attendance. See notes for explanation.

5 The maximum number of pupils attending was reached about 1855, and the lowest number occurs in 1880.

6 The number of academies increased during the last fifteen years of the nineteenth century.

Development of a New Type

A comparison of the academies of the last quarter of the nineteenth century with those that preceded shows a marked difference in several important characteristics.

1 The amount of total revenue received from state aid dropped from 4 per cent in 1870 to less than 1 per cent in 1900,[40] which shows that the financial tie between incorporated academies and the State was very much weaker than in any previous period. The State had abandoned its policy of fostering academies as a part of the public school system.

2 The relative amount of revenue received from tuition fees decreased from 69 to 35 per cent, which was probably due to the increase in the number of boarding schools and the revenue received for board and room rent. The reports of the Regents furnish some evidence on this point. Prior to 1890, the amount of revenue received from board and room rent was not reported separately. In that year, 22 per cent of the total revenue was received from those two sources. Such a large proportion could not have been obtained from those sources in 1860, because in that year 84 percent of the revenue was received from state aid and tuition, leaving but 16 per cent for all other sources. It is not probable that the amount received from board and room rent in 1870 was as much as 22 per cent, because the state aid and tuition that year amounted to 73 per cent, leaving but 27 per cent for all other sources. In 1890, 47 academies reporting to the Regents were boarding schools, in 1895 there were 50, and in 1900, 61. It seems, however, that the relative number of boarding schools decreased between 1890 and 1900. In the latter year 16 per cent of the revenue was obtained from board and room rent, and 44 per cent of the academies reported amounts received from those sources, as compared with 22 and 48 per cent respectively for the former year.

3 The tuition rate for pupils attending academies increased from

---

[40] Cf. table 15.

$21 to $57. It appears from this that there was an appeal in the later period to the wealthier classes.

4 Most of the academies incorporated before 1875 had passed out of existence before the close of the century, and a new group entered the University. Of the 137 regular academies reporting to the Regents in 1900, only 38, or 27.7 per cent had reported in 1875; and 59.1 per cent of the 137 had been incorporated or recognized after 1890.[41] Such changes were not characteristic of the earlier period. Of the 97 academies reporting in 1875, only 10 per cent had been incorporated in the preceding decade.[42] There had been periods when a large number of schools were admitted to the University in a few years,[44] but not with a corresponding dropping out of those already in.

5 Many of the more recently established academies were denominational or sectarian schools, whereas very few of the older academies were under denominational control. The Regents, March 2, 1874, according to a request from the Assembly, made a special report on certain matters affecting academies, in which they stated: " There are two academies whose trustees are elected by denominational bodies.[45] The law of 1873, specifying that no academy under denominational control should be granted a share of the state aid, made it necessary to decide the number which should be deprived of a share of the appropriation. It was accordingly stated that four academies were under trustees elected by denominational bodies, and were to be considered sectarian.[46] This number was about 4 per cent of all academies then reporting.

The Constitution adopted in 1893 made it necessary for the Regents again to specify what academies were under denominational control, as there was a clause preventing all such schools from receiving State aid. At that time 50 institutions, 21 Protestant and 29 Roman Catholic, were classed as denominational schools, and the other 75 academies reporting as undenominational.[47] Within twenty years there had been a change of from 2 or 4 denominational schools to 50, or of from 2 or 4 per cent to 40 per cent.

---

[41] Regents Rep'ts, 1876, p. 358–74; 1900, p. 1008, 1022, 1036, 1050.
[42] Regents Rep't, 1886, p. 691–709.
[44] Cf. table 13.
[45] Assembly Document, 1874, no. 78, p. 5.
[46] University Convocation Proceedings, 1873, p. 118.
[47] Regents Rep't, 1894, p. 1277.

It is evident that the old-time academy, cherished as a community enterprise and fostered by the State, had nearly passed out of existence by the close of the nineteenth century. As a means of public secondary education, high schools had taken its place; while academies of a new kind were meeting special demands not provided for by high schools.

Data Concerning Individual Academies

A complete explanation of the academy system in the State of New York during the nineteenth century would require a statement of the more significant facts concerning each academy, considered independently. A correct impression of the situation can not be gained from a general description, because comparatively few assertions that will apply to every institution or even to a majority of them can be made about the system as a whole. Diversity in organization, in curriculums, method of instruction, administration, purpose, means of support, relation to the State and community, and in nearly every respect, was a characteristic of academies. The laws of the State and the ordinances of the Regents, which produced some degree of uniformity, were often not specific, but defined minimum standards and prescribed only certain features of the system; so academies were left free to develop in various ways. Moreover, the Legislature increased the irregularity of the system by granting special privileges to certain academies. Nor were academies restricted much by academic or social traditions. They were a new kind of institution in a new nation, exercising a spirit of adventure, experimentation and discovery.

The advent of high schools in the second half of the century, and the gradual fusion of academies with them produced a confusion of names and almost every possible variety of school between the typical academy and the typical high school. The condition of an individual school in various years can be determined, but the whole system can not be accurately represented in general terms.

It is not the purpose to present here, however, a detailed account of every academy subject to the visitation of the Regents. Brief data concerning each academy that at any time reported to the Regents, such as is included in the catalog of names, locations and important dates, so far as determined, contained in table 17, will afford a more detailed view of the situation than is furnished by the preceding description.

TABLE 17

A catalog of academies at any time before the twentieth century reporting to the Regents, with some of the important dates for each

(For explanations and notes see end of table.)

NAME	LOCATION	DATE OF INCORPORATION OR ADMISSION BY REGENTS	DATE LAST REPORTED UNDER NAME GIVEN	ADDITIONAL DATA
Academy at Little Falls.....	Little Falls....	1844	1873	Merged in high schoo' in 1873
Academy of Dutchess County	Poughkeepsie..	1792	1868	Merged in high school in 1874
Academy of Mount St Vincent	New York.....	1890	Reporting	
Academy of Notre Dame....	Albany........	1896	1898	
Academy of the Sacred Heart	Syracuse......	1889-91	Reporting	
Academy of the Holy Names.	Albany........	1899	Reporting	
Adams Collegiate Institute..	Adams........	1855	1899	Called Hungerford Collegiate Institute from 1864 to 1884
Addison Academy..........	Addison.......	1849	1869	Merged in high school in 1869
Adelphi Academy of Brooklyn	Brooklyn......	1869	Reporting	
Albany Academy...........	Albany........	1813	Reporting	
Albany Female Academy....	Albany........	1828	Reporting	
Albany Female Seminary....	Albany........	1828	1866	
Albion Academy...........	Albion........	1841	1877	Merged in high school in 1876
Alexander Classical School..	Alexander......	1839	1843	Name changed to Genesee and Wyoming Seminary in 1845
Alfred Academy...........	Alfred (Center)	1843	Reporting	Became a part of "Alfred University" in 1857
All Saints Academy (All Saints Academic School of Manhattan)	New York.....	1898	Reporting	
Almond Academy..........	Almond.......	1872	1877	
A. M. Chesbrough Seminary.	North Chili....	Changed	Reporting	Name changed from Chili Seminary in 1885
Amenia Seminary..........	Amenia.......	1836	1881	Reincorporated in 1874
Ames Academy............	Ames.........	1839	1875	Merged in high school in 1872
Amsterdam Academy.......	Amsterdam....	Changed	1894	Name changed from Amsterdam Female Seminary in 1865
Amsterdam Female Seminary	Amsterdam....	1841	1865	Name changed to Amsterdam Academy in 1865
Andes Collegiate Institute...	Andes.........	1862	1893	Merged in high school in 1893 (?)
Angelica Academy..........	Angelica.......	1859	1869	
Antwerp Liberal Literary Institute	Antwerp.......	1856	1870	Name changed to Black River Conference Seminary in 1870
Arcade Academy...........	Arcade........	1862	1870	Merged in high school in 1867
Argyle Academy............	Argyle........	1841	1892	Merged in high school in 1892 (?)
Astoria Institute...........	Astoria........	1844	1848	
Auburn Academy...........	Auburn.......	1815	1866	Merged in high school in 1866
Auburn Female Seminary....	Auburn.......	1840	1849	
Augusta Academy..........	Augusta.......	1842	1877	
Augustinian Institute.......	Carthage......	1895	Reporting	
Aurora Academy...........	East Aurora...	1839	1883	Merged in high school in 1884
Avon Academy.............	Avon.........	1841	1844	Merged in high school in 1881
Ball Seminary..............	Hoosic Falls...	1843	1862	Merged in high school in 1863
Ballston Academy..........	Ballston.......	1808	1824	Burned in 1866
Batavia Female Academy....	Batavia.......	1839	1842	
Bedford Female Institute...	Bedford.......	1855	....	Did not report to Regents; closed in 1880

NAME	LOCATION	DATE OF INCOR- PORATION OR ADMISSION BY REGENTS	DATE LAST REPORTED UNDER NAME GIVEN	ADDITIONAL DATA
Berkeley Institute for Young Ladies	Brooklyn......	1886	Reporting	
Bethany Academy..........	Bethany.......	1842	1863	Closed about 1872
Binghamton Academy.......	Binghamton...	1842	1872	Merged in high school in 1861
Black River Conference Seminary	Antwerp......	Changed	1873	Name changed to Northern New York Conference Seminary in 1873 (see Antwerp Liberal Literary Institute)
Black River Literary and Religious Institute	Watertown....	1838	1846	Name changed to Jefferson County Institute in 1846
Blooming Grove Academy...	Blooming Grove	1811	1824	A private school from 1869 to 1874
Bridgehampton Literary and Commercial Institute	Bridgehampton	1875	Reporting	
Bridgewater Academy.......	Bridgewater...	1828	1837	
Brockport Collegiate Institute	Brockport.....	1842	1867	Merged in "Brockport Normal School" in 1867
Brookfield Academy........	Brookfield.....	1847	1877	Merged in high school in 1880
Brooklyn Collegiate and Polytechnic Institute	Brooklyn......	1857	1889	Authorized to confer degrees in 1869. Name changed to Polytechnic Institute of Brooklyn; academic department in 1889
Brooklyn Female Academy..	Brooklyn......	1847	1852	Name changed to Packer Collegiate Institute in 1853
Brownville Female Seminary	Brownville.....	1849–60	Did not report to Regents	
Buffalo Academy of the Sacred Heart	Buffalo........	1899	Reporting	
Buffalo Female Academy....	Buffalo........	1851	1887	Name changed to Buffalo Seminary in 1888 (?)
Buffalo Literary and Scientific Academy	Buffalo........	1830	1845	
Buffalo Seminary..........	Buffalo.......	Changed	Reporting	Name changed from Buffalo Female Academy in 1888 (?)
Cambridge Washington Academy	Cambridge....	1815	1873	Merged in high school in 1873
Canajoharie Academy.......	Canajoharie...	1828	1868	Merged in high school in 1876
Canandaigua Academy......	Canandaigua...	1795	1896	
Canisteo Academy..........	Canisteo......	1868	1896	
Canton Academy...........	Canton........	1840	1868	Merged in high school in 1869
Carlisle Seminary...........	Carlisle.......	1853	Did not report to Regents; closed in 1855	
Cary Collegiate Seminary....	Oakfield.......	1845	Reporting	
Cascadilla School..........	Ithaca........	1893	Reporting	
Cathedral Academy.........	Albany........	1892	Reporting	
Cathedral School of St Mary.	Garden City...	1890	1891	
Cathedral School of St Paul..	Garden City...	1890	1891	
Catskill Academy..........	Catskill.......	1804	1822	
Cayuga Academy...........	Aurora........	1801	1860	Name changed to Cayuga Lake Academy in 1860
Cayuga Lake Academy......	Aurora........	Changed	1898	Name changed from Cayuga Academy in 1860
Cazenovia Seminary........	Cazenovia.....	Changed	Reporting	Name changed from Central New York Conference Seminary in 1874
Central New York Conference Seminary	Cazenovia.....	Changed	1874	Name changed from Oneida Conference Seminary in 1870 (see Cazenovia Seminary)
Chamberlain Institute.......	Randolph.....	Changed	Reporting	Name changed from Randolph Academy Association in 1866

NAME	LOCATION	DATE OF INCORPORATION OR ADMISSION BY REGENTS	DATE LAST REPORTED UNDER NAME GIVEN	ADDITIONAL DATA
Champlain Academy........	Champlain....	1842	1872	Merged in high school in 1873
Champlain Institute........	Port Henry....	1894	Reporting	
Charbonneau Institute......	Rouse Point...	1895	Reporting	
Chautauqua Collegiate Institute	Stockton......	1857	Not organized	
Cherry Valley Academy.....	Cherry Valley..	1796	1895	Closed from 1866 to 1881
Chester Academy...........	Chester.......	1844	1872	Merged in high school in 1869
Chili Seminary.............	North Chili....	1869	1885	Name changed to A. M. Chesbrough Seminary in 1885
Christian Brothers Academy of Albany	Albany........	1869	Reporting	
Cincinnatus Academy.......	Cincinnatus....	1857	1896	
Clarence Academy..........	Clarence......	1854	1870	Merged in high school in 1869
Clarkson Academy..........	Clarkson......	1835	1856	
Claverack Academy........	Claverack.....	1839	1854	Name changed to Claverack Academy and Hudson River Institute in 1854
Claverack Academy and Hudson River Institute	Claverack.....	Changed	1895	Name changed from Claverack Academy in 1854. Authorized to confer degrees in 1869. Name changed to Hudson River Institute in 1895
Clermont Academy.........	Clermont......	1839	1839	Reported one year only
Clifton Springs Female Seminary	Clifton Springs.	1890	1898	
Clinton Academy...........	East Hampton.	1787	1868	Closed about 1881
Clinton Grammar School....	Clinton.......	1828	1893	Houghton Seminary branched off from this school in 1881–82
Clinton Liberal Institute....	Clinton (Fort Plain)	1836	Reporting	Removed to Fort Plain in 1879
Clinton Seminary..........	Clinton(Whitesboro)	1842	1844	Name changed to Whitestown Seminary in 1844
Clover Street Seminary......	Brighton......	1849	1857	Sold in 1858
Colgate Academy..........	Hamilton......	Changed	Reporting	Name changed from Grammar School of Madison University in 1873
Columbia Academy........	Kinderhook....	1797	1805	Closed in 1805
Conrad Poppenhusen Association	College Point..	1890	1893	Also classed as a special institution and reported in other years
Cook Academy.............	Havanna (Montour Falls)	1872	Reporting	
Cooperstown Seminary and Female Collegiate Institute	Cooperstown...	1854	Did not report to Regents	Sold in 1859
Cortland Academy..........	Homer........	1819	1873	Merged in high school in 1873
Cortlandville Academy......	Cortlandville...	1843	1869	Merged in " Cortland Norma School " in 1868
Coxsackie Academy.........	Coxsackie.....	1839	1875	Merged in high school in 1880. Charter renewed in 1863
Dansville Seminary.........	Dansville......	1853–60	1883	Merged in high school in 1885
Dean Academy.............	Binghamton...	1872	Did not report to Regents	
De Lancey Institute........	Westmoreland..	1842	1847	Sold in 1852
De Lancey School	Geneva.......	1888	Reporting	
Delaware Academy.........	Delhi........	1820	Reporting	
Delaware Literary Institute..	Franklin......	1839	Reporting	
Deposit Academy...........	Deposit.......	1867	1875	Merged in high school in 1876
De Ruyter Institute........	De Ruyter.....	1838	1871	Reincorporated in 1847; merged in high school in 1877
De Veaux School...........	Niagara Falls..	1890	Reporting	
Drew Seminary for Young Women	Carmel.......	1895	Reporting	Department of a college

NAME	LOCATION	DATE OF INCORPORATION OR ADMISSION BY REGENTS	DATE LAST REPORTED UNDER NAME GIVEN	ADDITIONAL DATA
Dundee Academy...........	Dundee.......	1855	1867	
Dundee Preparatory School..	Dundee......	1882–89	1895	
D'Youville Academy........	Plattsburg.....	1892–96	Reporting	
East Bloomfield Academy....	East Bloomfield	1840	1876	
East Genesee Conference Seminary	Ovid..........	Changed	1872	Name changed from Ovid Academy in 1864; merged in high school in 1873
East Hamburg Friends Institute	East Hamburg.	1872	1877	
East Springfield Academy...	East Springfield	1880–82	Reporting	
Ellenville High School.......	Ellenville......	1856	....	Did not report to Regents; merged in " Ulster Female Seminary " in 1867
Ellington Academy.........	Ellington......	1853	1867	Merged in high school in 1872
Elmira Academy...........	Elmira........	1840	1866	Merged in high school in 1859
Elmira Collegiate Seminary..	Elmira........	1853	....	Did not report to Regents; merged in " Elmira Female College " in 1855
Erasmus Hall..............	Flatbush......	1787	1895	Merged in high school in 1896
Essex County Academy.....	Westport......	1838	1843	Corporation dissolved in 1867
Evans Academy............	Peterboro.....	Changed	1896	Name changed from Peterboro Academy in 1864
Fairfield Academy..........	Fairfield.......	1803	1882	Name changed to Fairfield Seminary in 1883
Fairfield Seminary..........	Fairfield.......	Changed	Reporting	
Falley Seminary............	Fulton........	Changed	1885	Name changed from Falley Seminary of Black River Conference in 1857
Falley Seminary of Black River Conference	Fulton........	Changed	1857	Name changed from Fulton Academy in 1849 (see Falley Seminary)
Farmers' Hall..............	Goshen.......	1790	1866	
Fayetteville Academy.......	Fayetteville....	1839	1854	Merged in high school in 1883 (?)
Fayetteville Seminary.......	Fayetteville....	1857	....	Did not report to Regents; merged in high school in 1883
Female Academy of the Sacred Heart	Kenwood......	1891	Reporting	
Female Academy of the Sacred Heart...........	New York.....	1891	Reporting	
Female Academy of the Sacred Heart...........	Rochester.....	1891	Reporting	
Female Institute of Visitation.	Brooklyn......	1891	Reporting	
Florence Institute..........	Mechanicville..	1889	1889	Reported one year only
Flushing Institute..........	Flushing......	1890	Reporting	
Fonda Academy............	Fonda........	1845	1848	
Fort Covington Academy....	Fort Covington.	1831	1875	Merged in high school in 1853
Fort Edward Collegiate Institute	Fort Edward...	Changed	Reporting	Name changed from Washington County Seminary and Collegiate Institute in 1865
Fort Plain Seminary and Female Collegiate Institute	Fort Plain.....	1853–55	1879	
Franklin Academy..........	Malone.......	1831	1895	Merged in high school in 1867
Franklin Academy..........	Prattsburg.....	1824	1877	Merged in high school in 1870
Franklin School of Buffalo...	Buffalo........	1894–99	Reporting	
Fredonia Academy..........	Fredonia......	1830	1867	Merged in " Fredonia Normal School " in 1866
Friends' Academy..........	Locust Valley..	1898	Reporting	
Friends' Academy..........	Union Springs..	1860	1876	Name changed to Oakwood Seminary in 1876
Friendship Academy........	Friendship....	1849	1894	

NAME	LOCATION	DATE OF INCOR- PORATION OR ADMISSION BY REGENTS	DATE LAST REPORTED UNDER NAME GIVEN	ADDITIONAL DATA
Fulton Academy............	Fulton........	Changed	1848	Name changed from Fulton Female Seminary in 1842 (see Falley Seminary of Black River Conference)
Fulton Female Seminary....	Fulton........	1839	1842	Name changed to Fulton Academy in 1842
Gaines Academy............	Gaines........	1830	1842	Sold in 1844
Galway Academy............	Galway........	1839	1863	
Galway Academy............	Galway........	1845	....	Did not report to Regents
Genesee Conference Seminary	Pike..........	1856	1859	Name changed to Pike Seminary in 1859
Genesee and Wyoming Seminary	Alexander.....	Changed	1886	Name changed from Alexander Classical School in 1845
Genesee Valley Seminary....	Belfast........	1857–62	1877	
Genesee Wesleyan Seminary.	Lima.........	1836	Reporting	
Geneseo Academy..........	Geneseo.......	Changed	1875	Name changed from Livingston County High School Association in 1846
Geneva Academy...........	Geneva.......	1813	1824	Merged in " Geneva College" in 1824
Genoa Academy............	Genoa........	1847	1852	
German American School of Morrisania	Morrisania.....	1865	....	Did not report to Regents
German Martin Luther Seminary (German Martin Luther College)	Buffalo........	1893	1893	Reported one year only as an academy. Classed as a special school
Gilbertsville Academy, and Collegiate Institute	Gilbertsville...	1841	1895	
Glens Falls Academy........	Glens Falls....	1842	Reporting	
Gloversville Union Seminary (Gloversville Union Academy)	Gloversville....	1855	1868	Merged in high school in 1868
Gouverneur High School.....	Gouverneur....	1829	1840	Name changed to Gouverneur Wesleyan Seminary in 1840
Gouverneur Wesleyan Seminary	Gouverneur....	Changed	1889	Name changed to Gouverneur Seminary in 1889 (see Gouverneur High School)
Gouverneur Seminary.......	Gouverneur....	Changed	1894	Merged in high school in 1895
Grammar School of Columbia College	New York.....	1838	1858	Became private
Grammar School of Madison University	Hamilton......	1853	1873	Name changed to Colgate Academy in 1873
Grammar School of New York Central College	McGrawville...	1858	1858	Reported one year only
Grammar School of the University of the City of New York	New York.....	1838	1853	
Granville Academy.........	Granville......	1830	1864	Sold in 1870
Greenbush and Schodack Academy	East Greenbush	1841	1853	
Greenville Academy.........	Greenville.....	1816	1898	
Griffith Institute (Griffith Academy)	Springville.....	Changed	1877	Name changed from Springville Academy 1866; merged in high school in 1876
Groton Academy...........	Groton........	1839	1872	Merged in high school in 1872
Hackley School.............	Tarrytown.....	1900	Reported in 1901	
Halfmoon Academy........	Halfmoon.....	1851	1876	
Hamilton Academy.........	Hamilton......	1824	1859	Merged in high school in 1869
Hamilton Female Seminary	Hamilton......	1856	1863	
Hamilton Oneida Academy..	Kirkland......	1793	1812	Merged in Hamilton College in 1812
Hartford Academy..........	South Hartford	1866	1876	
Hartwick Seminary.........	Hartwick......	1816	Reporting	
Hebrew Technical School (Hebrew Technical Institute)	New York.....	1894	1898	Also classed as a special school

NAME	LOCATION	DATE OF INCOR-PORATION OR ADMISSION BY REGENTS	DATE LAST REPORTED UNDER NAME GIVEN	ADDITIONAL DATA
Hedding Literary Institute..	Ashland.......	1854	....	Did not report to Regents; merged in "Ashland Collegiate Institute" about 1858
Hempstead Institute........	Hempstead....	1858	....	Did not report to Regents
Hempstead Seminary.......	Hempstead....	1839	1847	
Herkimer Academy (Herkimer County Academy)	Herkimer......	1840	1847	
Hobart Hall..............	Holland Patent	1840	1857	
Hogansburgh Academy......	Hogansburgh..	1889	Reporting	
Holley Academy............	Holley........	1850	1868	Merged in high school in 1868
Holy Angels, Academic Department	Buffalo........	1898	Reporting	
Holy Angels Academy.......	Buffalo........	1894	Reporting	
Holy Cross Academic School.	Albany........	1897	Reporting	
Holy Cross Academy of Manhattan	New York.....	1898	Reporting	
Houghton Seminary.........	Clinton.......	Changed	Reporting	Organized as a separate department of Clinton Grammar School in 1881–82
Hubbardsville Academy.....	Hubbard's Corners	1850	1853	
Hudson Academy..........	Hudson.......	1807	1888	
Hudson River Institute.....	Claverack.....	Changed	Reporting	Name changed from Claverack Academy and Hudson River Institute in 1895
Hungerford Collegiate Institute	Adams........	Changed	1882	(See Adams Collegiate Institute)
Ingham Collegiate Institute..	Le Roy.......	1853	1857	Name changed to "Ingham University, Academic Department" in 1857
Ingham University, Academic Department	Le Roy........	Changed	1892	Name changed from Ingham Collegiate Institute in 1857
Institute of Sisters of St Joseph	Buffalo........	1892	Reporting	
Ithaca Academy............	Ithaca........	1826	1875	Merged in high school in 1884
Ives Seminary..............	Antwerp.......	Changed	Reporting	Name changed from Northern New York Conference Seminary in 1874
Jamestown Academy........	Jamestown....	1839	1865	Merged in high school in 1866
Jane Gray School...........	Mt Morris.....	1868	1875	
Jefferson Academy..........	Jefferson......	1833	1850	
Jefferson County Institute...	Watertown....	Changed	1865	Name changed from Black River Literary and Religious Institute in 1846; merged in high school in 1865
Johnstown Academy........	Johnstown.....	1794	1869	Merged in high school in 1870
Jonesville Academy.........	Jonesville......	1850	1869	Corporation dissolved in 1871
Jordan Academy...........	Jordan........	1842	1875	Merged in high school in 1867
Keeseville Academy.........	Keeseville.....	1839	1872	Merged in high school in 1873
Keuka Institute............	Keuka Park (Keuka College)	1890	Reporting	
Kinderhook Academy.......	Kinderhook....	1828	1895	
Kingsborough Academy.....	Kingsborough..	1839	1858	Merged in common school in 1863
Kingston Academy.........	Kingston......	1795	1880	Merged in high school in 1864
Knoxville Academy.........	Knox.........	1842	1868	
Lancaster Academy.........	Lancaster.....	1846	1846	Reported one year only
Lansingburg Academy.......	Lansingburg...	1796	Reporting	
La Salle Academy..........	New York.....	1896	Reporting	
La Salle Institute...........	Troy..........	1880–91	Reporting	

NAME	LOCATION	DATE OF INCOR-PORATION OR ADMISSION BY REGENTS	DATE LAST REPORTED UNDER NAME GIVEN	ADDITIONAL DATA
Laurel Bank Seminary	Deposit	1854	....	Did not report to Regents
Lawrenceville Academy	Lawrenceville	1861	1889	
Le Roy Academic Institute	Le Roy	1864	1891	
Le Roy Female Seminary	Le Roy	1841	1851	
Lewiston High School Academy	Lewiston	1828	1848	Closed about 1875
Liberty Normal Institute	Liberty	1849	1885	
Livingston County High School (Livingston County High School Association)	Geneseo	1829	1845	Name changed to Geneseo Academy in 1846
Lowville Academy	Lowville	1808	Reporting	
McAuley Academic School	Keeseville	1891–96	Reporting	
Macedon Academy	Macedon (Macedon Center)	1845	Reporting	
Manlius Academy	Manlius	1839	1869	Merged in high school in 1870
Marathon Academy	Marathon	1866	1869	Merged in high school in 1879
Marion Collegiate Institute	Marion	1855–58	Reporting	
Marshall Seminary of Easton	Easton	1863	1895	
Martin Institute	Martinsburg	1870	1875	
Mayville Academy	Mayville	1839	1864	Merged in high school in 1868
Mechanicville Academy	Mechanicville	1861	1888	
Mendon Academy	Mendon	1839	1848	
Mexico Academy	Mexico	Changed	1895	Name changed from Rensselaer Oswego Academy in 1845
Middlebury Academy	Wyoming	1819	1888	Merged in high school in 1839
Millville Academy	Millville	1841	1856	
Monroe Academy	Henrietta	1827	1840	Probably merged with the following
Monroe Academy	Henrietta	1843	1870	Merged in high school in 1871
Montgomery Academy	Montgomery	1791	1831	
Monticello Academy	Monticello	1852	1881	
Moravia Institute	Moravia	1840	1869	Merged in high school in 1868
Moriah Academy	Moriah	1841	1851	Name changed to Sherman Academy in 1873
Mount Beacon Academy (Mount Beacon Academic Association)	Fishkill-on-Hudson	1890	1893	
Mount Pleasant Academy	Mount Pleasant (Sing Sing) (Ossining)	1827	Reporting	
Mount St Mary's Academy	Newburgh	1888	Reporting	
Munro Academy	Elbridge	1839	1855	Name changed to Munro Collegiate Institute in 1855
Munro Collegiate Institute	Elbridge	Changed	Reporting	Name changed from Munro Academy in 1855
Naples Academy	Naples	1859–62	1880	Merged in high school in 1881
Nassau Academy	Nassau	1858	1875	
Nazareth Academy	Rochester	1891	Reporting	
Newark Valley Academy	Newark Valley	1889	1891	Merged in high school in 1891
New Berlin Academy	New Berlin	1844	1881	Merged in high school in 1881
Newburgh Academy	Newburgh	1805	1852	Merged in high school in 1853. At first a common school
New Paltz Academy	New Paltz	1836	1885	Reincorporated in 1845
New York Central Academy	McGrawville	1864	1857	Merged in high school in 1868
New York Conference Seminary	Charlotteville	1850	1866	Name changed to New York Conference Seminary and Collegiate Institute in 1867
New York Conference Seminary and Collegiate Institute	Charlotteville	Changed	1875	Name changed from New York Conference Seminary in 1867

NAME	LOCATION	DATE OF INCOR-PORATION OR ADMISSION BY REGENTS	DATE LAST REPORTED UNDER NAME GIVEN	ADDITIONAL DATA
New York Military Academy	Cornwall - on - Hudson	1890–93	Reporting	
New York Preparatory School	New York	1894–96	1895	
North Granville Female Seminary	North Granville	1854	1862	Merged in North Granville Ladies' Seminary in 1862
North Granville Ladies' Seminary	North Granville	1862	1875	Name changed to North Granville Seminary in 1875
North Granville Seminary...	North Granville	Changed	1893	Name changed from North Granville Ladies' Seminary in 1875
North Hebron Institute	North Hebron..	1854	1868	
North Salem Academy	North Salem...	1790	1862	Sold in 1884
Northern New York Conference Seminary	Antwerp	Changed	1874	Name changed to Ives Seminary in 1874 (See Black River Conference Seminary)
Norwich Academy	Norwich	1843	1875	Merged in high school in 1873
Nunda Academy	Nunda	1868	1876	Merged in high school in 1876
Nunda Literary Institute	Nunda	1845	1862	
Oakwood Seminary	Union Springs..	Changed	Reporting	Name changed from Friends' Academy (Union Springs) in 1876
Ogdensburg Academy	Ogdensburg....	1839	1857	Merged in high school in 1857
Olean Academy Association..	Olean	1853	1853	Name changed to Olean Academy in 1853
Olean Academy	Olean	Changed	1868	Name changed from Olean Association in 1853; merged in high school in 1868
Oneida Conference Seminary.	Cazenovia	Changed	1870	Name changed from Seminary of the Genesee and Oneida Conferences in 1835 (see Central New York Conference Seminary)
Oneida Institute of Science and Industry	Whitesboro....	1829	1843	Closed in 1844
Oneida Seminary	Oneida	1857–59	1872	
Onondaga Academy	Onondaga Valley	1813	1890	Merged in high school in 1866
Ontario Female Seminary....	Canandaigua...	1828	1875	Sold in 1878
Orleans Academy	Orleans	1851	Did not report to Regents	
Otsego Academy	Cooperstown...	1796	1808	Burned in 1869
Ovid Academy	Ovid	1830	1863	Name changed to East Genesee Conference Seminary in 1864
Owego Academy	Owego	1828	1869	Merged in high school in 1869
Oxford Academy	Oxford	1794	1896	
Oyster Bay Academy	Oyster Bay....	1803	1835	Merged in common school in 1835
Packer Collegiate Institute...	Brooklyn	Changed	Reporting	Name changed from Brooklyn Female Seminary in 1853
Palmyra High School	Palmyra	1833	1837	Closed in 1848
Park Academy	Prohibition Pk., S. I.	1893	1894	
Parma Institute	Parma	1859	1875	
Peekskill Academy (Peekskill Military Academy)	Peekskill	1839	Reporting	
Penfield Seminary	Penfield	1857	1869	Sold to common school in 1871
Perry Academy	Perry	1854	1875	Merged in high school in 1874 (?)
Perry Center Institute	Perry Center...	1843	1845	
Peterboro Academy	Peterboro	1853	1864	Name changed to Evans Academy in 1864
Phipps Union Seminary	Albion	1840	1875	
Piermont Academy	Piermont	1842	Did not report to Regents	

NAME	LOCATION	DATE OF INCORPORATION OR ADMISSION BY REGENTS	DATE LAST REPORTED UNDER NAME GIVEN	ADDITIONAL DATA
Pike Seminary.............	Pike..........	Changed	Reporting	Name changed from Genesee Conference Seminary in 1859
Plattsburg Academy........	Plattsburg.....	1829	1870	Merged in high school in 1867
Polytechnic Institute of Brooklyn, Academic Department	Brooklyn......	Changed	Reporting	Name changed from Brooklyn Collegiate and Polytechnic Institute in 1889
Pompey Academy..........	Pompey.......	1811	1895	
Poughkeepsie Collegiate School	Poughkeepsie..	1839	1841	
Poughkeepsie Female Academy	Poughkeepsie..	1837	1865	
Pratt Institute High School..	Brooklyn......	1894	Reporting	
Prattsville Academy........	Prattsville.....	1850	1852	Merged in common school in 1859
Princetown Academy.......	Princetown....	1853	1854	
Prospect Academy.........	Prospect......	1851	1868	Burned in 1879
Randolph Academy Association	Randolph.....	1851	1865	Name changed to Chamberlain Institute in 1866
Raymond Collegiate Institute	Carmel........	1859	Did not report to Regents	
Red Creek Union Academy..	Red Creek.....	1846	1866	
Red Creek Union Seminary..	Red Creek.....	1867	1895	
Red Hook Academy........	Redhook.....	1829	1842	
Rensselaer Oswego Academy.	Mexico........	1833	1844	Name changed to Mexico Academy in 1845
Rensselaer Institute.........	Troy..........	1846	1852	Merged in Rensselaer Polytechnic Institute in 1861
Rensselaerville Academy.....	Rensselaerville.	1845	1896	
Rhinebeck Academy........	Rhinebeck.....	1841	1856	
Richburg Academy.........	Richburg......	1850	1866	Merged in high school in 1873 (?)
Richmondville Union Seminary and Female Collegiate Institute	Richmondville..	1854	Did not report to Regents	
Ridgebury Academy........	Minisink......	1840	1846	
Riga Academy.............	Riga..........	1840	1863	
Riverdale Institute........	Yonkers.......	1863	1866	Closed in 1871
Rochester Athenaeum and Mechanical Institute	Rochester.....	1892	1893	Also classified as a special school and reported in other years
Rochester Collegiate Institute No. 1	Rochester.....	Changed	1851	Name changed from Rochester High School No. 1 in 1838
Rochester Collegiate Institute No. 2	Rochester.....	1865	....	Did not report to Regents
Rochester Female Academy.	Rochester.....	1839	1889	
Rochester High School No. 1.	Rochester.....	1831	1837	Name changed to Rochester Collegiate Institute No. 1 in 1838
Rockland Academy.........	Nyack........	1878	Did not report to Regents	
Rockland County Female Institute	Nyack-on-Hudson	1855	1868	
Rogersville Union Seminary.	South Dansville	1853	1891	
Round Lake Academy.......	Round Lake...	1897	1898	
Round Lake Summer Institute	Round Lake...	1889–90	Reporting	Also classified as a special school
Rural Academy............	Montgomery...	1852	Not organized	
Rural Seminary............	East Pembroke.	1856	1891	
Rush Academy of the Methodist Episcopal Zion Conference	Twelfth Township	1864	Not organized	
Rushford Academy.........	Rushford......	1852	1868	Merged in high school in 1867
Rutgers Female Institute...	New York.....	1840	1866	Merged in Rutgers Female College in 1867
St Agnes Female Seminary..	Brooklyn......	1895	Reporting	
St Ann's Academic School...	Hornellsville...	1894	Reporting	
St Austin's School..........	West New Brighton	1886	Reporting	
St Bernard's Academy......	Cohoes........	1890	Reporting	
St Brigid Academic School of Manhattan	New York.....	1900	Reporting	

NAME	LOCATION	DATE OF INCORPORATION OR ADMISSION BY REGENTS	DATE LAST REPORTED UNDER NAME GIVEN	ADDITIONAL DATA
St Catharine's Academic School of New York	New York.....	1900	Reporting	
St Cecilia's Academic School of New York	New York.....	1900	Reporting	
St Elizabeth's Academy.....	Allegany......	1895	Reporting	
St Faith s School..........	Saratoga Spgs.	1893	Reporting	
St Francis Xavier's Academic School	Brooklyn......	1895	Reporting	
St Gabriel's Academy of Manhattan	New York.....	1898	Reporting	
St Gabriel's School.........	New York.....	1894	Reporting	
St James's Academy of Brooklyn	Brooklyn......	1897	Reporting	
St Joachim's Academic Institute	Watertown....	1894	1896	
St John's Academic School..	Greenbush.....	1895	1896	
St John's Academic School of Goshen	Goshen........	1900	Reported in 1901	
St John's Academic School of Schenectady	Schenectady...	1898	Reporting	
St John's Academy.........	Albany........	1896	Reporting	
St John's Academy of Rensselaer	Rensselaer.....	1895	Reporting	
St John's Catholic Academy.	Syracuse......	1888–90	Reporting	
St John's Military School....	Manlius......	1890	Reporting	
St Joseph's Academic School.	Batavia.......	1897	Reporting	
St Joseph's Academic School.	Binghamton...	1894	Reporting	
St Joseph's Academic School.	Brasher Falls...	1891–96	Reporting	
St Joseph's Academic School.	Mount Vernon.	1900	Reporting	
St Joseph's Academy........	Albany........	1892	Reporting	
St Joseph's Academy........	Flushing......	1892	Reporting	
St Joseph's Academy........	Troy..........	1896	Reporting	
St Joseph's Academy and Female Industrial School	Lockport......	1890	Reporting	
St Lawrence Academy.......	Potsdam......	1816	1869	Merged in " Potsdam Normal School " in 1868
St Lawrence Academy of Manhattan	New York.....	1898	Reporting	
St Margaret's School........	Buffalo........	1885	Reporting	
St Mary's Academic School..	Dunkirk.......	1894	Reporting	
St Mary's Academy.........	Ogdensburg....	1890	Reporting	
St Mary's Academy and Industrial Female School	Buffalo........	1895	Reporting	
St Mary's Academy of Hoosick Falls	Hoosick Falls..	1894	Reporting	
St Mary's Academy of Hudson	Hudson.......	1900	Reported in 1901	
St Mary's Academy of Little Falls	Little Falls....	1898	Reporting	
St Mary's Catholic Institute.	Amsterdam....	1883–87	Reporting	
St Patrick's Academy........	Catskill.......	1892	Reporting	
St Patrick's Academy of Troy.	Troy..........	1898	Reporting	
St Paul's Academy of Oswego.	Oswego.......	1899	Reporting	
St Peter's Academy.........	Rome.........	1890	Reporting	
St Peter's Academy.........	Troy..........	1889–91	Reporting	
St Philomena's Academic School	Brushton......	1894	Reporting	
St Stanislaus Academic School	Keeseville.....	1895	Reporting	
St Teresa's Ursuline Academy	New York.....	1896	Reporting	
St Thomas' Academic School of New York	New York.....	1900	Reporting	
St Thomas Aquinas Academy.	Brooklyn......	1896	Reporting	
Sag Harbor Institute........	Sag Harbor....	1848	1862	Merged in high school in 1862
Sand Lake Academy........	Sand Lake.....	1846	1856	Closed about 1874
Sans Souci Seminary........	Ballston.......	1864	1867	
Saugerties Academy........	Saugerties.....	1854	1864	
Sauquoit Academy..........	Sauquoit......	1849	1894	Merged in high school in 1894 (?)
Schenectady Academy......	Schenectady...	1793	1795	Merged in Union College in 1795
Schenectady Academy.......	Schenectady...	1818	1837	A revival of the Schenectady Academy of 1793 and used as a preparatory school of Union College

NAME	LOCATION	DATE OF INCOR-PORATION OR ADMISSION BY REGENTS	DATE LAST REPORTED UNDER NAME GIVEN	ADDITIONAL DATA
Schenectady Lyceum and Academy	Schenectady...	1839	1855	
Schenectady Young Ladies' Seminary	Schenectady...	1839	1839	Reported one year only
Schoharie Academy.........	Schoharie......	1839	1872	Merged in high school in 1873
Schuylerville Academy......	Schuylerville...	1840	1866	Merged in high school in 1878 (?)
Scientific and Military Academy of the Western District	Whitesboro....	1829	Did not report to Regents	
Seminary of the Genesee Conference	Cazenovia.....	1828	1829	Name changed to Seminary of the Genesee and Oneida Conferences in 1829
Seminary of the Genesee and Oneida Conferences	Cazenovia.....	Changed	1835	Name changed to Oneida Conference Seminary in 1835 (see Seminary of the Genesee Conference)
Seneca Falls Academy.......	Seneca Falls...	1839	1875	Merged in high school in 1867
Seward Female Seminary of Rochester	Rochester.....	1840	1853	
Seymour Smith Academy....	Pine Plains....	1874-79	1896	
Sherburne Union Academy...	Sherburne.....	1840	1856	Merged in high school in 1867
Sherman Academy..........	Moriah........	Changed	1892	Name changed to Sherman Collegiate Institute in 1892 (see Moriah Academy)
Sherman Collegiate Institute.	Moriah........	Changed	Reporting	Name changed from Sherman Academy in 1892
Sodus Academy............	Sodus.........	1855	Reporting	
Spencertown Academy......	Spencertown...	1847	1873	Merged in high school in 1870
Spring Mills Academy.......	Spring Mills...	1861	1864	
Springville Academy........	Springville.....	1830	1865	Name changed to " Griffith Academy " in 1866
S. S. Seward Institute.......	Florida........	1848	1895	
Stamford Seminary.........	Stamford......	1872	1877	
Starkey Seminary..........	Starkey.......	1848	Reporting	
Staten Island Academy......	New Brighton..	1885	Reporting	
Steuben Academy..........	Steuben.......	1828	1829	Closed in 1830
Stillwater Academy........	Stillwater.....	1839	1853	Reincorporated in 1848
Sullivan County Academy...	Bloomingburg..	1831	1832	
Susquehanna Seminary......	Binghamton...	1854	1860	
Syracuse Academy.........	Syracuse.....	1839	1844	
Temple Grove Seminary.....	Saratoga......	1869-79	Reporting	
Ticonderoga Academy.......	Ticonderoga...	1858	Did not report to Regents; merged in union free school in 1872	
Trinity School............	New York.....	1895	Reporting	
Troupsburg Academy.......	Troupsburg....	1861	1865	Burned about 1870
Troy Academy.............	Troy..........	1839	Reporting	
Troy Female Seminary......	Troy..........	1838	Reporting	
Trumansburg Academy.....	Trumansburg..	1854-58	1876	Merged in high school in 1879
Unadilla Academy..........	Unadilla......	1852	1893	Merged in high school in 1893 (?)
Union Academy............	Stone Arabia...	1795	1796	
Union Academy............	Granger.......	1855	Not organized	
Union Academy of Belleville.	Belleville......	Changed	Reporting	Name changed from Union Literary Society in 1859
Union Hall................	Jamaica.......	1792	1893	Intermittent in reports
Union Literary Society......	Belleville......	1830	1859	Name changed to Union Academy of Belleville in 1859
Union Village Academy......	Union Village..	1840	1868	Merged in high school in 1868
University Preparatory School	Ithaca........	1895	Did not report to Regents	
Ursuline Convent...........	Bedford Park..	1895	Reporting	
Ursuline Seminary..........	New Rochelle..	1898	Reporting	
Utica Academy.............	Utica.........	1814	1875	Merged in high school in 1853

NAME	LOCATION	DATE OF INCORPORATION OR ADMISSION BY REGENTS	DATE LAST REPORTED UNDER NAME GIVEN	ADDITIONAL DATA
Utica Catholic Academy	Utica	1891	Reporting	
Utica Female Academy	Utica	1839	Reporting	
Vernon Academy	Vernon	1839	1875	Merged in high school in 1865
Wagner Memorial Lutheran College	Rochester	1892	Reporting	
Wallkill Academy	Middletown	1842	1875	Merged in high school in 1868
Walton Academy	Walton	1854	1869	Merged in high school in 1868
Walworth Academy	Walworth	1843	Reporting	
Warnersville Union Seminary and Female Institute	Warnersville	1854	Did not report to Regents	
Warrensburg Academy	Warrensburg	1860	1888	Merged in high school in 1889 (?)
Warwick Institute	Warwick	1854	1895	Merged in high school in 1868
Washington Academy	Salem	1791	Reporting	Merged in high school in 1853
Washington Academy	Warwick	1811	Not organized	
Washington County Seminary and Collegiate Institute	Fort Edward	1854	1864	Name changed to Fort Edward Collegiate Institute in 1865
Waterford Academy	Waterford	1839	1847	Merged in high school in 1871 (?)
Waterloo Academy	Waterloo	1842	1846	Merged in high school in 1855
Watervliet Collegiate Institute (Watervliet Academy)	Watervliet	1898	Reporting	
Watkins Academy	Watkins	1860–62	1872	Merged in high school in 1863
Waverly Institute	Waverly	1858	1872	Merged in high school in 1872
Wayne County Collegiate Institute	Newark	1855	1860	Name changed to Wayne and Ontario Collegiate Institute in 1860
Wayne and Ontario Collegiate Institute	Newark	Changed	Did not report to Regents. Name changed from Wayne County Collegiate Institute in 1860	
Webster Academy	Webster	1850–58	1878	Merged in union school in 1876 (?)
Westerleigh Collegiate Institute	West New Brighton	1891–96	Reporting	
Westfield Academy	Westfield	1839	1873	Merged in high school in 1868
West Hebron Classical School	West Hebron	1855	Did not report to Regents. Merged in high school in 1858	
Westtown Academy	Westtown	1840	1847	
West Winfield Academy	West Winfield	1851	1883	Merged in high school in 1884
Whitehall Academy	Whitehall	1848	1864	Sold in 1867
White Plains Academy	White Plains	1830	Did not report to Regents	
Whitesboro Academy	Whitesboro	1813	1849	Made intermittent reports
Whitestown Seminary	Whitesboro	Changed	1885	Name changed from Clinton Seminary in 1844
Williamsville Academy	Williamsville	1867	1869	Merged in high school in 1875 (?)
Wilson Academy	Angelica	1881–86	1896	Merged in high school in 1897
Wilson Collegiate Institute	Wilson	1846	1869	Merged in high school in 1869
Windsor Academy	Windsor	1849	1870	Merged in high school in 1871
Woodhull Academy	Woodhull	1868	1884	Merged in high school in 1879
Worrall Hall	Peekskill	1890	1895	
Yates Academy	Yates	1842	1890	
Yates County Academy and Female Institute	Penn Yan	1830	1836	Closed about 1848
Yates Polytechnic Institute	Chittenango	1853	1872	Merged in high school in 1868

4

Explanations: 1 The word " Reporting " is used to indicate that the school was in operation at the close of the nineteenth century.

2 Names inclosed in quotations are for schools not in the University, or not recognized at the time by the Regents.

3 In case a school used two names simultaneously, or was located in more than one place or a place with two names, such duplicate names are inclosed in parentheses.

4 The date of incorporation or admission by Regents is not given for names included in the list that do not represent the entrance of a school but only a change in the name of an academy entered at some previous date.   Cross references with the dates of changes are given in such instances, and instead of the entrance date the word " Changed " is used.

5 Where two dates are given for the incorporation or admission by Regents, the first is the date of provisional and the second that of permanent admission.

Notes: 1 The above catalog does not contain the names of: (a) Academies incorporated by the Legislature or general law and not recognized by the Regents, (b) high schools and free academies, (c) a few special schools reported with academies after 1890, (d) a few foreign schools reporting to the Regents, (e) schools of college rank.

2 Certain academies continued to report under the same name a number of years after they had merged in high schools. This fact is shown in the table.

3 Some of the academies that were promoted to college rank continued to maintain an academic department of the college. In these cases, the academy is considered to have both merged in a college and to have been continued as an academy often with a change in name.

Continuity of Academies

The extent to which academies under the Regents may be regarded as permanent institutions is shown in table 17.   Some that were incorporated were not even organized, others continued only a few years; but a number lasted over a half century, and a few for over a hundred years.   A summary of these facts is contained in table 18.

TABLE 18

(Compiled from table 17)

Number of years that the several academies continued in operation under the Regents.

Note: The time from which an academy was incorporated or recognized by the Regents until it last reported as an academy is taken as the number of years that it was in operation under the Regents.   The fact that it might have been established a number of years before it entered the University, or have continued to report to the Regents as a high school after it ceased as an academy, is not considered here.   The large number in operation for less than ten years is partly accounted for by the fact that a large number included in the list were incorporated near the close of the nineteenth century.

Number in operation less than one year.....	33	From 55 to 60 years...............7	
From 1 to 5 years.....................	68	From 60 to 65 years..............11	
From 5 to 10 years.....................	74	From 65 to 70 years..............4	
From 10 to 15 years.....................	44	From 70 to 75 years..............6	
From 15 to 20 years.....................	35	From 75 to 80 years..............3	
From 20 to 25 years.....................	19	From 80 to 85 years..............6	
From 25 to 30 years.....................	30	From 85 to 90 years..............1	
From 30 to 35 years.....................	20	From 90 to 95 years..............2	
From 35 to 40 years.....................	20	From 95 to 100 years.............3	
From 40 to 45 years.....................	12	From 100 to 105 years............4	
From 45 to 50 years.....................	20	From 105 to 110 years............1	
From 50 to 55 years.....................	11		

Some academies that ceased reporting to the Regents as represented in table 17 were continued privately or in some form of public school or college, and in the latter form continued to report to the Regents, if the public school or college was in the University.   Others ceased to exist when they left the University.   The disposition that was made of the academies that ceased to report as academies to the Regents is summarized in the following table.

TABLE 19

Summary of academies in the University during the eighteenth and nineteenth centuries

Number of academies incorporated by the Regents..................	299
Number of academies incorporated by the Legislature and recognized by the Regents..	121
Number of academies incorporated under the general law and recognized by the Regents..	14
Number incorporated by the Legislature and not recognized by the Regents .... 86[d]	
Number incorporated under the general law and not recognized by the Regents... 5	

Whole number of academies that were at any time under the Regents	434[a]
Number that were in operation in 1900............................	137[b]
Number that were extinct in 1900................................	297
Number of those extinct that had merged in colleges........... 9	
Number of those extinct that had merged in normal schools..... 4	
Number of those extinct that had merged in high schools........ 98	
Number of those extinct that had merged in common schools.... 6	
Number of those extinct that had merged in private schools..... 5	
Number of those extinct not accounted for.................... 175[c]	

297

Conclusions

1 The close relation between the development of the academy system under the Regents and the state aid to those institutions is evidenced by the large numbers that were incorporated when the appropriations were increased, and by the advanced requirements of the State and Regents that accompanied increased appropriations.

2 The most important effect of state aid to academies was the strengthening of the authority of the Regents over them. The chief penalty that the Regents could inflict was to withhold from an academy that failed to observe the ordinances its share of the public funds. State aid also tended to keep tuition rates lower, and make possible institutions in localities that could not have otherwise maintained them.

3 In addition to state aid, academies received financial support from tuition fees, endowment funds, and in rare instances from taxation. The proportion of total revenue received from taxation

---

a Excluding all duplicate names included in table 17.
b Excluding three special schools, one foreign school, Washington Academy and Ten Broeck Free Academy which may be considered high schools and including three academies that were incorporated in 1900 and did not report until the following year.
c Some of these probably merged in high schools near the close of the nineteenth century.
d This number is somewhat indefinite, because it is not possible to decide in every case whether an institution incorporated by the Legislature should be called an " Academy."

decreased during the nineteenth century; in 1825 it was about 21 per cent and in 1900 only 0.6 per cent. Academies were compelled to depend more upon endowments and, in case of boarding schools, fees paid for board. Annual tuition fees increased from $9 in 1825 to $57 in 1900.

4 The first form of state aid was land grants and appropriations by special legislation to individual schools. The next step was temporary appropriations to all academies alike. Permanent funds affording a definite annual revenue for academies were the outgrowth of temporary aid, and began in 1813. Local taxation was tried in a number of instances in the earlier period, and was made general in 1872. But tax support of academies was not supported by public opinion, and after the measure was defeated in 1873 it was never again attempted.

5 It was the tax law of 1873 that determined in a large measure the relation of the high schools and the academies. Since the former were supported by taxation and the latter were not, their functions and management were to be thereafter different. This led to the development of a new type of academy which differed from the old-time academy in at least five respects: (a) The new type of academy could not depend upon the State for any considerable part of its revenue. (b) The number of boarding academies was greater than in previous years. (c) The tuition rate was about three times higher than in the old-time academy. (d) While the total number of academies was about the same, the same institutions were not found in the lists of the academies. Only 27.7 per cent of the academies reporting to the Regents in 1900 had been recognized in 1875. Even in cases where the same name was retained the nature of the institution often changed. (e) The new academies were largely denominational. In 1873 only 4 per cent of the academies were sectarian; in 1893 40 per cent of them were sectarian.

6 It was the intention of the Regents to make the academies permanent institutions, but this effort was only partly successful. A number of the academies recognized by the Regents reported as academies only a few years, and comparatively few were in operation more than fifty years. However, a number of those that ceased reporting as academies did not pass out of existence, but were changed into high schools, normal schools, and even into colleges.

CHAPTER V

Curriculums and Methods

Part I   Curriculums

The act of 1787, which fixed the legal status of academies and placed the Regents in control of them, did not prescribe a curriculum nor designate any subjects as required; but gave the trustees of each school power to adopt a course of study, subject to ratification and revision by the Regents.   The third article of the act specified that the Regents should visit academies, and " examine into the State and System of Education and Discipline therein."[1]   The trustees were given power by the same act to "make Bye-Laws for the Admission, Education, Government and Discipline of the Scholars or Sudents." [2]   In other words, they were granted the authority to prescribe courses of study for their respective academies.   That it was intended that the Regents should decide upon any part of the curriculum of an academy, or make their ruling apply to all schools, is evident from the following clause: " The Trustees thereof shall lay before the Regents of the said University, from Time to Time, the Plan or System proposed to be adopted, for the Education of the Students in each of the said Academies respectively, in order that the same may be revised and examined by the said Regents, and by them be altered or amended, or approved and confirmed, as they shall judge proper." [3]

To what extent the subject matter taught in academies should be uniform was left by the law of 1787 to the discretion of the Regents. Before 1817 there was no ordinance or law requiring academies to teach any particular subject; but each institution was left free to choose its own curriculum.   In that year the Regents passed a resolution requiring all academies that received state aid to teach the classics and other college entrance subjects.   It was decided to distribute the money appropriated by the State on the basis of the number of pupils in each academy pursuing subjects required for college entrance.[4]   The entrance requirements of colleges at that time, practically uniform for all, may be judged by those of Columbia, which were: Latin, the ability to read Virgil; Greek,

---

[1] Pratt, Annals of Public Education in the State of New York, in University Convocation Proceedings, 1875, p. 264.
[2] Ibid., p. 269.
[3] Loc. cit.
[4] Minutes of the Regents, April 7, 1817. Quoted by Hough, p. 446.

the Greek Testament; and arithmetic.[5]   All academies that hoped to share in the funds distributed by the Regents were then required to teach Latin, Greek and mathematics.   The Regents explained that by this act they sought to hold the academies to advanced studies, by rewarding those giving instruction in the more advanced subjects, and discouraging the practice of confining the instruction chiefly to elementary studies.   But opposition to using the funds for the encouragement of the classics at the expense of the advanced English studies arose.   The literature committee of the Senate showed in its report that, since the Regents paid nothing for pupils pursuing only the more practical studies, the tendency was for schools to discourage the study of such studies, or to charge an unfair rate of tuition for them.[6]   The Legislature modified the rule of the Regents in 1827 by a law which required that the appropriation of the State be distributed in proportion to the number of pupils enrolled in classical or advanced English studies, or in both.   This act is of special significance, because it was the only law ever passed prescribing subjects of study, and remained in force until virtually annulled by the acts passed in 1877 and 1880, a period of fifty years, establishing examinations.[7]   It occurred in the revised statutes in the following words: " Every such distribution shall be made in proportion to the number of pupils in each academy, who, for four months during the preceding year, shall have pursued therein, classical studies, or the higher branches of English education, or both.   No pupil in any such seminary, shall be deemed to have pursued classical studies, unless he shall have advanced at least, so far as to have read in Latin, the first book of Aeneid; nor to have pursued the higher branches of English education, unless he shall have advanced beyond such knowledge of arithmetic, (including vulgar and decimal fractions,) and of English grammar and geography, as is usually obtained in common schools."[8]   The Regents passed an ordinance the next year in accordance with this law, but defining more in detail what the admission requirements should be; which were one-half of Corderius, one-half of Historia Sacra, one-third of Viri Romae, and two books of Caesar's Commentaries for the classical department;[9] and for the higher English studies, the following was the requirement:

---

[5] Broome, A Historical and Critical Discussion of College Admission Requirements, p. 39, 41.
[6] Senate Jour., 1827, p. 226.
[7] Laws of 1877, chap. 425, par. 6; Laws of 1880, chap. 514, par. 1.
[8] 1 R. S. 458, par. 24, 25.
[9] Regents Instructions, 1834, p. 24.

No students, in any such academy, shall be considered scholars in the higher branches of English education, within the meaning of this ordinance, until they shall, on examination duly made, be found to have attained to such proficiency in the arts of reading and writing, and to have acquired such knowledge of the elementary rules or operations of arithmetic, commonly called notation, addition, subtraction, multiplication and division, as well in their compound as in their simple forms, and as well in vulgar and decimal fractions as in whole numbers, together with such knowledge of the parts of arithmetic commonly called reduction, practice, and the single rule of three direct, and simple interest, as is usually acquired in the medium or average grade of common schools in this State; and until they shall also, on such examination, be found to have studied so much English grammar as to be able to parse correctly any common prose sentence in the English language, and to render into good English the common examples of bad grammar given in Murray's or some other like grammatical exercises; and shall also have studied, in the ordinary way, some book or treatise in geography, equal in extent to the duodecimo edition of Morse's, Cumming's, Woodbridge's or Willett's geography, as now in ordinary use.

These acts established definite entrance requirements to studies of academic rank in all Regents academies. The law specified one subject in classical studies, and was silent in regard to the curriculum of the English department. The Regents supplemented the law by prescribing English composition and declamation for both classical and English students.[10] Neither the Legislature nor the Regents said anything about the content of the English course further than composition and declamation. The reason for this omission is explained by the Regents committee on distribution, which reported in 1829: that the difficulty of including all subjects that should be credited, and the desire to allow the Regents more freedom in deciding from time to time on various subjects had prevented any fixed curriculum being specified.[11] Practically all subjects offered, except Latin, Greek, elementary geography, elementary arithmetic, English grammar, and the entrance studies for the classical department, were accepted by the Regents as advanced English studies. The more important of these as enumerated in 1829 were: history (all kinds), geometry, algebra, botany, rhetoric, natural philosophy, moral philosophy, logic, chemistry, bookkeeping, surveying, mensuration, navigation, astronomy, trigonometry, constitution of United States and of New York, Grecian and Roman antiquities, advanced arithmetic, advanced geography, French, German, Spanish, and other modern languages.[12]

---

[10] Ordinance of the Regents, passed March 18, 1828. Regents Instructions, 1834, p. 24.
[11] Regents Instructions, 1834, p. 19.
[12] Loc. cit.

Although the law of 1827 remained in force until 1877, it never interfered with progress, because it fixed only a minimum requirement beyond which the Regents were free to act. By the law of 1877, the Regents were given authority to hold examinations in such studies " as in the judgment of the Regents, will furnish a suitable standard of graduation from the said academies and academic departments of union schools, and admission to the several colleges of the State."[13] This virtually placed the Regents in complete control of the curriculum of academies by establishing a new basis of authority. Heretofore, the only reward of a school for complying with the ordinances of the Regents was a share in the funds appropriated by the State, but now the advantage of offering instruction leading to a Regents diploma, which admitted the holder to the colleges of the State, was added for the benefit of those schools that followed the prescribed course. The power of the Regents over the curriculum was still further increased three years later by a law providing that one-fourth of the funds appropriated might be distributed on the basis of the number of students who had during the year received the Regents diploma.[14]

The following outline is a brief sketch of the subjects required for entrance to academic rank and the curriculums prescribed by laws and ordinances during various periods from 1817 to the close of the century.[15]

Required by law		Required by ordinance		YEAR
Higher English studies	Classical studies	Higher English studies	Classical studies	
There was no law concerning entrance or curriculum until 1827		Entrance		1817[16]
		None	None	
		Curriculum		
		None	Latin Greek Arithmetic	
Entrance		Entrance		
Elementary arithmetic		Reading	Latin equal to: One-half of Corderius	
Elementary geography	None	Writing		
English grammar		Elementary arithmetic	One-half of Historia Sacra	1828[17]
		Elementary geography	One-third of Viri Romae	
		English grammar		

[13] Laws of 1877, chap. 425, par. 6.
[14] Laws of 1880, chap. 514, par. 1.
[15] The law of 1827 required that an academy should offer either classical studies, higher English studies, or both; but no school was *required* to offer both.
[16] Minutes of the Regents, April 7, 1817.
[17] Laws of 1827, chap. 228. Regents Instructions, 1834, p. 24, 25.

Required by law		Required by ordinance		YEAR
Higher English studies	*Classical studies*	*Higher English studies*	*Classical studies*	
Curriculum			Two books of Caesar's Commentaries	
Indefinite	Virgil's Aeneid, first book	**Curriculum**		
		English composition and declamation	Virgil's Aeneid, first book / English composition and declamation	
		Entrance		
The same as in 1828		Same as in 1828	Same as for higher English studies and: Latin equivalent to the Latin reader / One-third of Cornelius Nepos / Two books of Caesar's Commentaries	1853[18]
		Curriculum		
		English composition and declamation / Reviews in spelling, reading and writing	The same as in higher English studies and Virgil's Aeneid, first book	
		Entrance		
The same as in 1828		Reading / Writing / Elementary arithmetic / Elementary geography / English grammar / Spelling	The same as in higher English studies	1864[19]
		Curriculum		
		The same as in 1853[20]	The same as in higher English studies and: First book of Virgil, or equivalent in Caesar, Sallust, or Cicero	
		Entrance		
The law of 1827 was virtually annulled by the acts of 1877 and 1880, and all control of the curriculum delegated to the Regents		The same as in 1864, except writing is omitted	The same as for higher English studies	1879[21]

Curriculum

(The same for both higher English and classical studies)

1 Algebra	Any four of the following (14–20)
2 Plane geometry	14 English literature
3 Physiology	15 Moral philosophy
4 Natural philosophy	16 Science of government
5 Rhetoric and English composition	17 General history
6 American and general history	18 Zoology
7 Chemistry	19 Plane trigonometry
	20 Drawing
Any four of the following (8–13)	The following may be substituted for Nos. 12 to 20 inclusive, or any of them:
8 Botany	
9 Physical geography	21 Latin
10 Physical astronomy	22 Greek
11 Mental philosophy	23 French
12 Bookkeeping	24 German
13 Geology	

[18] Regents Instructions, 1853, p. 62, 63.
[19] University Manual, 1864, p. 61–62.
[20] This part of the curriculum is not found in the University Manual of 1864, but is repeated in the Manuals of 1870 and 1882, and was a part of the information that the academies were required to report until 1869, after which time these subjects were probably no longer required. See Regents Rep'ts, 1864–69.
[21] Regents Rep't, 1879, p. x, xi.

Required by ordinance		YEAR
Higher English studies	Classical studies	
Entrance		
The same as in 1879	The same as in 1879	
Curriculum		
Algebra	Algebra	
American history	American history	1889[22]
Physical geography	Plane geometry	
Physiology	Caesar (Bks. 1-4)	
Rhetoric	Sallust's Cataline	
Plane geometry	Virgil's Aeneid,	
Any eight additional,[23]	(Bks. 1-6)	
four from each group		
	Virgil's Ecologues	
I	Cicero, 6 Orations	
Bookkeeping	Latin composition	
Civil government	Xenophon's Anab.	
English literature	(Bks. 1-3)	
History of England	Homer's Iliad, (Bks.	
History of Greece	1-3)	
History of Rome		
Mental philosophy		
Moral philosophy		
Political economy		
II		
Algebra (higher)		
Astronomy		
Botany		
Chemistry		
Drawing		
Geology		
Physics		
Plane trigonometry		
Solid geometry		
Zoology		

It will be seen from the preceding tabulation that the subjects required for entrance to academic standing remained practically unchanged throughout the entire period. There were some changes in the entrance studies for the classical subjects, and by 1864 all Latin requirements for entrance had disappeared. For higher English studies, geography, English grammar and arithmetic remained throughout, and spelling and writing fluctuated. Before 1879, the prescribed curriculum consisted chiefly of reviews in elementary subjects, English composition and declamation with the addition of the first book of Virgil's Aeneid or its equivalent in the classical studies. The subjects announced by the Regents in 1879 and 1889 as they appear in the tabulation above were not changed materially during the remainder of the century.[24]

Subjects Reported to Have Been Taught by Academies

The few subjects required by law and ordinances previous to 1879 were but a small portion of the curriculums in actual use in

[22] University Manual, 1889, p. 72.
[23] Some of the classical studies could be substituted for some of these under certain restrictions. See Regents Manual, 1889, p. 72.
[24] Cf. Regents Rep't, 1900, p. 1251-61.

academies. Most of the subjects taught were chosen freely by each school, and included a wide range of studies in nearly every field of knowledge. These subjects and the number of academies in which each was taught during the years indicated, are enumerated in table 20.

TABLE 20

The number of academies (including high schools) offering the various subjects for the years indicated.

This table shows how the logical divisions of physics were first taught as separate subjects, and were later combined with natural philosophy, which was called physics after 1880.

Note: These figures are complete up to 1870 except for the year 1795 for which the report contains the curriculums of only four of the nine academies reporting to the Regents that year. Beginning with 1870, the figures refer to the number of different kinds of textbooks (different autho £) used in the schools reporting. For some elementary subjects, a few schools probably used texts of two or more authors, and hence would be counted two or more times; for example, the number of schools teaching arithmetic in 1870 is given as 215, with the total number of schools reproting 184; so 31 schools are counted twice, or if some reported three or more authors used the number is less than 31. This discrepancy is probably confined to elementary subjects, and in no case is it large.

TABLE 20

SUBJECTS	1787	1795	1801	1805	1808	1812	1817	1826	1830	1835	1840	1845	1850	1855	1860	1865	1870	1875	1879	1885	1890	1895	1900
Number of schools (including high schools after 1850) reporting studies	2	9	5	10	19	21	25	33	58	66	127	153	166	164	192	202	182	216	b237	261	335	504	705
Algebra							19	19	47	66	127	153	163	163	187	196	196	222	247	367	295	477	702
Anatomy		2									2		50	117	156	144	127	182	215	258	308	e	e
Arithmetic	2			10	19	21	33	33	58	66	110	129	151	152	149	135	119	124	157	144	264	443	696
Astronomy	2	2	4	7	16	1		8	24	42	88	110	136	145	158	173	144	179	182	192	158	321	174
Bookkeeping					21				30	30	30	113	116	134	139	139	123	131	155	144	242	288	448
Botany									1	1	2		19	63	29	20	6		b172	156	206		373
Calculus		3			8		8	8	29	63	118	138	130	142	152	142	122	141			165	206	263
Chemistry				4	8			1	2	3	1		19	63	29		6					275	407
Chronology							11	1	51	66	127	153	163	163			12	9	3				
Composition									2	3	7	8	20	42		22	12	32	3				
Conic sections								1	5	7	22	29	34	64	75	67	33			52	141	313	484
Criticism, ele. of	2								51	63	114	143	150	152					84				
Declamation or elocution								2	8	15	22	22	15	5									
Drawing											4		2				13	16					
Ecclesiastical history									2	5	2	2	38	104	20	20							
Electricity												5											
Engineering		3	5								2	4	10	32	29		13		29				
Engineering, civil			10	8	19	21	22	33	58	66	127	153	163	163	186	194	211	228	259	243	282	399	683
English, elem.																			157		198	237	380
English literature																				42			
Ethics		2				2	5	5	4	7	10	11	25	44	48	42	37	30	125	121	100	133	294
Evidence of Christianity		2	1	1	4	3	a3	9	30	46	112	124	148	150	168	173	163	147	213	205	241	386	682
French			5		16	16	22		58	66	127	153	150	162	175	191	243	275	156	218	276	405	595
Geography									1	1	2		51	62	79	85	61	95	114	129	179	212	300
Geography, physical				7					1	3	36	44	11	51	60	50	41	30					
Geology										2	4	5	7	40									
Geometry, analytical								15	44	66	119	140	152	160	188	180	175	199	216	135	281	386	610
Geometry, descriptive											1									83	117	127	291
Geometry, plane									1	2	3	9	36	73	103	101	129	140	162	202	227	228	537
Geometry, solid		4		4	8	3		1	1	64	8	132	19	42	59	47	39	38					
German				9			24	33	58	4	111	7	152	137	159	149	153	162	170	157	168	139	239
Grecian antiquities	2				19	20		16	46	66	3	2	4										
Greek		4									127	106	104	132	117	109	81	114	149	118	215	253	412
Hebrew																							48
History of England	1									1	2							79	112	57	44	107	156
History of France																				64	113	184	329
History, general																							
History of Greece										1	2									80		231	409
History of literature																	13	16					
History of New York																			188	238	153	190	330
History of Rome																157	137	169			292	451	698
History of United States									29	45	96	93	86	130	164								

Subject																				
Hydrostatics, pneumatics																				
Hygiene																				
Italian																				
Logarithms																				1
Logic	641	33	26	238	32	31	51	54	99	32	5	2	4	16	1			8	4	
Leveling	622	38	315	124	207	203	101	181	117	15	18	4	9	58	33	11	5	15	9	2
Latin					70	5	47	46	15	9	42	46		5	1	24	20	10		4
Law (civics)									94	24	47	148	61	2	12	1				
Mapping									52	41	3	42	161							
Mathematics									49	14	47	42	1	39						
Mechanics		5							161	161	3	5		5						
Mensuration									33	30				12						
Meteorology						15	35	28	2	3				6	16				7	3
Mineralogy				47	21	39	22	21	89	32	5	3		1						
Music									81	41	30	23	18	18				16		
Mythology					46	10		28	38	15				6						
Natural history					39	15	35	21	26	10	21	20	18	18	1					
Natural theology					20	27	59	52	9	10	24	15	6	18						
Navigation					19	16	28	29	50	41	27	19	19	19						
Optics					12	27	39	31	34	22	20	17	14	14				1		1
Orthography, spelling						16	36	41	34	21	13	13	6							
Painting							30	46	46	26	9	4								
Penmanship, writing									91	13										
Perspective					182	164	16	14	163	163	153	127	66	66	2				10	2
Philosophy, mental, intellectual		51	192	188	9	10	6	94	4	6	14	9	6		33	23	21	18	4	4
Philosophy, moral		48	65	68	72	61	81	88	163	163	153	127	66							
Philosophy, natural				46	60	53	78	158	99	99	4	1	1	11	4	5	1	2	1	
Phonography				7	204	16	192	176	80	82	103	90	30	36	15	7	4	3	1	
Physics				215	6				158	158	72	73	33	66	46	16				1
Physiology											147	127	66							
Political economy		51	29	29	19	17	31	29	137	120	70	29	2	2						
Pronunciation			65	205	222	196	171	185	187	27	22	16	16	2						2
Reading					157	130	199	182	163	22	153	127	66	66	33	23	21	18	4	
Rhetoric	520	379	290	249	228	52	148	137	163	163	153	127	58	66	15	11	5	8		
Roman antiquities					55	55	57	73	125	97	105	101	16	58						
Spanish					3	5	11	15	17	18	14	14	16	9	2					
Stenography	63	25								10	4	4	9	6						
Surveying			918	855	855	968	89	31	123	103	100	90	51	51	38	11			1	
Teaching, principles of			85	85	79	85	103	108	80	12	18	18	12	8						
Technology					2				8	11	8	8	3	1						
Trigonometry	193	73	59	119	118	90	94	142	126	83	52	92	118	26	9	4			4	
Zoology	171	91	102	44	24	17	15	19	6	4	1	48	48	28	9					

a Called modern foreign language.
b For the year 1880.
c See anatomy.
d Economics.
e Reported with physiology after 1885.
f Afterward reported with anatomy and physiology.
g Includes leveling from '60.

The following subjects were also taught for a short time in a few schools as designated:

	1826	1830	1835	1840	1845	1850	1855	1870	1875
Acoustics		1							
Architecture			2	2	1	1			3
Biblical antiquities			1	3	2				
Biography			1						
Calisthenics					3	1			
Carpentry					4	14	35		1
Chemistry, agricultural				2	4	1			1
Commerce					2	1			
Conchology		1	1						
Dialing									
Domestic economy				1		1	4	4	3
Embroidery			3		2	1	2		
Extemporaneous speaking		1							
Fencing, military tactics		2							
Fluctions	1	1							
Geography, ancient, biblical						2			
Geography, political						1			
Gymnastics					4	31	94		
Hydraulics	1								
Magnetism	3				1	1			
Mental arithmetic			1	1		1			
Philosophy					3				
Phreno-mnemotechny		1	2	1	3	1			
Psychology									
Theology									
Topography									
Waxwork									
Nautical astronomy									
Statistics									

Note: The sources from which this table was compiled are indicated below.

For 1787: First Annual Report of Regents, M. S.
  " 1795: Senate Journal, 1796, p. 56, 57.
  " 1801: Senate Journal, 1802, p. 113-14.
  " 1805: Assembly Journal, 1806, p. 297.
  " 1808: Senate Journal, 1809, p. 177.
  " 1812: Assembly Journal, 1813, p. 496.
  " 1817: Senate Journal, 1818, table opposite p. 320.
  " 1826: Senate Journal, 1827, appendix B, table.
  " 1830: Senate Document, v. 1, no. 50, table opposite p. 6.
  " 1835: Regents Report, 1836, p. 31-36.
  " 1840: Regents Report, 1841, p. 69-70.
  " 1845: Regents Report, 1846, p. 119-28.
  " 1850: Regents Report, 1851, p. 172-85.
  " 1855: Regents Report, 1856, p. 287-305.
  " 1860: Regents Report, 1861, p. 222-72.
  " 1865: Regents Report, 1866, p. 262-73.
  " 1870: Regents Report, 1871, p. 395-414.
  " 1875: Regents Report, 1876, p. 439-52.
  " 1879: Regents Report, 1880, p. 453-63.
  " 1885: Regents Report, 1886, p. 676-82.
  " 1890: Regents Report, 1891, p. 1080-86.
  " 1895: Regents Report, 1900, p. 1251-61.
  " 1900: Regents Report, 1900, p. 1251-61.

The numbers in the column headed 1895 are too low, because the records do not include the textbooks used in only four or fewer schools for that year.

Note: A number of subjects occur in table 21 that are not included in the above table, because they were not taught in the years specified.

The curriculums of the first two incorporated academies present, at their beginning in 1787, some significant features. They furnish a clue to the relationship between the eighteenth century Latin grammar school and the academies of the following century. Erasmus Hall and Clinton Academy were both organized with two departments; each with separate subject matter, the Latin or classical and the English departments. The curriculums of the two academies were as follows: [25]

	Classical departments		English departments
Erasmus Hall	Clinton Academy	Erasmus Hall	Clinton Academy
Latin	Latin	English	English
Greek	Greek	language	grammar
Geography	Geography	Reading	Reading
History,	Mathematics	Writing	Writing
general	Natural	Arithmetic	Arithmetic
	philosophy	Bookkeeping	Accountantship
	Logic	Elocution	Public
		French	speaking
			French

It will be noticed that the classical department differed from the Latin grammar school of an early type only in containing more subject matter in its curriculum. In addition to the classics, the classical departments included mathematics and sciences, but it was not unlike the grammar schools of the second part of the eighteenth century in this respect, because many of those taught geography and mathematics. These academies were then organized to give the same kind of education that the grammar schools gave to those who desired it.

The English departments seem to have been planned to give an elementary and practical education to those who were not preparing for college. To this extent the academies departed from the grammar schools and were the harbingers of the many academies that followed.

In the absence of any legal necessity, the two curriculums are surprisingly similar. In the English departments, the same studies, except that they differed in terminology, were offered; and the principal subjects of the classical were the same. This was probably due to common conditions and needs, the same location and educational situation in which both were placed.

The curr.culums of Erasmus Hall and Clinton Academy served as models for the incorporated academies of the State for the first quarter of the nineteenth century. For a period of nearly forty

[25] Assembly Jour., 1788, p. 97.

years, only nine more subjects were taught in academies.[26] Of the fourteen subjects in the curriculums of the original academies, all except two (logic and elocution) continued through to the end of the nineteenth century; though writing was not reported after 1880,[27] and natural philosophy underwent changes in organization of subject matter and name.

The classical and the English departments organized in 1787 were recognized by law in 1827, made a part of the organization of the University by the Regents, and continued in 1889 under the names of Latin course and English course.[28]

The relation between the subjects that the academies claimed to teach and the studies prescribed by law and ordinance was very close and definite. The required subjects were always few, and were in such close agreement with the demands of the clientele of the academies that there would have been no reason to neglect them. The danger of principals and trustees making false reports for the sake of securing a larger share of the funds distributed by the Regents was mitigated by requiring every report to be accompanied by an affidavit declaring it to be correct. For these reasons, it is evident that very few academies failed to meet the requirements specifying a part of the curriculum.

Between 1817 and 1827, when the Regents required only college entrance subjects, Latin, Greek and arithmetic, only a few of the academies were of such an elementary grade that they were not able to offer those subjects, as is shown by table 21.

TABLE 21

This table shows what subjects were required by law and ordinance previous to 1865, the number of academies that claimed to teach those subjects, and the number that failed to meet the requirement.

Academies and high schools reporting	1817	1826	1830	1835	1840	1845	1850	1855	1860	1865
porting..................	25	33	58	66	127	153	166	165	192	212
Subjects taught										
Latin....................	24	33	58	64	117	148	161	161	181	194
Greek...................	24	33	....	....	....	....	....	....	....	....
Arithmetic..............	23	33	....	....	....	....	....	....	....	....
Composition.............	....	....	51	66	127	153	163	163	....	....
Declamation.............	....	....	51	63	114	143	150	152	....	....
Reading.................	....	....	....	....	....	....	....	163	182	187
Spelling................	....	....	....	....	....	....	....	163	....	....
Writing.................	....	....	....	....	....	....	....	163	....	....
Academies failing to meet requirements.............	2	0	7	0	0	0	3	13	11	35

[26] Cf. table 24.
[27] Cf. table 20.
[28] University Manual, 1889, p. 72.

From 1826 to 1853, composition was the only subject absolutely required of all academies, but Latin was required of all that offered a classical course; and declamation of all except female academies. Composition is then made the basis for estimating the number that failed to meet the requirements during that period. From 1853 to 1864, the required curriculum included reviews in reading, spelling and writing as well as the usual English composition; also declamation for all students. During these years a somewhat larger number of schools failed to report the required subjects; but this number was relatively small.

The close cooperation between the academies and the Regents, and the strong influence that the Regents exercised over the incorporated academies, are well illustrated by the facts presented in the above table.

Continuity and Development of Subjects as Illustrated by Table 20

The subjects that appear in table 20 may be divided, in respect to their continuity, into three groups: (1) Those that continue throughout after they first appear; for example, algebra, English, French and Latin; (2) subjects.that disappear for a period after they enter, but reappear later and continue to the close of the century; for example, composition, drawing, history of England, history of New York, stenography; (3) those that do not continue through to the close of the century, most of which enter about 1826, and drop out about 1875, occupying the middle section of the table. Of these there are two kinds: (a) Those that disappear in name, but whose subject matter is embodied by means of reorganization and reclassification into other studies that continue; for example, anatomy, electricity, natural philosophy.[29] (b) Subjects that seem to disappear entirely; for example, calculus, Hebrew, logic.

The gradual development and organization of a subject by a synthesis of its divisions, that were first taught as separate subjects, to form one comprehensive study, are illustrated in the case of physics. Mechanics was first taught in 1830, optics entered the curriculum in 1831, hydrostatics in 1832, magnetism in 1839, electricity in 1843, pneumatics in 1844, hydraulics in 1850, and statics and dynamics in 1852.[30] The number of academies teaching each of those sciences, except the last named, and the way they were included in natural philosophy after 1855, are represented by the table below. In 1857, the Regents first reported these sciences with natural philosophy,[31]

[29] Cf. table 22.
[30] Cf. table 23.
[31] Regents Rep't, 1857, p. 254-71.

and in 1879 the word "physics" was substituted for natural philosophy.

TABLE 22

(The data for this table were taken from table 20)

This table shows how the logical divisions of physics were first taught as separate subjects, and were later combined with natural philosophy, which was called physics after 1880.

SUBJECTS	YEARS										
	1830	1835	1840	1845	1850	1855	1860	1865	1870	1875	1880
Electricity............	...	...	...	5	38	104	...	...	...	...	...
Hydraulics............	...	...	...	...	1	...	...	...	...	...	...
Hydrostatics.........	...	...	2	5	32	99	...	...	...	...	...
Magnetism...........	...	...	...	4	31	94	...	...	...	...	...
Mechanics...........	1	...	3	5	32	89	...	...	...	...	...
Optics...............	...	...	4	9	26	91	...	...	...	...	...
Pneumatics with hy-drostatics..........	...	...	...	5	32	99	...	...	...	...	...
Natural philosophy...	46	66	127	147	158	158	176	192	168	204	...
Physics..............	...	...	...	...	...	...	...	...	...	...	215

Another science that passed through a similar process before reaching its present form, is physiology. Anatomy first appeared in 1837, physiology was reported in 1835 for the first time, and hygiene in 1849. They were all entered for a period under the term "anatomy," and later reported as physiology.[32] Civics was taught in the early part of the century as "Constitution of the United States, and the State of New York," and later as various forms of law.[33]

Table 21 indicates that, during the fifty years from 1825 to 1875, the curriculum was most crowded. A large number of subjects fall entirely or chiefly in this section of the table. The disappearance of some of these subjects that were merged into some comprehensive unit, by a process illustrated in table 22, is only apparent; but others, perhaps because there was no demand for them, were no longer taught in any form. Hebrew, Italian, meteorology and Spanish are types of the latter kind. Still others disappeared entirely from the academies, and were continued in colleges; for example, calculus, descriptive and analytical geometry, and engineering.

The following subjects, together with the twenty-nine appended

---

[32] Cf. table 20.

[33] Under the same title appeared, "Duties of Officers, Select and Revised Statutes, Conkling's Manual, Criminal and Mercantile Law, Blackstone," but except in the last case all seem to be what is now called civics. Regents, Rep'ts, 1836, p. 33; 1841, p. 70, 72.

to table 20, practically all appeared in the curriculum after 1825, and dropped out again before 1879.[34]

Calculus	Mechanics
Chronology	Mensuration
Conic sections	Meteorology
Criticism, elements of	Mineralogy
Declamation	Music
Ecclesiastical history	Mythology
Electricity	Natural history
Engineering	Natural theology
Engineering, civil	Navigation
Evidences of Christianity	Optics
Geometry, analytical	Orthography, spelling
Geometry, descriptive	Painting
Grecian antiquities	Penmanship
Hebrew	Perspective
History of literature	Philosophy, natural
Hydrostatics, and pneumatics	Phonography
Hygiene	Pronunciation
Italian	Reading
Leveling	Roman antiquities
Logarithms	Spanish
Mapping	Technology

About seventy subjects were discontinued before 1879, and only four were added after that time, so the curriculum of secondary schools contained something like sixty-six fewer subjects during the last quarter of the century than in previous years. In 1850, eighty subjects were taught in secondary schools as compared with thirty-four subjects in 1900. It is evident from these data that the curriculum was much more crowded at the middle of the century than at the close.

TABLE 23

This table shows when, according to Regents Reports, various subjects entered the curriculums of incorporated academies in the State of New York. The date corresponding to each group of subjects is placed at the head of the column to which it refers. The arrangement is chronological.

1787	Greek	*1796*
Arithmetic	History	Spelling,
Bookkeeping	Latin	orthography
Declamation,	Logic	*1797*
elocution	Mathematics	Arts and sciences
English	Natural philosophy	Astronomy
French	Reading	*1799*
Geography	Writing	Rhetoric
		1801
		Surveying

----
[34] Cf. table 20.

1804
Composition
English Literature
Moral philosophy

1817
Belles letters

1825
Algebra
Chemistry
Fluxions
Geometry,
   plane and solid
German
Higher mathematics
Logarithms
Philosophy
Spanish
Stewart on the mind
Trigonometry

1826
Chronology
Criticism,
   elements of
Drawing
Geography,
   ancient and biblical
Law (civics)
Mental arithmetic
Military tactics
Navigation
Painting
Philosophy,
   intellectual, (mental)

1827
Blair's lectures
Botany
Conic sections
Ethics
Evidences of Christianity
Evidences,
   Parley's
Fine needle-work
Globes
History of United States
Mapping
Mensuration
Metaphysics

Military education
Music
Philosophy of language
Roman antiquities
Watts on the mind

1828
Ath. Ex. (?)
Engineering
Fencing and military
   tactics
Geography,
   physical
Geometry,
   analytical
Geometry,
   descriptive
Grecian antiquities
Italian
Jewish antiquities
Mineralogy
Natural theology
Needle-work
Ornamental needle-work
Perspective
Philosophy,
   natural and chemical
Zoology

1829
Hebrew
History,
   Tytler's
Mythology
Natural and moral
   chemistry

1830
Architecture
Calculus
Dialing
Ecclesiastical history
Geography,
   political
Geology
Mechanics
Natural history
Technology
Theology
Topography

1831
Biography
History of New York
Intellectual arithmetic
Nautical astronomy
Optics
Philosophy,
   vegetable
Stenography
Statistics
Teaching,
   principles of
Technology,
   mathematical
Trigonometry,
   plane and spherical

1832
Biblical antiquities
Classical biography
Ev. religion
Elements of taste
Hydrostatics
Mnemonics
Music,
   vocal
Political economy

1833
Lectures on English
   language
Laws of interpretation

1834
Extemporaneous speaking
Leveling
Pronunciation

1835
Engineering,
   civil
Physiology

1836
Embroidery

1837
Anatomy
Dancing
Phrenology

1838
Chaldee
Meteorology

1839
Magnetism

1840
Conchology

1841
Calisthenics
Constitution,
  New York
Constitution,
  United States
History of England
History of France
Isoperimetry

1842
Chemistry,
  agricultural
1843

Electricity
Waxwork

1844
Archaeology
Carpentry
Pneumatics (with
  hydrostatics)
Phreno-mnemotechny

1846
Phonography

1847
Ornithology
Psychology

1849
Gymnastics
Hygiene

1850
Acoustics
Domestic economy

Hydraulics

1851
Draughting

1852
Statics and dynamics

1867
History of literature

1874
Commerce

1879
Physics

1881
History of Greece
History of Rome

1885
Geometry,
  solid

Summary of the number of subjects introduced into the academies in different years, as shown in the above table:

1787	14	1837	3
1796	1	1838	2
1797	2	1839	1
1799	1	1840	1
1801	1	1841	6
1802	1	1842	1
1804	2	1843	2
1817	1	1844	4
1825	11	1846	1
1826	10	1847	2
1827	17	1849	2
1828	16	1850	3
1829	4	1851	1
1830	11	1852	1
1831	11	1867	1
1832	8	1874	1
1833	2	1879	1
1834	3	1881	2
1835	2	1885	1
1836	1		

TABLE 24

This table contains the list of subjects, arranged alphabetically, found in the curriculums of the nineteenth century academies, with the date when each subject first appeared in the reports.

SUBJECT	YEAR	SUBJECT	YEAR
Acoustics	1850	English, elementary, grammar etc.	1787
Algebra	1825	English literature	1804
Archaeology	1844	Ethics	1827
Architecture	1830	Evidences of Christianity	1827
Anatomy	1837	Evidences, Parley's	1827
Arithmetic	1787	Ev. religion	1832
Arts and sciences	1797	Extemporaneous speaking	1834
Ath. Ex.(?)	1828	Fencing and military tactics	1828
Astronomy	1797	Fine needle-work	1827
Belles letters	1817	Fluxions	1825
Biblical antiquities	1832	French	1787
Biography	1831	Geography	1787
Blair's lectures	1827	Geography, ancient and biblical	1826
Bookkeeping (accountantship)	1787	Geography, physical	1828
Botany	1827	Geography, political	1830
Calculus	1830	Geology	1830
Calisthenics	1841	Geometry, analytical	1828
Carpentry	1844	Geometry, descriptive	1828
Chaldee	1838	Geometry, plane	1825
Chemistry	1825	Geometry, solid	1885
Chemistry, agricultural	1841–42	German	1825
Chronology	1826	Globes	1827
Classical biography	1832	Grecian antiquities	1828
Commerce	1874	Greek	1787
Composition	1804	Gymnastics	1849
Conchology	1840	Hebrew	1829
Conic sections	1827	Higher mathematics	1825
Constitution, New York	1841	History of England	1841
Constitution, United States	1841	History of France	1841
Criticism, elements of	1826	History, general	1787
Dancing	1837	History of Greece	1881
Declamation (elocution)	1787	History of literature	1867
Dialing	1830	History of New York	1831
Domestic economy	1850	History of Rome	1881
Drawing	1826	History, Tytler's	1829
Draughting	1851	History of United States	1827
Ecclesiastical history	1830	Hydraulics	1850
Electricity	1843	Hydrostatics	1832
Elements of taste	1832	Hydrostatics and pneumatics	1844
Embroidery	1836	Hygiene	1849
Engineering	1828	Intellectual arithmetic	1831
Engineering, civil	1835		

SUBJECT	YEAR	SUBJECT	YEAR
Isoperimetry	1841	Philosophy	1825
Italian	1828	Philosophy, intellectual (mental)	1826
Jewish antiquities	1828		
Latin	1787	Philosophy of language	1827
Law (civics)	1826	Philosophy, moral	1804
Laws of interpretation	1833	Philosophy, natural	1787
Lectures on English language	1833	Philosophy, natural and chemical	1828
Leveling	1834		
Logarithms	1825	Philosophy, vegetable	1831
Logic	1787	Phonography	1846
Magnetism	1839	Phrenology	1837
Mapping	1827	Phreno-mnemotechny	1844
Mathematics	1787	Physics	1879
Mechanics	1830	Physiology	1835
Mensuration	1827	Political economy	1832
Mental arithmetic	1826	Pronunciation	1834
Metaphysics	1827	Psychology	1847
Meteorology	1838	Reading	1787
Military education	1827	Rhetoric	1799
Military tactics	1826	Roman antiquities	1827
Mineralogy	1828	Spanish	1825
Mnemonics	1832	Statics and dynamics	1852
Music	1827	Stenography	1831
Music, vocal	1832	Stewart on the mind	1825
Mythology	1829	Statistics	1831
Natural history	1830	Surveying	1801
Natural and moral chemistry	1829	Teaching, principles of	1831
Natural theology	1828	Technology	1830
Nautical astronomy	1831	Technology, mathematical	1831
Navigation	1826	Theology	1830
Needle-work	1828	Topography	1830
Optics	1831	Trigonometry	1825
Orthography (spelling)	1796	Trigonometry, plane	1831
Ornamental needle-work	1828	Trigonometry, spherical	1831
Ornithology	1847	Watts on the mind	1827
Painting	1826	Waxwork	1843
Penmanship (writing)	1787	Zoology	1828
Perspective	1828		

Note: The sources from which tables 23 and 24 were compiled are referred to below:
For 1787, First Annual Report of Regents. M.S.
" 1796, Senate Journal, 1797, p. 85.
" 1797, Assembly Journal, 1798, p. 224.
" 1799, Assembly Journal, Nov. 1800, p. 27.
" 1801, Senate Journal, Jan. 1802, p. 114.
" 1802, Senate Journal, 1803, p. 117.
" 1804, Assembly Journal, 1805, p. 305.
" 1817, Senate Journal, 1818, table opposite p. 320.
" 1825, Senate Journal, 1826, table opposite p. 612.
" 1826, Senate Journal, 1827, appendix B, table.
" 1827, Senate Journal, 1828, appendix B, table.
" 1828, Senate Journal, 1829, p. 431.
" 1829, Legislative Document, 1830, v. 3, p. 216.
" 1830, Senate Document, 1831, v. 1, no. 50, table opposite p. 6.
" 1831, Senate Document, 1832, v. 2, no. 72, table opposite p. 14.
" 1832, Senate Document, 1833, v. 2, no. 70, table opposite p. 8.

For 1833, Senate Document, 1834, v. 2, no. 83, table opposite p. 12.
" 1834, Senate Document, 1835, v. 2, no. 70, p. 31–52.
" 1835, Regents Report, 1836, p. 31–36.
" 1836, Regents Report, 1837, p. 55–60.
" 1837, Regents Report, 1838, p. 54–60.
" 1838, Regents Report, 1839, p. 70–75.
" 1839, Regents Report, 1840, p. 71–77.
" 1840, Regents Report, 1841, p. 69–75.
" 1841, Senate Document, 1842, no. 55, p. 91–98.
" 1842, Regents Report, 1843, p. 106–13; also p. 122.
" 1843, Regents Report, 1844, p. 110–18.
" 1844, Regents Report, 1845, p. 118–27.
" 1846, Regents Report, 1847, p. 116–27.
" 1847, Regents Report, 1848, p. 132–42.
" 1849, Regents Report, 1850, p. 157–70.
" 1850, Regents Report, 1851, p. 172–85.
" 1851, Regents Report, 1852, p. 192–207.
" 1852, Regents Report, 1853, p. 187–202.
" 1867, Regents Report, 1868, p. 529–45.
" 1874, Regents Report, 1875, p. 487–505.
" 1879, Regents Report, 1880, p. 453–63.
" 1881, Regents Report, 1882, p. 256–59.
" 1885, Regents Report, 1886, p. 676–82.

It is remarkable that a large number of the subjects, nearly two-thirds, found in the curriculums of the incorporated academies of the State of New York during the nineteenth century, first appeared in the decade preceding 1835. Some of those that arose later were not new in substance, but only new names for what had been taught in a different form. Physics was only another name for natural philosophy, and the history of Greece and Rome had probably been presented during the middle of the century as Grecian and Roman antiquities, or as general history. The fact that eighty-three academies were teaching solid geometry the first year that it was reported, makes it certain that it had been taught some years previously with plane geometry, or with some other study. These facts represent a tendency to divide a general field of knowledge, once taught as one subject, into its logical factors, making a special subject of each; which is the reverse of the process indicated by table 22.

No attempt has been made in arranging the subjects in table 23 or in table 24 to discriminate between names of those that represent the same subject matter, and to exclude those entries that might refer to the same subject already included in the table under a slightly different title; because it is not safe to assume what titles are duplicates. For example, military tactics and military education probably refer to the same thing. Elements of criticism, elements of taste, and powers of interpretation are three that seem to differ only in name. Needle-work, fine needle-work, and ornamental needle-work might have been considered simply as needle-work.

Part II   Methods

Information about the methods of instruction in academies, during the greater part of the period when they were prominent, must be obtained from incidental remarks and fragmentary records, or inferred from what the records contain about subject matter, equipment, entrance requirements and the like. However, from 1835 to 1851, the Regents received annual reports on the "mode of instruction" practised in academies. These contain sufficient data to substantiate some conclusions in regard to the methods then practised; and since academies were a well-developed type of institution at that time, this information will afford an insight into the methods that prevailed during the whole century.

In 1834, academies were asked to report on "courses and modes of instruction,"[35] and were urged not to neglect to state to what extent they drilled their pupils in elementary studies and correct pronunciation. It was suggested that less time be spent on such classical studies as Grecian and Roman antiquities, and that more attention be paid to subjects of a more practical kind. In commenting upon the "mode of instruction," the Secretary of the Regents, Gideon Hawley, said that "the leading objects to be pursued in every institution for the education of youth, are now generally conceded to be, to make study voluntary and agreeable to the pupil; to cause it to act directly on his *understanding*, and through that medium on his *memory*; to cultivate his inventive faculty, by exercises in composition and other processes requiring him to originate thought; and to learn him to apply the knowledge and skill thus acquired to practical purposes most likely to occur to him in after life."[36] He requested that trustees and teachers of academies report what special means they were using to accomplish the aims he mentioned.

It is impossible to judge in every case, from the reports made in response to these instructions by local officials from year to year, when they were describing the practices that prevailed in their schools and when they were merely discussing theories. Even when they state that they teach by a certain method, we can not be sure that they followed it as closely as the report indicates. They were also probably influenced somewhat by the views expressed by Secretary Hawley, but this was not true of all of them, because they often expressed opinions in opposition to his ideas.

The number of schools from which remarks on method and other similar topics were contributed from year to year, the number of pages of print devoted to those reports, and the references to them in the Regents Reports are indicated in table 25.

---

[35] Regents Instructions, 1834, p. 5, 8, 9.
[36] Ibid., p. 9.

TABLE 25

Year for which report was made	Number of schools	Reference to Regents Reports dated	Year for which report was made	Number of schools	Reference to Regents Reports dated
1834	30	1835, p.33–69	1842	9	1843, p.137–51
1835	38	1836, p.54–74	1843	17	1844, p.135–56
1836	27	1837, p.78–103	1844	9	1845, p.141–54
1837	32	1838, p.79–105	1845	7	1846, p.140–50
1838	38	1839, p.100–31	1846	7	1847, p.140–54
1839	32	1840, p.86–105	1847	5	1848, p.156–71
1840	37	1841, p.84–114	1848	7	1849, p.155–69
1841	17	1842, p.122–50	1849	1	1850, p.185–201

By systematically scoring the frequency of typical expressions that point to certain aims, psychological views and practices, an estimate of the prevalence of methods then in use has been made. The conclusions reached by this process are sketched in the next few pages.

Aims and psychological theories. Among the aims expressed and implied, that of mental discipline, training the mind, is most conspicuous; and its psychological correlative, mental faculties, was the theory generally held. In more than one-third of the reports referred to in table 25, this aim and theory are evident by such expressions as: "teach children to reason; develop the intellect; train them to think; train the mental faculties; the memory is to retain, the understanding is to comprehend, and the reason to arrange and express ideas; [37] no matter what is taught, the important thing is how it is learned." An even clearer statement of this view is furnished by one of the contributors, who says: "The mind is composed of different faculties or powers; among the most important of these are memory and the reasoning faculties. The course of study pursued is designed to call into exercise and cultivate both these powers, as nearly as may be in an equal degree." [38]

Often where no such direct assertion appears, the formal discipline aim is evident in the general and special methods advocated.

The formation of correct habits, either of thinking or conduct, ranked next to mental discipline as an aim, but did not receive more than one-fifth of the attention given the latter. At one academy, diligence, promptness and accuracy were the principal ends of instruction; and as such virtues are usually considered a result of habit, they may be included in the aim of habit formation.

The acquisition of knowledge as the desideratum in all instruction was advanced almost as often as the habit-formation aim. The mind must be filled, the memory loaded with information, it was

---

[37] Regents Rep't, 1838, p. 84
[38] Ibid., p. 116.

claimed. In expressing this aim, one writer says: "The great purposes of education are to store the mind (which in this sense is but another name for memory) with useful knowledge; and in the process of doing so, to give increased energy, activity and precision to the mental faculties." [39]

That one of the principal ends to be sought in education is the development of character, was mentioned about twenty times in all the articles written. The importance of character was recognized by advocates of formal discipline, and thought to be one of the benefits that would flow from a "trained mind," but character as an aim does not often occur in the reports.

Harmonious development was not put forth as a definite, conscious aim, but three or four writers advocated a general training of all the powers and faculties, and the moral nature as well as the mind and body, it was claimed, should receive attention.

Fitting the young for social service was mentioned not more than twice in such a way that indicated the authors were conscious of what is now called the social aim. But preparation for citizenship, in the sense of being able to vote intelligently, was a common notion the first half of the nineteenth century.

Besides the general aims enumerated above, a number of specific aims, relating to some one subject, or to a limited range of thought and conduct, are scattered throughout the contributions. An adequate means of expression in language; thoroughness in learning subject matter; the ability to think for one's self; and to become a good grammarian, were all brought in as aims.

None of the writers discussed educational aims to determine which were the more valuable, but mentioned them only incidentally to preface a remark or explain some device or plan that they were supporting.

Drill. Each of the general aims mentioned has an appropriate method by which it is best realized. Since training the mind to think was the chief goal, drill was used above all other means for reaching that goal. Such expressions as: "regularly exercised in spelling, in pronunciation, and in all elementary studies," occur in over half of the articles. Much of the prominence of persistent drill as reported for elementary subjects was evidently due to the ordinance requiring all pupils of academic rank to be practised frequently in those studies. But after making allowance for such influence, the emphasis upon drill in all subjects was undoubtedly great. Those

---

[39] Regents Rep't, 1839, p. 126.

who wished to make good grammarians drilled their pupils for that purpose, and the need of persistent repetition of *paradigms* in Latin and Greek was frequently pointed out. For many teachers, this process seemed to be the panacea for all ignorance, whether the aim was training the mind, forming correct habits, or filling the head with useful knowledge.

Lectures. The reports indicate that there was scarcely an academy in which some sort of lecture method was not used. About half of the contributors refer directly to lectures. It seems that all subjects that did not lend themselves readily to drill work were taught by lectures, which were delivered by the principal of the academy, professional men living near, or any intelligent visitor. Lawyers, doctors, preachers, professors and others were welcomed by the authorities to " hold a course of lectures." The subjects embraced all departments of knowledge, but the sciences especially were taught by lectures. Lecture table experiments were generally used in natural philosophy, which included all the mathematical sciences, and in chemistry; but there is nothing said about individual experiments performed independently by the pupils. Illustrative materials and mechanical devices were used in lectures on astronomy, geography, geology and similar subjects. Cabinets of minerals were at times mentioned in this connection, and specimens of plant and animal life were to be found in many academies.

Moral and religious instruction was also often carried on by the lecture method. The virtues of a Christian and the duties of a citizen were explained in this way. The frequency of these lectures in the reports is about one-fourth that of the scientific lectures. As a rule they were made a part of the " opening exercises."

A third class of lectures were those intended to impart general knowledge, to help fill the mind. They dealt with all kinds of information not otherwise presented, such as meteors, current topics, law and inventions. The principles of teaching was a subject on which lectures were delivered.

Incentives. The means that were used to arouse pupils to activity, to furnish a motive for study, were referred to in about one out of every ten reports. The incentive most frequently discussed was emulation. There was a division of opinion on the advisability of encouraging pupils to try to excel one another, but those who maintained the affirmative side were in the majority by about five to one. Those on the negative side said that emulation caused enmity, distrust and other evils, and a higher motive should be found. One

man, probably having in mind the custom of "turning down," said
that emulation caused too much moving about and disturbance in
the schoolroom. Rewards, prizes and honors, which were often conferred at the close of public examinations, were a natural part of the
system in which emulation was a leading motive.

Other means, not so often mentioned, of inducing pupils to study
were that the studies should be made pleasant; some easy mode of
instruction should be employed. These notions were also opposed
by champions of effort, who quoted, "There is no royal road to
learning." The way in which interest could be aroused and the work
made pleasant was not definitely explained, except in connection with
some device or petty method.

Rote vs reason. One of the most frequently discussed points of
method was the question of the relative proportions of subject matter
that should be taught by rote and by an "appeal to the understanding." In no instance was either extreme favored, but five or six men
came very near claiming everything for the memory method. As a
rule it was thought that axioms, principles, definitions, theorems,
mathematical tables, rules of grammar, paradigms, important dates
and the like should be taught by rote. However, there is no evidence
of any considerable attention given to memorizing poetry and literary
gems.

The solution of problems in mathematics and scientific truths
were conceded to the rational method. The Secretary of the University condemned the practice of teaching mathematical theorems
by rote, and claimed that in general where "deductive processes and
association of thought" can be used, an appeal should be made to
the reason. But he granted that "ultimate principles, tables and
various other useful information" which had been once intelligently
understood should be fixed in the memory by drill.[40] Since the
memory, or rote, system of teaching is but one aspect of the process
of drill, the prevalence of the latter practice would indicate rote
work. But much that is expressed in the articles contained in the
Regents Reports on this topic, is probably a discussion on theory
rather than a statement of practice.

Analytical method. Another method that found a place in a few
academies was called the analytical, or inductive method; and the
word synthetic was once used in the same sense. It was said that
this process would cause pupils to think for themselves, and would
lead them to effective study by training them how to sift the prin-

---

[40] Regents Instructions, 1845, p. 85–90.

cipal thoughts from pages of print. Making outlines of articles read in the lesson assignments was one way in which this method was used to train pupils to analyze. In the recitation, pupils were asked to recite the main points in a topic, and in written work, abstracts of chapters or subjects were prepared. It appears that a decided departure was made by those who followed this method from the drill and memory exercises. It was mentioned, however, only by those teaching in strongest and most progressive academies of that period, notably those in Albany.

Questions. The custom of asking questions was probably an essential part of every recitation, but it is mentioned as a distinct method something like twenty times only in all the discussions. The questions printed at the close of lessons in textbooks, question books on certain subjects designed as an aid in reviews, and the interrogative method received attention. One academy announced a special interrogative system introduced by Mr Wood of Edinburgh.[41] Printed questions at the close of lessons were condemned by all who mentioned them, on the grounds that they produced a mechanical response; but the question books were considered by some a valuable help. The ordinary use of questions in recitations was disregarded, and the subject came up only when the contributors wished to advance some new plan or device, or criticise some scheme in vogue.

Devices, petty and special methods. That part of the Regents instructions to academies on what the reports should contain referred to remarks by trustees and teachers, and requested them to describe any unusual means of instruction that they had adopted.[42] Perhaps

---

[41] The details of this plan were not explained.

[42] The title under which all such remarks by school officials were printed was: " Schedule No. ——, containing extracts from the remarks submitted by the trustees of several academies in their reports to the Regents of the University, for the year —— on the peculiar modes of instruction adopted by them, and on other special matters relative to education." The latter clause was not added until 1841. See Regents Reports, 1835, p. 53; 1841, p. 84.

In regard to those reports, the Regents offered the following explanation: " The Regents, in this and in former reports, in presenting these general and sometimes speculative views of education, as well as occasionally criticisms or commendations of elementary books or modes of instruction, do not assume to assert as their own, the opinions expressed in the various returns selected for publication. These are given as the views of enlightened and experienced persons employed in actual instruction, which if even in some degree inaccurate, must have a share of utility in inviting the attention of those engaged in the same pursuits to the consideration of topics important to the best interests of society; but which, if correct, are of the highest and most direct utility, in diffusing valuable information among those, who being practically in the business of instruction, may make an immediate and beneficial application of the knowledge thus communicated. See Regents Rep't, 1836, p. 6.

it was due, in part, to this invitation to communicate "peculiar modes of instruction" that so many devices, special systems, and petty methods are found in the reports. One-third of all the articles on method contained some plan supposed by its author to be original, ingenious and capable of wonderful results. One taught all history of the world with the important dates by a mnemonic chart. Another claimed to have removed all drudgery from composition work by a skilful arrangement and organization of materials. A device by which pupils could readily exchange written work, and correct one another's mistakes, and another for the use of maps in history study, were among the contrivances advanced. One man advocated the doctrine of "strike while the iron is hot." A part of his argument was that grammar, writing, rules and elementary subjects in general should be learned early in life. He said such subjects were "well adapted to the powers of the unfolding intellect; for the power of imitation and remembrance, upon which these primary studies depend, is greatest previous to the full development of the reflective faculties." [43] Three or four writers approved the use of interlinear translations in the study of Latin, and one was sure that Latin could be learned correctly only by writing and speaking it. But some opposed any such easy plans for learning Latin, claiming that "knowledge must be dug out."

Apparatus and equipment. Some of the many devices referred to above were worked out by means of special apparatus. Schenectady had a building that "combined the advantages of a private house and a school." [44] The rooms were circular in shape with low

---

[43] Regents Rep't, 1843, p. 147.

[44] "Schenectady Lyceum and Academy. Peculiar efforts have been made to adapt the building to the purposes of instruction. In this last respect it differs, it is believed, from every other building for academic purposes in this State, or rather did thus differ when first erected, for it is reported that other buildings within the last two or three years have been erected on a plan copied after the Schenectady Lyceum. In the internal arrangements an attempt has been made to combine the advantages of private apartments with a public schoolroom. The seats are arranged around the circumferences of an octagonal room, and separated by partitions, so that each pupil who faces the wall occupies a seat where he is liable to no interruption, and he is at the same time immediately under the eye of and near his instructor, to whom he can apply at intervals for assistance, and for relaxation at the close of every hour. The desks of the instructors are so situated as to command a view of all the pupils in the room. In the principal room, which is on the first floor of the building, there are fifty of these recesses; but as these are arranged around the circumference of the room, there is space left (whenever the occasion require the accommodation of more than fifty pupils in the room,) for more than 20 additional pupils. The location of these additional pupils between the scholars in front of them and the instructor in their rear, does not prevent the latter from

partitions radiating from the center where the teacher sat.   The
pupils each occupied a separate compartment and could not see one
another, but the teacher at the center could see all the pupils.   In
another academy there was a device for ventilation, whereby the fresh
air was admitted through an opening under the stove and the impure
air escaped from a window.   Such an arrangement was then unusual;
most of the writers, who mentioned ventilation, said that the doors
and windows were used for that purpose.

The equipment used for general work included blackboards, maps,
globes and slates.   Blackboards were probably in common use in
practically all the academies.   Seventy-five of the articles contain
the word " blackboard," either incidentally or especially emphasizing
its value.   One writer said he did not approve of the use of a blackboard, because it would not secure independent work.

Illustrative materials in the form of specimens of stones, cabinets
of minerals, drawings, charts and diagrams were noticed, especially
in connection with lectures on science.

The rod and ferule, not much in evidence, are revealed in discussions of discipline, and seem to have been growing unpopular.   All
use of those aids to teaching was disclaimed by at least ten academies.
But the opponents of this tendency did not fail to express their
views.   One cited the " Biblical injunction " as an argument against
abolishing corporal punishment, and another said: "A state may
indeed exist without a king, and a church without a bishop, but not
a school without a strap or ferule."[45]   These kinds of expressions,

---

exercising the same inspection and care over them that he does over other
scholars, more especially as his seat and that of his assistants are on a platform raised several feet above the level of the floor.   Immediately in front
of the platform there are benches, on which the different classes take their
seats during their recitations and examinations; and for the purpose of
declamation they ascend the platform before alluded to.   This room is
lighted by seven large gothic windows, besides several small rose windows.
It is used by the principal of the academy and his assistants, who have
charge of the classical departments.   The lower story of the lyceum, in its
internal divisions, fitness and convenience, corresponds to the first story as
above described.   The second story is designed and used as a lecture room,
has a platform, desk, and a sufficient number of seats to accommodate 150
pupils.   It is for the accommodation of the pupils of the young ladies' academy of this city, as well as for those of the lyceum, during the delivery of
lectures.   The whole building has the form of an octagon, and the style of
architecture is modern Gothic.   The walls are of brick, rough cast, and in
imitation of dark granite, and are surrounded by a battlement of eight pin-
nacles.   The belfry rising from the centre of the roof terminates in a tur-
ret."   Senate Document, 1839, No. 56, p. 110-11.
    It is known that Lowville Academy used a similar building as early as
1825.   See Hough, Historical and Statistical Record, p. 655.
    [45] Regents Rep't, 1846, p. 143.

however, were rare. Those that had dispensed with the ferule gave a number of other incentives that they had tried; precept, lectures on morals, self-government (but in only one case in the sense of student self-government), Bible study, public censure and praise, deportment marks and written reports to parents, "merit system," suspension and expulsion. In one academy, each pupil who had been guilty of some offence was required to write an essay dealing with his fault and the corrective virtue.

Miscellaneous notions. A few scattered ideas of some significance, but not frequent enough to indicate any considerable practice, occur in the reports. Some of these are thrown together here.

One writer criticised the monitorial method, and another explained his practice of employing advanced students as assistants, but with these two exceptions, nothing was said about the monitorial system. Some attention was paid to teaching current events. "Ideas not words" was demanded, and the necessity of connecting ideas and words was recognized. "From the simple to the complex" was quoted by one man. Correlation of subjects, especially history and geography, was not uncommon. Reviews and examinations were a part of the instruction in a number of academies. What is now called vocational education found a few representatives among teachers previous to 1850, as is evidenced by the phrases: "Prepare the pupil for the business or vocation he is to follow when he leaves school; fit him for life; meet the needs of the pupil; make the instruction practical." An academy in Albany was provided with movable seats, apparently similar to chair-desks.

Daily routine. Enough information is furnished in the remarks printed by the Regents to afford an insight into the daily routine of the typical academy. The school day began at about 8 o'clock in the morning, and closed at 4 in the afternoon, with an intermission of an hour at noon. Reading from the Bible, prayer and sacred music, and at some academies lectures on a wide range of topics, constituted the program for the opening of the daily session.

Conclusions

1 Incorporated academies were legally free to act independently in selecting their curriculums. However, after 1817 those that received state aid were required to offer Latin, Greek and arithmetic; and after 1827 "higher English studies," which in general were sciences, history or modern language, could be offered instead of or in addition to Latin, Greek and arithmetic. This arrangement

5

left the academies practically free to teach any secondary subjects without losing cast. Complying with an act passed in 1877, the Regents established a system of advanced examinations, which placed a number of restrictions upon accredited curriculums, but did not prescribe one fixed curriculum for all Regents academies. This situation remained about the same until the close of the century. The requirements for entrance to studies of secondary rank were in general about what is now required for entrance to a high school, except that until after 1853 elementary Latin was required for entrance to the classical departments.

2 The freedom that academies were allowed in selecting curriculums was manifested in the wide range of subjects that they offered. Practically every school subject was at some period taught. During the middle of the nineteenth century when the number of subjects taught was greatest, eighty different studies appeared in the curriculums of the academies. Seventy-one subjects were introduced after 1825 and dropped before 1879. The decrease in the number of subjects is partly accounted for by a synthesis and reorganization of subject matter. Nearly all the academies met the few requirements of the law and ordinances.

3 The wide range of subject matter offered by academies from 1825 to 1875, and the elimination of many subjects indicate an experimental stage in secondary education. One of the chief services of the academies resulted from their freedom to experiment with various processes and plans, and in that way discover the ones most suited to secondary education in this country. The curriculums of our modern high schools were developed largely in academies.

4 Methods of instruction that prevailed in academies were determined for the most part by the faculty theory of psychology that was almost universally held at that time. Hence, one of the chief aims was to discipline the mind and to store the memory with useful facts. Emulation was the principal incentive, but attempts to appeal to a sense of duty and an intellectual interest were not lacking. Drill and memory work were emphasized; but some of the better schools sought to develop an ability to acquire thought from the printed page by the method of logical analysis. The lecture method, especially in connection with experimental and objective work in sciences, was used in nearly all academies. Moral and religious instruction was a prominent feature, and was carried on in connection with the "opening exercises."

CHAPTER VI

Educating Teachers for the Common Schools

How to provide an adequate supply of competent teachers for elementary rural and small village schools is a vital problem, which nearly all the states of our country are now attempting to solve. Until the middle of the nineteenth century, only a few of the states made any effort to train teachers. During the second half of that century, normal schools were generally established to meet the demand for competent teachers. Near the close of the century educational leaders began to realize that practically all the teachers prepared in normal schools were being employed by city systems or secondary schools. The small elementary schools were receiving no direct benefit from the normal schools. This condition led to the problem of establishing schools for the preparation of all common school teachers.

At the present time, when the educators of the Nation are being confronted with this question, it is interesting to notice that New York since 1835 has supplied a large portion of her common school teachers by means of teacher-training departments in secondary schools. This was early made possible by the excellent system of academies that characterized the State, and the close supervision that the Regents exercised over them. New York is entitled to the claim of being the first state of this country to provide a system for training common school teachers. How these departments were established, organized and administered; and the results they achieved are sketched on the following pages.

The early academies made no special provisions or definite attempts to train teachers for schools of a lower grade. Such teachers were at first only a by-product. This instruction was incidental, unorganized, unrecognized by the State, and even unnoticed for a time by the academy officials themselves. With the organization of a permanent system of public elementary schools and the resulting demand for competent teachers, the academies were recognized as a means of meeting the growing need. With the intention of promoting the instruction of common school teachers by that means the state aid to academies was increased. Later the Regents organized teachers departments in certain selected academies; until 1849 a great many plans for educating teachers were advanced, and a number of them were tried. Since the reorganization of teachers departments in secondary schools in 1849, they have been continued upon a definite, well-organized and essentially permanent plan. The standards of scholarship in them have gradually advanced, and the State has increased its appropriations to them as the system of public education has grown. As the public high schools developed, the teachers departments were gradually shifted to them. The transfer of all such work in secondary schools from the Regents to the Superintendent of Public Instruction in 1889 may be considered the close of teachers departments in academies, because very few of them found it profitable to continue such courses after that time. An account of the period previous to 1849, when the teacher-training work was yet in the experimental stage, will first be given; then the second period of that work, when they were more permanently organized, from 1849 to 1889, will be described.

First Period—Previous to 1849

The instruction of common school teachers was considered one of the functions of the early academies in all parts of this country. The trustees of Franklin's Academy at Philadelphia, in their application to the common council of the city for aid, stated as one of the purposes of their institution:

That a number of the poorer sort will hereby be qualified to act as schoolmasters in the country, to teach children reading, writing, arithmetic and the grammar of their mother tongue, and being of good morals and known character may be recommended from the Academy to the country schools for that purpose — the country suffering very much at present for want of good schoolmasters, and obliged frequently to employ in their schools vicious imported servants or concealed Papists, who by their bad examples and instructions often deprave the morals or corrupt the principles of the children under their care.[1]

" The Moravian School, established in 1807 at Nazareth Hall, had a ' special department for the preparation of teachers.' " [2] James B. Carter of Massachusetts opened a seminary for general instruction, and for particular instruction of teachers.[3] " The Rev. Joseph Emerson's seminary for young women at Byfield and Saugus, 1818–24, received about one thousand pupils, many of them young school teachers." [4] " In 1830 a seminary was opened by Samuel R. Hall, in connection with the Phillips Academy at Andover, for the special preparation of teachers for the common schools." [5] Chancellor Brown draws a general conclusion from the evidence; " But there was a great lack of even moderately well-prepared teachers, and the academies were looked to for an improvement in this respect." [5]

---

[1] Wickersham, History of Education in Pennsylvania, p. 60.
[2] Com'r of Ed. Rep't, 1898–9, v. 2, p. 2327.
[3] Ibid., p. 2264.
[4] Brown, The Making of our Middle Schools, p. 254.
[5] Ibid., p. 250.

The academies in the State of New York followed this general rule. Soon after the establishment of a state system of common schools in 1813, the fact that the State should prepare teachers for those schools was recognized. In his message to the Legislature in 1818, Governor DeWitt Clinton suggested that young men be trained for teachers of common schools in Lancasterian seminaries.[6] The Regents, three years later, were confident that the academies furnished the means for preparing teachers. In their report to the Legislature they say:

This consideration (aid to poor but talented boys) probably induced the legislature to confine the annual distributions of a great part of the literature fund, to academies; and when it is recollected, that it is to those seminaries that we must look for a supply of teachers for the common schools, as well as for the occasional rescue of humble merit from obscurity, the regents trust they shall be enabled to extend the sphere of their bounty, and of their usefulness, and by such additional appropriations to the literature fund, as the finances and resources of the state may warrant.[7]

These two views, the one that teachers should be prepared in institutions especially established for that purpose, the other that the existing academies should be used for that purpose, are typical of all the plans that were proposed or tried during the first half of the nineteenth century. DeWitt Clinton, during the ten years that he was Governor, consistently advocated the first in connection with his unsuccessful attempt to organize all elementary schools on the monitorial plan.[8] In 1826 he recommended a seminary for the instruction of teachers, and in 1827 and 1828 he advocated a school in each county for the training of teachers.[9] But he failed to foresee that the monitorial system of instruction was fundamentally wrong. The Legislature did not act upon his plans. The use of academies for that purpose, the second type of plan mentioned above, was to be tried first.

Both the Regents and the Legislature were convinced that common school teachers should be trained in the incorporated academies. The former in 1823 declared that the distribution of state aid to the academies insured " a supply of competent teachers for the common schools." [10] A report of the literature committee of the Senate in 1826, refers to the lack of competent teachers, the unwillingness

---

[6] Senate Jour., 1818, p. 6.
[7] Senate Jour., 1821, p. 269.
[8] Senate Jour., 1819, p. 9. Charles Z. Lincoln, Messages from the Governors, v. 2, p. 1048; v. 3, p. 61, 116, 159, 212.
[9] Ibid., v. 3, p. 116, 159, 212.
[10] Senate Jour., 1823, p. 379.

of trustees to employ good teachers, and after pointing out that 7642 teachers are needed in the State, continues: "It is obvious that the suggestion of the Governor in his message,[11] respecting the establishment of an institution expressly for the purpose of educating teachers, will not answer the exigencies of the case. It is entitled to much weight, however, as a means, in conjunction with others, to effect the object. But in the view which the committee have taken, our great reliance for nurseries of teachers must be placed on our colleges and academies." [12]   The same year the Regents said in their annual report, "Teachers for common schools must generally be derived from the academies." [13]   The literature committee of the Senate the next year reported: "The colleges and academies ought to furnish competent instructors, and indeed to them we are indebted, but chiefly to the academies, for the qualified instructors now employed. . . . Competent teachers of common schools, must be provided; the academies of the State furnish the means of making that provision." [14]

The Legislatu.e preferred this latter plan to the one proposed by the Governor, and passed an act in 1827 entitled, "An act to provide permanent funds for the annual appropriation to Common Schools, to increase the Literature Fund, and to promote the education of teachers." [15]   But the law does not specify even in a general way how the education of teachers was to be effected. It increased the literature fund by $150,000, which meant an increased annual appropriation to the incorporated academies. By this means alone, the legislators apparently thought, the education of teachers would be brought about. In every other respect the law left the work of training teachers where it had been before. It was still voluntary, incidental and unorganized.

The law of 1827 was not considered adequate and final by those most interested. The discussions on the subject for the next seven years brought out many schemes for the preparation of teachers, some proposing institutions especially for that purpose, and others depending on the academies. The Regents and State Superintendent held the latter view. The former, the year after the law was passed, reported: "The Legislature having, by the act before referred to, declared it to be one of their primary objects, in the great increase

---

[11] Messages from the Governors, v. 3, p. 116.
[12] Senate Jour., 1826, p. 158.
[13] Senate Jour., 1826, p. 612.
[14] Senate Jour., 1827, p. 226.
[15] Session Acts, 1827, chap. 228.

made by them of the literature fund, ' *to promote the education of teachers,*' the Regents, equally with the Legislature, being impressed with a sense of the paramount importance of this great object, will always cooperate in promoting its speedy accomplishment." [16] The superintendent's report the same year was in harmony with this view. He said that the law would tend to multiply the number of well-qualified teachers, and " encourage the academies in becoming nurseries of teachers." [17] The next year he was of the opinion that the " higher seminaries of learning" had to be depended upon to supply the 8600 district schools with teachers.[18] His reports for the following two years show even more emphatically that he favored the plan of using the academies for educating teachers.[19]

But the advocates of special schools for teachers also agitated their cause during this period. Governor DeWitt Clinton in his message to the Legislature in 1828 advised a monitorial school for each county for the instruction of teachers.[20] Two years later a petition to the Legislature from the city of Rochester stated that the academies were not meeting the demand for teachers, and outlined an elaborate system of state schools for them.[21] The petitioners based their conclusions upon the information received from a circular letter sent to the town inspectors of Monroe county. Their plan briefly stated was: (1) The establishment of three state " seminaries " for the education of teachers. These were to be conducted on the manual labor plan, with one hundred young men not less than 15 years of age, chosen by competitive examination, enrolled in each. (2) After completing the three years of the normal, the young men should return to their home counties and conduct a central model town school, where the teachers of the town would learn by observation. There was to be one of the latter model schools in each town. The states of Prussia and Saxony are mentioned in this connection as examples of efficiency in training teachers. In addition to pointing out the advantages of the proposed system, the petition summed up the arguments against grafting teachers departments upon academies. First, only a *very small* number of common school teachers were being educated in academies; from one-fourth to one-tenth, probably an average of one-eighth. Second, the acad-

---

[16] Senate Jour., 1828, appendix B, p. 4.
[17] Assembly Jour., 1828, appendix C, p. 6.
[18] Ibid., 1829, p. 387.
[19] Legislative Documents, 1830, v. 1, no. 30, p. 8, 9, 10. Assembly Documents, 1831, v. 1, no. 15, p. 11, 12.
[20] Messages from the Governors, v. 3, p. 212.
[21] Legislative Documents, 1830, v. 4, no. 387.

emies were not primarily concerned with such work, and probably never paid any attention to the "art of teaching." Third, the expense of attending an academy prevented many teachers from profiting by study in them.[22]

The Superintendent of Common Schools and the Regents present the opposite view, which in outline is: (1) The teachers prepared by the State would probably not be paid a sufficient amount by the trustees of the districts to justify their remaining in the profession. They would engage in other work, and the purpose of the State would be defeated. To prevent this the State would have to provide for their employment, which would be contrary to a democratic form of government.[23] (2) The State had contributed so much to building up the academies, and was appropriating a large amount to them annually, so that she might expect some service from them such as educating teachers.[24] (3) State normals would have to be paid for by a state tax, and people object even to a local tax for common schools.[24] (4) The academies have failed to supply enough teachers, because the schools would not pay an adequate salary.[24] (5) The academies had the advantage of well-equipped laboratories and libraries, and teachers attending them would be benefited by all the courses taught in those institutions.[25] (6) The number and location of the academies were such as to make them adequate for the purpose.[25]

The Regents show that for two years before 1834 some of the academies had maintained teachers departments in which professional instruction was given,[26] and that year they express the advantages of a law authorizing them to make an additional appropriation to such schools.[27]

These views were probably held by the majority of the leading men of the times. Governor Marcy called the attention of the Legislature to the necessity of training teachers, and added that "upon them (academies) we must, in a great measure, depend for competent teachers of the common schools."[28] The judgment of the Governor and educational leaders found expression in the law of

---

[22] Op. cit., passim.

[23] Legislative Documents, 1830, v. 1, no. 31, p. 9, 10; Senate Document, 1832, v. 2, no. 72, p. 10, 11.

[24] Assembly Documents, 1831, v. 1, no. 15, p. 11, 12.

[25] Senate Documents, 1832, v. 2, no. 72, p. 11, 12.

[26] Regents Rep't, 1832, p. 11; ibid., 1833, p. 7.

[27] Regents Rep't, 1834, p. 9.

[28] Senate Jour., 1834, p. 14.

1834, under which was organized the first state system for preparing common school teachers in this country. It reads:

An act concerning the Literature fund. § 1 The revenue of the literature fund now in the treasury, and the excess of the annual revenue of said fund hereafter to be paid into the treasury, over the sum of twelve thousand dollars, or portions thereof, may be distributed by the regents of the university, if they shall deem it expedient, to the academies subject to their visitation, or a portion of them, to be expended as hereinafter mentioned.

§ 2 The trustees of academies to which any distribution of money shall be made by virtue of this act, shall cause the same to be expended in educating teachers of common schools, in such manner and under such regulations as said regents shall prescribe.[29]

The organization, supervision and all details of the contemplated instruction was left to the Regents, who appointed a committee May 22, 1834,[30] to draw up a plan, which was later adopted by them,[30] for establishing teachers departments in academies. This plan, although used in its unmodified form but six years, is of importance because of its completeness and judicious provisions, many of which are embodied in state laws, concerning the education of teachers, at the present time. Its principal features were:

1 Eight academies, one in each senatorial district, were designated as recipients of the special grant upon the conditions of the law. It was explained that if the available sum of $10,040 were distributed to all academies, the amount to each would be too small to be effective. It was also thought best to reserve $6000 of the sum for emergencies.

2 Four thousand dollars was apportioned to the selected academies the first year for the purchase of library books and laboratory apparatus. The part of this sum given to each institution was to be determined by its relative needs; the average to each would have been $500, but for the first year it was less.

3 Four hundred dollars was granted annually to each of the eight academies, irrespective of the number of pupil-teachers enrolled or the length of term they were taught, which was to reimburse the academies for the extra expense incurred on account of the teachers departments. It was the judgment of the Regents that if the appropriations were made the same to each, " without reference to the number of pupils in training," the emphasis would be placed upon high scholarship rather than upon numbers of pupils.

---

[29] Session Acts, 1834, chap. 241.
[30] Regents Rep't, 1835, p. 81.

4 The requirements for admission to the teachers departments
were the same as those for admission to the higher English
departments.[31]

5 The curriculum prescribed for the proposed departments was:
English, writing and drawing, arithmetic and bookkeeping, geography
and general history, history of the United States, geometry, trigonometry, mensuration and surveying, natural philosophy and the
elements of astronomy, chemistry and mineralogy, constitution of
the United States and of the State of New York, parts of the laws
of the State of New York, moral and intellectual philosophy, the
principles of teaching.

6 The time required for the completion of the course was fixed
at three years of eight months each, because the prescribed course
could not be learned in less time.

7 Each of the selected schools should possess a library valued at
not less than $200.

8 The laboratory apparatus recommended for each department
was valued at $309, and included the following: orrery, numerical
frame and geometrical solids, globes, movable planisphere, tide
dial, optical apparatus, mechanical powers, hydrostatic apparatus,
pneumatic apparatus, chemical apparatus, 100 specimens of mineralogy, electrical machine, instruments to teach surveying, map of
the United States, map of the State of New York, atlas, telescope,
quadrant.

9 Complete annual reports were required on the organization,
equipment, support and progress of the departments.

10 Those graduated from the course were to receive a diploma,

----

[31] Regents Instructions, 1834, p. 24.   This requirement was as follows:
"No students, in any such academy, shall be considered scholars in the
higher branches of English education, within the meaning of this ordinance,
until they shall, on examination duly made, be found to have attained to
such proficiency in the arts of reading and writing, and to have acquired
such knowledge of the elementary rules or operations of arithmetic, commonly called notation, addition, subtraction, multiplication and division, as
well in their compound as in their simple forms, and as well in vulgar and
decimal fractions as in whole numbers, together with such knowledge of the
parts of arithmetic commonly called reduction, practice, the single rule of
three direct, and simple interest, as is usually acquired in the medium or
average grade of common schools in this State; and until they shall also,
on such examination, be found to have studied so much of English grammar
as to be able to parse correctly any common prose sentence in the English
language, and to render into good English the common examples of bad
grammar given in Murray's or some other like grammatical exercises; and
shall also have studied, in the ordinary way, some book or treatise in geography, equal in extent to the duodecimo edition of Morse's, Cumming's,
Woodbridge's or Willett's geography, as now in ordinary use."

which, however, would not be a license to teach, from the officers of the various academies.

11 The eight academies selected were: first district, Erasmus Hall; second district, Montgomery; third district, Kinderhook; fourth district, St Lawrence; fifth district, Fairfield; sixth district, Oxford; seventh district, Canandaigua; eighth district, Middlebury. Equipment, endowment and location were the determining factors in making the selection.

12 The rate of tuition for the course was left to the discretion of the local authorities, but the Regents recommended that it be made as low as possible.

13 It was advised that the pupils of the teachers departments be required to sign a statement that they intended to teach in the common schools of New York.[32] This practice was discontinued the next year.[33]

The principal criticisms of the above system were: (1) The pay of common school teachers was too low to justify a young man spending three years in preparation for such work.[34] (2) The Regents requirements were far in excess of the legal requirements for a certificate to teach.[35] (3) An unwillingness of students to assume the serious obligation, which they thought was included in the pledge to teach.[36] It is evident that the graduates from these departments would have been far better qualified than the teachers then demanded by the common schools. However, before the work was well developed a change in administration was made, which probably did more to hinder the teacher-training work and to lead finally to its temporary abandonment than all causes combined.

Governor Marcy recommended this change in the following words:

The members of this Board [the Regents] are widely dispersed over the State, serve without compensation, and rarely assemble in the recess of the Legislature. There would seem to be a fitness in giving the immediate direction and supervision of these departments to the same authority that superintends the common schools.[37]

The Legislature passed a law in accordance with the Governor's views:

The institutions in which departments for the instruction of common school teachers are or shall be established, shall make to the Superintendent

---

[32] Regents Rep't, 1835, p. 81–110.
[33] Regents Rep't, 1836, p. 15.
[34] Regents Rep't, 1836, p. 94, 99.
[35] Ibid., p. 101.
[36] Ibid., p. 98.
[37] Governor's Message, Assembly Jour., 1837, p. 14.

of Common Schools an annual report of the conditions of those departments, in such form and containing such information as he may from time to time require; and in respect to the organization and management of the departments and the course of study therein, the said institutions shall be governed by such direction as he may prescribe; and he may direct the said forms and direction to be printed by the state printer.[38]

During the six years from the enactment of this law until all appropriations for teacher-training in academies ceased, the system was administered by three superintendents, Dix, Spencer and Young, whose principal position was Secretary of State; and who did not follow the same policy in the work. The first thought it would be better to decrease the number of departments to four;[39] the second organized teachers departments in sixteen academies instead of eight;[40] and the third thought that the departments were doing no special good, and ordered the appropriations to them to cease.[41] Under such a vacilliating management, not always free from political influence, the best results could not be expected. Governor Seward said: "The office of inspector of common schools is unhappily always involved in the political organization of parties;"[42] and previously Governor Marcy had expressed a regret that the common schools were not in charge of an officer especially qualified for that duty.[43] It is evident that the transfer of the teachers departments to the common school system in 1837 was not a wise arrangement, as it subjected them to the control of a political office that was frequently changing in personnel and policy.

Soon after the eight teachers departments were established under the law of 1834, there was a widespread demand for an extension of the system or of some other additional means of preparing teachers. Governor Marcy said in his message to the Legislature in 1838 that some further provision should be made for supplying teachers for the common schools.[44] The same year the Assembly committee on colleges, academies and common schools reported that the system instituted by the Regents in 1835 should at once be sufficiently extended to adapt it to the "exigences of the State."[45] The Superintendent the previous year favored founding eight more teachers departments in academies and meeting the expense from the revenue

---

[38] Session Acts, 1837, chap. 241, par. 4.
[39] Sup't Rep'ts, 1837, p. 22; 1838, p. 22; 1839, p. 26; 1840, p. 17; 1841, p. 21.
[40] Ibid., 1842, p. 16.
[41] Rep't of Sup't, 1844, p. 30.
[42] Messages from the Governors, v. 3, p. 743.
[43] Assembly Jour., 1837, p. 14.
[44] Messages from the Governors, v. 3, p. 652.
[45] Assembly Documents, 1838, no. 236, p. 8.

of the United States deposit fund,[46] which had just been received and devoted by the Legislature to the cause of education. He repeated the same opinion the next year.[47]

It was probably in response to these demands that the Legislature included a clause in the appropriation act of 1838, which required every academy that received the sum of $700 or more a year to maintain a department " for the instruction of common school teachers," under the direction of the Regents.[48] This provision was indefinite, inadequate and in every way ill advised, whether considered theoretically or judged by its results. The Superintendent pointed out its chief defects the year after it was enacted: (1) It did not consider local needs. It might leave a large section of the country unsupplied with a means of instructing teachers, and multiply normal departments in some other section. (2) It did not require the academies that it affected to supply themselves with suitable equipment for the departments. (3) There would be no inducement for such schools to lower tuition rates to pupil-teachers, or to make the departments efficient in any way. (4) Since the appropriations for academies were made equal in each senatorial district regardless of population or the number of pupils in attendance, and the amount paid to the academies of some districts per pupil was much more than that paid to academies in other districts, where the population was greater and hence a larger number of academies to share the sum received by the district, the tendency would be to provide the departments where the population was sparsest and where the smallest number of teachers were needed. (5) The nature of the work done by some schools affected by the law was inconsistent with the education of teachers, such as the grammar school of Columbia College, and the New York Deaf and Dumb Institution.[49] It appears from the reports of the academies required by this law to train teachers that the measure was practically useless.[50] Professor Potter of Union College, who was appointed by the Superintendent in 1840 as a special inspector of teacher-training departments, after enumerating the defects of the law of 1838 said: " It is apprehended that these conditions will be found, in practice, to have rendered the law nearly inoperative."[51]

---

[46] Sup't Rep't, 1837, p. 22, 23.
[47] Ibid., 1838, p. 21, 22.
[48] Session Acts, 1838, chap. 237, par. 9.
[49] Sup't Rep't, 1839, p. 24, 25, 26.
[50] — See p. 146-7.
[51] Sup't Rep't, 1841, p. 118.

Although each year the Superintendents recommended changes in the system introduced by the Regents in 1835,[52] the plan was not modified until 1841.[53] The provision of 1838 did not in any way interfere with the original eight departments. The report of Professor Potter, mentioned above, and that of Mr Little,[54] appointed for the same purpose as was Professor Potter, advised that the number of departments be increased.

The Regents in 1841 provided for a larger number of teachers departments, a change that had been urged from a number of sources for several years.[55] They directed that $300 should be paid annually to each of sixteen designated academies, which should maintain a teachers department, as specified by the Superintendent, for six months of the year between May 15th and December 15th.[56]

The requirements adopted by the Superintendent in accordance with this resolution were: (1) Every pupil-teacher enrolled in the departments was required to sign a pledge that he would teach at least one year after leaving the department. (2) No male pupil was admitted to the departments under the age of 18, and no female under the age of 16. (3) Practice teaching was made a required part of the course of study for all those enrolled in the departments; and this teaching was to be done in the presence of the preceptor of the academy and under his direction.[57] But two years after the reorganization of these departments, they were deprived of all state aid and state control. Those responsible for the change were considering the introduction of some system of state normal schools, which had been advocated by DeWitt Clinton, and which were then attracting much attention. Some were in favor of state normals in addition to the academical departments then in operation,[58] and others thought it would be best to invest all the resources of the State, donated to training teachers, in one or more state normals.[59]

The suggestion of Governor Marcy in 1838, that county normal schools might be better than academical departments,[60] was not acted upon; and Governor Seward the next year said: " We seem at last to have ascertained the only practicable manner of

---

[52] Sup't Rep'ts, 1837, p. 22; 1838, p. 21; 1839, p. 26; 1840, p. 17.

[53] Sup't Rep't, 1841, p. 124–27.

[54] Sup't Rep't, 1838, p. 18.

[55] Cf. p. 140–1 ante.

[56] Assembly Documents, 1842, v. 1, no. 12, p. 16.

[57] Hough, Historical and Statistical Record, p. 548, 549.

[58] Sup't Rep't, 1841, p. 120, 121. Potter's Report, ibid., p. 21, 22.

[59] Messages from the Governors, v. 3, p. 652; Assembly Documents, 1844, no. 135, p. 72; Sup't Rep't, 1843, p. 17, 18.

[60] Messages from the Governors, v. 3, p. 652.

introducing normal schools into our country. It is by engrafting that system upon our academies."[61] But sentiment in favor of state normals grew rapidly. The Superintendent (Spencer) advised that " one model school or more " be established in central parts of the State ;[62] in voicing this, he followed the view of Professor Potter that a state normal be maintained at Albany.[63] The report of a committee of the assembly, 1844, declared that the previous efforts of the State to train teachers had been a failure,[64] and outlined a plan, that was afterward embodied in law, for a normal school at Albany. One of the most pronounced opponents of the academical teachers departments, and an ardent advocate of state normals, was Colonel Young, then State Superintendent of Common Schools. He pointed out in what particulars the former had failed: (1) The academies not appointed and having received no extra reward from the State for educating teachers, had done as much in that respect as those especially designated and paid for that service. (2) The pledge required of pupil-teachers was unfair and useless. (3) " The great cause of failure seems to be that the bounty of the State is diffused over too great a surface."[65] He advanced a plan for four normals in different parts of the State, and a central normal at Albany.[65]

The teachers institutes, that were begun at this period, were welcomed as a cheap and quick means of training instructors for the common schools; and no doubt were influential in bringing about the abandonment of teachers departments in academies. One of the first institutes was held in September 1842, by F. B. Sprague, deputy superintendent in Fulton county, at Kingsboro.[66] It was conducted for eight weeks in both fall and spring, and was called a " private normal " by the founder.[66] This form of instruction became popular, and in the year that the state normal was established, nineteen institutes were conducted, at which 1448 pupil-teachers received instruction.[67] The next year it was announced that " comparatively a brief period of time only is necessary to supply every school district in the State with competent and well-qualified teachers."[68]

---

[61] Ibid., p. 743.
[62] Sup't Rep't, 1841, p. 21, 22.
[63] Ibid., p. 121.
[64] Assembly Documents, 1844, no. 135, v. 5, *passim.*
[65] Sup't Rep't, 1843, p. 17, 18.
[66] Sup't Rep't, 1844, p. 289 ff.
[67] New York District School Journal, v. 6, April 1845, p. 12.
[68] Ibid., v. 5, March 1845, p. 323.

The law establishing the state normal (1844) withdrew the state aid from teachers departments provided in 1834,[69] and they were no longer officially maintained. The regulation of 1838 was still effective, but was disregarded by the Superintendent, and no reports concerning the education of teachers were any longer received from academies, until the reestablishment of teacher-training courses in them under the law of 1849.

Results Accomplished by Teachers Departments during the First Period (1787–1849)

Prior to 1835, while the instruction of teachers was incidental and unorganized, no records were kept of the number of teachers that the academies prepared; but by indirect information it appears that a number of teachers was sent out by academies even during the early years. (1) The academies were practically the only schools, except the two or three colleges, at which an education beyond the mere rudiments could be obtained. (2) The instruction of common school teachers was considered one of the functions of academies at that time. (3) An expression of the Regents in 1821 indicates that it had been customary to consider the secondary schools the proper place for the instruction of teachers. They say: "When it is recollected, that it is to these seminaries that we must look for a supply of teachers for the common schools, . . . the Regents trust they shall be enabled to extend the sphere of their bounty, and their usefulness, and by such additional appropriations to the literature fund, as the finances and resources of the state may warrant." [71] (4) After some of the academies had organized teachers departments, the number of pupil-teachers was reported in a few instances. The Regents reported that St Lawrence and Canandaigua had organized such departments, and that the former during the year 1831 had sent out eighty teachers.[72] The total number of pupils in such departments that year was reported to be one hundred five,[73] and the next year forty-five[74] were reported. The following table[75] contains the statistics for the first year of the eight academical departments organized under the law of 1834.

---

[69] Session Acts, 1844, chap. 311.
[71] Senate Jour., 1820–21, p. 269.
[72] Regents Rep't, 1832, p. 11.
[73] Sup't Rep't, 1834, p. 18.
[74] Loc. cit.
[75] Compiled from Regents Rep't, 1836, p. 92 ff.

TABLE 26

| ACADEMY | RECEIVED FROM REGENTS FOR | | TUITION RATE | PUPIL-TEACHERS ENROLLED |
	Support	Equipment		
Canandaigua............	$400	$164	$4 a quarter.................	22
Erasmus Hall...........	400	184	1.25 a quarter...............	None
Fairfield................	400	309	3 a year....................	None
Kinderhook.............	400	286	Not reported................	None
Middlebury..............	None	285	6 to $16 a year.............	5
Montgomery.............	None	309	Not reported................	None
Oxford.................	400	282	3 for 15 weeks..............	25
St Lawrence.............	400	177	12 a year...................	66
Totals..............	$2 400	$1 996		118

In addition to those trained in the eight departments under the requirements of the Regents, table 27 shows those instructed independently. Even some of the schools in which the Regents had established a regular department reported pupil-teachers who for certain reasons did not enter the prescribed course. Such pupils are included in this table.

TABLE 27.[76]

ACADEMY	PUPIL-TEACHERS ENROLLED	REMARKS
Bridgewater.............	20	"Most of the common school teachers in this vicinity have attended the academy."
Delaware...............	20	
Gouverneur High School...	46	Of the students of the last seven years hundreds have probably become teachers. These were not in the regular department.
Kinderhook.............	15	
Lansingburg...	Not reported	"Many students . . . stay but one quarter; some fitting for teachers."
Lowville.....	Not reported	"Several of the students of the last year are now engaged in schools."
Monroe................	30	
Onondaga..............	12	
Oxford.................	18	"From 15 to 20 whose names are not included in the list of students in the department."
Palmyra High School.....	Not reported	"We are endeavoring . . . to follow the recommendation . . . for instruction of teachers."
Rensselaer..............	25	
Springville..............	5	Free tuition was granted to one pupil of each town in the county.
St Lawrence............	34	"Upwards of a hundred have left our school the past year to engage in teaching."
Union.................	45	"Between forty and fifty teachers have been instructed in this academy the past year."
Washington.............	Not reported [77]	
Yates Co. and Female S...	25	"Some 20 or 30 have been prepared for common school teachers the past year."
Total...............	295	

[76] Compiled from Regents Rep't, 1836, p. 54 ff.
[77] Washington Academy, Salem, sent an outline of their two year teachers course, and said, "There has been a teachers class in the academy during the fall term for the last four years." Regents Rep't, 1836, p. 61, 62.

These records give a total of 413 pupil-teachers that were instructed by the academies during the year 1835, 118 in the regular departments and 295 in addition. But this list does not include those in schools that did not report the number of such students in numbers; so the real total would be greater than 413. Detailed statistics, showing the results of teachers departments until they were discontinued in 1844, are presented in table 28.

The operation of the departments required by the law of 1838 is indicated by the results reported the year after its enactment. Twelve academies the preceding year had received more than $700 from the State, and so were required by law to maintain teachers departments. Two of these twelve, Canandaigua and Oxford, were among the eight that had been selected by the Regents in 1835, consequently they were receiving state aid for their teacher-training departments, and were not affected by the later law. Two more, the Grammar School of Columbia College, and the Grammar School of the University of the City of New York, did not report on that particular; no notice of their delinquency was taken at the time, and they were evidently regarded as special institutions exempt from the law. Four (Albany Female Academy, Troy Female Seminary, Erasmus Hall, and Amenia) reported that they had instructed no pupil-teachers, and some of them had not organized any definite departments for that purpose. Ithaca made no report. The remaining three, Genesee Wesleyan, Cortland and Rochester Collegiate Institute reported a total of 148 pupils in the required departments.[78] The corresponding totals for this class of academies for the next three years were 272, 281 and 163 respectively.

TABLE 28

ACADEMY	1835	1836	1837	1838	1839	1840	1841	1842	1843
Albany Female...........	....	....	....	....	L 0	L 0	L x	L x	L
Amenia.................	....	....	....	....	L 0	L 112	L x	L 25	L
Canandaigua...........	A 22	A 26	A 36	A 44	L A 50	A 61	A 46	A 50	A
Cortland..............	....	....	....	....	L 28	L 30	A 12	A 50	A
Delaware..............	....	....	....	....	....	....	A 19	A 16	A

[78] Sup't Rep't, 1840, p. 90.

ACADEMY	1835	1836	1837	1838	1839	1840	1841	1842	1843
Erasmus Hall	A 0	....	....	....	L 0	....	....	....	.....
Fairfield	A 0	A 0	A 16	A 53	A 38	A 56	A 13	A 23	A
Franklin, Prattsburg	....	....	....	....	....	....	A 14	A 33	A
Fredonia	....	....	....	....	....	....	A 31	A 45	A
Genesee Wesleyan	....	....	....	....	L 110	L 282	L 164	L 78	L
Grammar School of Columbia College	....	....	....	....	L x	L x	L 0	L 0	L
Grammar School of Univ. of City of N. Y.	....	....	....	....	L x	L x	L 0	L 0	L
Hamilton	....	....	....	....	....	....	A 26	A 34	A
Hobart Hall Inst	....	....	....	....	....	....	A 25	A 39	A
Ithaca	....	....	....	....	L x	....	A x	A 19	A
Kinderhook	A 0	A 1	A 20	A 25	A 23	A 29	A 18	A 29	A
Middlebury	A 5	A x	A 34	A 41	A 10	A 32	A 35	A 30	A
Montgomery	A 0	A 21	A 12	A 31	A 127	A 132	A 25	A 21	A
Oxford	A 25	A 28	A 35	A 35	L A 44	L A 75	L 57	L 48	.....
Rensselaer Oswego	....	....	....	....	....	....	A x	A 20	A
Rochester Col. Inst	....	....	....	....	L 10	....	A x	A 18	A
Rutgers Female Inst	....	....	....	....	....	L x	L 3	L 12	L
St Lawrence	A 66	A 102	A 96	A 106	A 104	A 107	A 52	A 73	A
Troy Female Seminary	....	....	....	....	L 0	L 0	L 57	L 0	.....•
Washington	....	A 36	A 35	A 39	A 20	A 26	A x	A 18	A
Number required	8	8	8	8	18	16	24	24	22
Number reporting	8	7	8	8	15	13	18	23	0
Pupils enrolled	118	224	284	374	564	942	597	681	0

Explanation: The numbers opposite the name of an academy represent the number of pupil-teachers enrolled for the several years. The letter L means that the academy was required by the law of 1838 to maintain a teachers department; and A shows that the school was appointed by the Regents and received a special appropriation for training teachers. The fact that an academy failed to report is designated by the letter x. In some instances an academy was affected by the law of 1838, and was also appointed by the Regents; for example Canandaigua and Oxford in 1839.

In addition to the number of pupil-teachers included in table 28,[79] there were some instructed in an irregular way, and not reported as belonging to the departments. The number of this kind the first year was 295. The numbers for the following years are as follows: 1836, Kinderhook, 14; Fairfield, 40; 1840, Rochester Collegiate Institute, 15; 1842, Gilbertville, 70, Hamilton 13, Livingston County High School, 35. By adding these amounts to the totals in table 28, the numbers in the following summary are obtained. The cost of the departments to the State is also included.

TABLE 29

YEAR	PUPIL-TEACHERS ENROLLED	COST TO STATE	YEAR	PUPIL-TEACHERS ENROLLED	COST TO STATE
1835	413	$4 396[80]	1839	564	$3 200
1836	278	3 200	1840	957	3 200
1837	284	3 200	1841	597	4 800
1838	374	3 200	1842	799	4 800

The appropriation was withheld from the sixteen appointed academies in 1843,[81] and no official reports on teachers departments were made for that year nor for the years following until 1850. A few schools[82] were still required under the provision of 1838 to maintain such departments, but the law was inoperative after 1842. However, the academies continued to educate teachers for the common schools. Evidence of this is found in the incidental references that occur in the reports of various academies to the Regents. From such information it appears that nineteen were continuing their teacher-training work the year they were abandoned by the State. These were:[83] Delaware: "A large and increasing number of students

[79] Owing to different interpretations of the reports from the academies, there are certain discrepancies in the statistics published by the Regents and the State Superintendents; e. g. the Regents Report, 1837, p. 8, gives a total of 228 pupil-teachers for the past year; and the Superintendent's Annual Report, 1841, p. 19, 20, gives 218 such pupils. The data furnished by individual academies was often indefinite: e. g. Kinderhook in 1842 (Superintendent's Report, 1842, p. 113 ff.) reported "15 or 20" pupil-teachers. Cf. Oxford, Union, and Yates County and Female Seminary, p. 145.
The data from which table 28 was compiled are recorded in the following reports: Regents, 1836, p. 92–104. Regents, 1837, p. 116–24. Superintendent's 1838, p. 109. Superintendent's 1839, p. 132–43. Superintendent's, 1840, p. 90. Superintendent's, 1841, p. 95. Superintendent's, 1842, p. 113–31. Regents, 1843, p. 198.
[80] $7200 was appropriated for this year, but only a part of it was distributed.
[81] Sup't Rep't, 1844, p. 30; Regents Rep't, 1850, p. 15.
[82] These numbers were: 1844, 6; 1845, 4; 1846, 3; 1847, 4; 1848, 4; 1849, 3.
[83] Regents Rep't, 1844, p. 138–52; also p. 129.

are prepared in this institution, every year, to become teachers of common schools." Delaware Literary Institute: " Over seventy teachers we have sent out during the year." Kinderhook: " The number of this description (teachers of common schools) in the academy during the past year, has been quite as large as usual." Gouverneur Wesleyan Seminary: " During the last two years, about eighty have so far completed the course, as to receive the license of the county superintendent of common schools to teach." Kingsboro: A normal school of two terms, two months each, was held. " Most of them (pupil-teachers) are now employed in teaching, to the great satisfaction of their patrons and pupils." Alfred: " Between fifty and sixty scholars who attended the last fall term are known to be engaged in teaching." Franklin: " There have been about 40 individuals who have been engaged as teachers in our common schools, who during a part of that year have been members of this institution." Thirteen (Hempstead, Kinderhook, Fairfield, Black River, Cherry-Valley, Clinton, DeLancey, Hamilton, Oneida, Oxford, Canandaigua, Onondaga and Albion) reported that they were using a textbook in the " principles of teaching." One of the latter (Kinderhook) is one of the first seven mentioned; so counting it but once, the total is nineteen. An indication of the extent of teacher-training during the period when no systematic reports were made, is afforded by the data published by the Regents on the text-books used in the academies. The number of academies that were using a text in the " principles of teaching " was as indicated by the figures in the table below.

TABLE 30

YEAR	NO. OF ACADEMIES	AUTHORITY
1843	14[84]	Regents Rep't, 1844, p. 129
1844	9	Ibid., 1845, p. 138
1845	12	Ibid., 1846, p. 139
1846	10	Ibid., 1847, p. 139
1847	10	Ibid., 1848, p. 155
1848	9	Ibid., 1849, p. 154
1849	11	Ibid., 1850, p. 184

The number of pupil-teachers enrolled in the academies using a textbook in the principles of teaching, as well as the number in the other academies, can not be ascertained. But the academies were probably instructing as many common school teachers as they had done prior to 1843 when they received state aid for that work. This inference is supported by the additional facts that the normal at Albany was supplying fewer than two hundred teachers a year[85] to

---

[84] In the same report (p. 15) this number is given as thirteen.
[85] New York District School Journal, 9: 182.

the schools of the State, whereas more than two thousand recruits were needed each year; and that the teachers institutes were limited in their scope and influence. The only other agency for providing common school teachers was the academies, and the extent of their service in this particular is not fully represented by the statistical records, which usually show only the number of pupils enrolled in the special teachers departments.[86]

Second Period — 1849 to 1889

Previous to 1849 the State pursued no definite well-established policy in regard to the training of teachers in secondary schools. Whatever was done was of an experimental character. The law was changed every few years to test in practice some new plan of maintaining teachers departments in academies. But with the reestablishment of those departments in 1849 on a broader and more permanent basis, the State proceeded with more confidence and decision. The discussions, criticisms and petitions that characterized the earlier period for the most part disappeared. The changes that were made in the organization and administration of the teachers departments during this second period were designed to make them more effective, not to limit their influence or to abolish them. They have been maintained continuously from their reestablishment to the present time.

Although some were of the opinion that the normal at Albany and teachers institutes were sufficient to supply the common schools with good teachers,[87] others recognized the error of this view. They foresaw that a normal school alone would not supply teachers in sufficient number to meet the demand. As early as 1826 the literature committee of the Senate pointed out the impossibility of training the necessary number of teachers in the normal then advocated by Governor DeWitt Clinton.[88] The year the State Normal School was established at Albany, a number of men called attention to the limitation of such schools. F. B. Sprague, deputy superintendent

---

[86] Pupil-teachers in the teachers departments in 1835 were 118; those not in the departments, 295. As a rule, only the former number is given in the reports.

[87] The State Normal School. "In conjunction with the establishment of teachers institutes in the several counties, and the efforts of the county and town superintendents, we are satisfied that comparatively a brief period of time only is necessary to supply every school-district in the State with competent and well qualified teachers." New York District School Journal, 5:323.

[88] Senate Jour., 1826, p. 158.

of Fulton county, who conducted the first county institute, reported:
" Let the bounty of the State be bestowed upon these schools [teach-
ers institutes] rather than upon our colleges and academies, and I
might add to the list the contemplated state normal schools.   The
two former have never fulfilled the expectations of the friends of
universal education, particularly as it regards qualifying teachers of
common schools, and the latter will fail of accomplishing the great
end in view, as they can not be numerous enough to meet the wants
of the community.   I would inquire how many of the 20,000 different persons, male and female, actually engaged in teaching in this
State every year, could be benefitted by three or four state normal
schools ? "[88a]

The report of the committee of the Assembly on colleges, academies and common schools the same year, which drew up the plans
for the normal at Albany, warned the people not to expect too much
of the new institution.   " The committee do not indulge an expecta-
tion that an adequate supply of well-trained teachers for our schools
can be furnished in a very brief period; this, whenever undertaken,
and under the most favorable auspices, must be the slow work of
years." [89]

The records of the state normal school for the first few years
after its establishment bear out these prophecies. During the first three
years of its operation, 254 students were graduated. Of this number
232 taught in the common schools of the State; 9 became teachers in
academies or select schools; the other 13 did not teach after leaving
the school.   In addition to these, the school had furnished 210
undergraduate students as teachers of common schools in the State,
and was instructing 200 pupils at the time the report was made.[90]
At the end of five years, 952 individuals had been enrolled at the
school, and 350 had been graduated.[91]   Assuming that all those
enrolled became teachers, the number would still fall below an
average of 200 a year, which was a striking contrast to the 20,000
teachers required for the schools. The academies before the normal
school was established had been instructing in their teacher-training
departments from 600 to 900 teachers a year.   These numbers
include those that returned from year to year, so the actual number
of individuals was somewhat less, but was far greater than the number instructed at the normal. Many others not enrolled in normal

[88a] Sup't Rep't, 1844, p. 292.
[89] Assembly Documents, 1844, v. 5, no. 135, p. 72.
[90] New York District School Journal, 1848, 9:7–8.
[91] Ibid., 9:182.

departments probably taught after leaving the academies. In the matter of expense, the normal did not appear to be so efficient as the teachers departments in academies. The former received $10,000[92] a year from the State, or about $50 for each pupil instructed. The latter never received more than $4800 a year from the State, or about $6 for each pupil instructed.

Such facts as these probably did not escape the notice of legislators and others interested in education. The need of further means of educating teachers was recognized in 1849 by a law, reestablishing teachers departments in academies for a period of two years, at the end of which time a similar provision was made, but making the departments permanent instead of for a period of years. The former act read as follows:

The treasurer shall pay, on the warrant of the Comptroller, out of the income of the United States deposit or literature fund, not otherwise appropriated, to the trustees of one or more academies, as the Regents of the University may designate, in each county in this State, the sum of two hundred and fifty dollars per year for the years 1850 and 1851, provided such academy or academies shall have instructed in the science of common school teaching for at least four months during each of said years at least twenty individuals, but no such one county shall receive a larger sum than two hundred and fifty dollars.[93]

It is of importance to notice that this law restored the administrative control of the teachers departments to the Regents, under whose authority they had been from their establishment in 1834 until an act of 1837 had placed them in charge of the Superintendent of Common Schools. The Regents then remained in administrative control of them until 1889. Other features of the law were: (1) $250 was paid annually to every academy selected; (2) to receive this grant an academy, after having been selected by the Regents, was required to meet two definite conditions: to instruct a class of not fewer than twenty pupils in the " science of common school teaching," and to continue that instruction for at least four months; (3) if two or more academies were appointed in the same county, the total sum appropriated to all of them should not exceed $250; (4) the law was limited to a period of two years, after which time its provisions would no longer be effective.

The Regents, acting under the authority conferred upon them by the act, adopted the following rules in regard to the teachers departments in the selected academies: (1) No more than one academy

---

[92] Session Acts, 1844, chap. 311.
[93] Session Acts, 1849, chap. 174, sec. 2. The title of the act is: " An act making appropriations for the support of common schools for the years 1849 and 1850."

would be appointed in any one county. Two reasons were given for this decision. It was thought that if a division of the funds given to a county were made, and the pupil-teachers of a county distributed to several schools, the departments thus organized would be too small and weak to be effective, and that the "object to be attained would be altogether considered a secondary one." It was also the opinion of the Regents that the best academies, which would be most adequately fitted to carry on the proposed departments, would not be willing to instruct a number of students, even though a small number of ten or less, for less than the full amount allowed to a county. (2) The curriculum was prescribed only in a general way. All the elementary subjects were included, and as many advanced subjects as could possibly be taught were recommended. It was suggested that the science of common school teaching required by law might be taught by lectures, by observation, or by practice teaching, as the local authorities might think best. (3) Pupils enrolled in the departments were to be instructed free of charge for the four months of the course. (4) All those who received this free instruction were required to sign a pledge that they intended to teach a reasonable time in the common schools of the State. (5) The Regents advised that no female pupil under the age of 14, and no male under the age of 16 be admitted to the departments. (6) The law did not require the four months specified to be four consecutive months, but the Regents urged the academies to avoid dividing the term when possible. (7) The question of employing an additional teacher for the department was left to the decision of the local authorities.[94]

Forty-four[95] academies, representing the same number of counties, were appointed to receive grants for maintaining teachers departments as the law provided. The principal consideration in making the choice among the schools that applied was the ability of the academy "to perform the required duty." In case two academies in the same county seemed equally well adapted for training teachers, preference was given to the one that was deprived of its expected appropriation in 1844.[96]

A comparison of these requirements with those issued by the Regents in 1835 shows a marked difference. The latter were intensive in character, and aimed to supply a limited number of teachers especially well qualified. The former were of an extensive kind,

[94] Regents Rep't, 1850, p. 14, 15, 16.
[95] Increased later to 45. Regents Rep't, 1851, p. 215, 216.
[96] Regents Rep't, 1850, p. 15, 17, 18.

which sought to reach a relatively large number of teachers, even at
the risk of preparing them less thoroughly. This change of policy
was probably due to the criticism of the earlier teachers departments,
and to the fact that a state normal meanwhile had been established
to afford an opportunity to teachers for a liberal professional
training. The literature committee of the Senate (1851) was of the
opinion that the normal school was to give special training, and that
the academies should instruct the great majority of teachers.[97]   So
the Legislature and the Regents were probably reflecting the opinion
of the majority when they planned an extensive rather than an
intensive system of teacher-training.

The academies appointed under this provision by the Regents were
required to report the following particulars: (1) The names and
ages of all pupils; (2) the exact number of weeks instruction was
given; (3) whether it was free or not; (4) whether the pupils had
signed the pledge; (5) whether an additional teacher was employed on
account of the teacher-training work; (6) whether pupil-teachers
were taught with the other pupils of the school; (7) whether the
term of instruction was continuous.[98]

After the first year's report of the result of this system of teachers
classes, the literature committee of the Senate stated that the work
of the departments had been highly gratifying; and recommended
that they be continued, but with a few changes in their organization,[99] which the results of the first year of their operation showed
were desirable. It was advised that the sum of $12.50 be allowed
for the instruction of each pupil-teacher for four months, and that
the Regents be given authority to "allot the monies appropriated
as the merits of each case may appear to them to deserve."[1]   The
previous year many schools appointed had done what they could to
comply with the law, that they instruct at least twenty pupils for not
less than four months of the year, but had failed in some particular.
The Regents thought these schools should not be compelled to lose all
their appropriations for instructing teachers because they had not
complied with some of the conditions. Upon the recommendations of
the Regents and the literature committee,[2] the Legislature authorized the Regents to use their own judgment in compensating
academies that had instructed teachers, but had not complied with

---

[97] Senate Documents, 1851, v. 9, no. 58, p. 13.
[98] Ibid., p. 3.
[99] Senate Document, 1851, v. 2, no. 58 *passim.*
[1] Senate Document, 1851, v. 2, no. 58, *passim.*
[2] Ibid., *passim.*

the law so as to deserve the maximum amount of $250.[3] But this irregularity of some academies had a more important result. It led to the recommendation of the literature committee of the Senate for a change in the teacher-training work, as mentioned above, and resulted in the passage of the following act which made the recommendation effective:

The Treasurer shall pay yearly, on the warrant of the Comptroller, out of the income of the United States deposit or literature fund, not otherwise appropriated, to the trustees of one or more academies in each county of the State, as the Regents of the University shall designate, the sum of twelve dollars and fifty cents for each scholar who shall have been instructed in such academy during at least four full calendar months in the science of common school teaching.[4]

This law differs from the previous provision in two respects. It is continuous in its effect, as indicated by the word "yearly," whereas the act of 1849 made appropriations for two years only. The sum of $12.50 is granted for each pupil instructed, instead of $250 for twenty or more pupils. The Regents also made several changes in their requirements, and added some rules to meet the new conditions. They appointed academies with the understanding that no school would receive pay for more than twenty pupils, or a total sum of $250. The age limits for entrance requirements was raised from 16 to 18 for males and from 14 to 16 for females.[5]

Since the instruction of teachers was voluntary on the part of the academies, and the Regents could not require them to accept an appointment and had no means of knowing what academies wished to undertake the work, the initiative in the matter was left to the academies themselves, as it had been previously. All schools that sought an appointment sent an application to the Regents, who selected certain schools out of those applying. It was the intention to distribute the opportunities for instruction of this kind to teachers evenly throughout the State,[6] but on account of an equal number of applications being sent from the various counties, this was not possible. In 1852, no application was received from nine counties; one was received from each of fourteen counties; two from each of twenty-one counties; and from three to five from each of fifteen counties.[7] The corresponding appointments were: fourteen acad-

[3] Session Acts, 1951, chap. 536, sec. 5.
[4] Ibid., sec. 4.
[5] Regents Rep't, 1852, p. 20.
[6] The laws specify that appointments are to be made to academies in each county of the State.
[7] Regents Rep't, 1852, p. 17, 18, 19, 20.

emies in fourteen counties; seventy-two academies in thirty-six counties;[8] and later Elmira Academy, in Chemung county,[9] making the total for the year eighty-seven.

The tendency at this time to regard the academies as the proper means for instructing teachers is indicated by a report of the literature committee of the Senate on a number of petitions to the Legislature from Washington, Warren and Saratoga counties asking that appropriations be made for union teachers institutes under the law of 1847. Among the reasons that the committee gave that the requests should be denied, the principal one was the following: " The provisions of chap. 536 of the Laws of 1851, appropriating to the trustees of such academies as the Regents of the University shall designate, the sum of twelve dollars and fifty cents for each scholar who shall have been instructed therein for a period of four months, in the *science* of common school teaching, are sufficiently ample for all the purposes in such act contemplated, and have virtually superceded any imaginable necessity for the existence or endowment of teachers' institutes." [10]

The academies found it difficult to obey that part of the law that required them to instruct teachers four months. The Regents decided that since nearly all the academies divided the year into four terms, and found it difficult to rearrange their courses, fourteen or fifteen weeks would constitute the four months so far as the spirit of the law was concerned.[11] This decision was evoked by inquiries from many of the schools in regard to the exact meaning of the term " four months." [12] The second form of the law used the expression " four full calendar months," and the Regents then refused to accept any shorter period as fulfilling the law.[13] The Fairfield Academy petitioned the Legislature that the time be reduced to fourteen weeks " in order to accommodate the arrangement of the trustees as to the length of their academic term." [14] The committee of the Assembly on colleges, academies and common schools to which the petition was referred, in making its report called attention to the difficulty that had been experienced in carrying out the provision in question. However, it was thought that if any change was to be made it should apply to all academies alike. The committee advised the Assembly

---

[8] Ibid., p. 18.
[9] Ibid., p. 21.
[10] Senate Documents, 1852, v. 2, no. 82, p. 2.
[11] Ibid., p. 4.
[12] Regents Rep't, 1851, p. 220.
[13] Regents Rep't, 1852, p. 21.
[14] Assembly Documents, 1852, no. 63, p. 1.

that the petition be not granted.[15]   In spite of this unfavorable report, the Legislature amended the act by substituting " one-third of the academic year " for " four full calendar months." The amount paid for each student was changed from $12.50 to $10.[16]

The following year (1853) the law was modified in two important respects: (1) The sum of $18,000 was appropriated definitely for "instruction of common school teachers in the academies designated by the Regents of the University."[17]   Previous to this time only surplus funds had been used for this purpose. (2) No academy was to be paid for more than twenty-five pupils.[18]   The new provision also specified that the pupil-teachers be pledged to teach, and that the trustees of the several academies be required to report to the Regents; but in these two particulars the law was only repeating what the Regents had always required.[19]   With the exception of two minor modifications, no changes were made in the law under which the Regents administered the teachers classes in academies for a period of twenty years.   These modifications were passed in 1855,[20] when the maximum number of students claimed by any one academy was reduced from twenty-five to twenty, although the Regents retained the authority to reduce the number below twenty; and in 1864, when the Regents were given permission to use $3000 of the whole amount appropriated for the instruction of teachers to pay the expenses of maintaining in the academies, selected courses in physiology and the laws of health.[21]   However, the latter provision was never put into operation, and it was not until 1885 that instruction in physiology and hygiene was made a part of the prescribed course in teachers classes.[22]

The ordinance of the Regents in regard to teachers classes remained practically unchanged.[23]   The appointments for the year 1853 were of two kinds, absolute and provisional.   All academies that received an absolute appointment were paid for their teachers classes first; then those with provisional appointments were paid if the funds were sufficient.   Ninety of the former and fourteen of the latter were made for the year.[24]   Three years later, out of 119

[15] Assembly Documents, 1852, v. 2, no. 63, p. 2, 3.
[16] Session Acts, 1852, chap. 235.
[17] Session Acts, 1853, chap. 219.
[18] Session Acts, 1853, chap. 402.
[19] Senate Documents, 1851, v. 2, no. 58, p. 3.
[20] Session Acts, 1855, chap. 410.
[21] Session Acts, 1864, chap. 556.
[22] Regents Rep't, 1885, p. 20.
[23] Regents Instructions, 1853, p. 117.
[24] Regents Instructions, 1853, p. 117.

applications from 48 of the 59 counties of the State, 113 appointments were made, and the number of pupils allowed to each academy was limited to 16. A large number of institutions was selected in order to distribute opportunities for instruction to teachers as widely as possible; and as a result it was necessary to limit the number of pupils in each so that the money appropriated would be sufficient.[25]

The ordinances continued to be modified in some of their details from year to year. In 1857 the number of classes was reduced to 90, and a more definite course of study adopted.[26] The course consisted of reading and orthography, writing, arithmetic, English grammar and geography. Any student who was proficient in some of these subjects could elect one or two of the following: algebra, geometry, natural history, natural philosophy, history of the United States, science of government, physiology. All pupils were required to study the theory and practice of teaching and to devote most of their time to elementary subjects, those named in the first group.[27] By the year 1882, two of the subjects of the second group had been transferred to the first; otherwise the curriculum remained the same.[28]

The rules for the admission of students to the teachers classes that were in force in 1864 will serve to illustrate the requirements in this respect for nearly the whole period. (1) "Pupils must be selected by the joint action of the trustees and principal of the academy." (2) The minimum age for males was 18, and for females 16. (3) Their entrance examination should indicate their ability to qualify for . teacher's certificate after pursuing the subjects of the teachers class. (4) "They should be residents of the county in which the academy is situated, and fairly distributed among the several towns." (5) They were required to pledge themselves to teach for a reasonable time.[29]

In 1873 the annual appropriation for teachers classes was increased from $18,000 to $30,000, the amount allowed to academies for each pupil-teacher was raised from $10 to $15, and the period of instruction was made thirteen weeks instead of one-third of the academic year. Instruction for not less than ten and not more than twenty weeks was paid for at the same rate.[30] Such changes had been

[25] Regents Rep't, 1856, p. 103, 104.
[26] Regents Rep't, 1857, p. 17, 18.
[27] Manual of the Regents of the University, 1864, p. 104, 105.
[28] University Manual, 1882, p. 168.
[29] Manual of the Regents of the University, 1864, p. 103.
[30] Session Acts, 1873, chap. 642, sec. 3.

previously suggested,[31] and the next year the Regents explained the necessity for increasing the sum paid for each pupil instructed in the teachers classes. " For several years past, applications from academies for appointment under this law (of 1855) have not been quite sufficient to exhaust the appropriation. The sum to be paid has not been equal to the rates of tuition established in some academies, in the subjects embraced in the prescribed course, and provision for the most efficient instruction has, in many instances, been regarded as a burden to be avoided, rather than a privilege to be sought." [32]

The increased appropriation provided by this act was based upon a fractional mill tax for the support of secondary schools,[33] which was repealed in 1874; so that only the $18,000 was available after the first year that the increased appropriation was made. This was true until 1877 when a new law was enacted. The academies appointed to instruct teachers classes under the revised law were paid one dollar a week for each pupil enrolled in the class, but the class was not to continue less than ten weeks, or it may continue longer at the discretion of the Regents provided that all the instruction should be in one academic term. Not fewer than ten nor more than twenty-five pupils could be included in any one class. The amount of $30,000 a year was again provided, and in other respects the law was similar to the preceding one.[34]

Two years later the source of revenue again failed. Losses occurred in the investment of the United States deposit fund, which according to law were made up from the income of the fund.[35] The amount paid for instructing the teachers classes dropped from $30,021 [36] in 1878 to $17,107 [37] in 1879, and for 1880 and 1881 it was $11,645,[38] and $3669 [39] respectively. This financial impediment was obviated by the Legislature in 1881.[40]

The following year, the teachers classes were reorganized and many improvements were instituted. The Regents recommended to the Legislature that a system of supervision be established, and

[31] Regents Rep't, 1869, p. 742.
[32] Regents Rep't, 1874, p. xv.
[33] Session Acts, 1872, chap. 736.
[34] Session Acts, 1877, chap. 425.
[35] Regents Report, 1879, p. x, 458.
[36] Regents Rep't, 1879, p. x, 458.
[37] Ibid., 1880.
[38] Ibid., 1881, p. 461.
[39] Ibid., 1882, p. 260.
[40] Session Acts, 1881, chap. 1.

that the classes be placed under the school commissioners in whose districts they were situated.[41]   The Legislature included both of these features in the law passed that year, and also specified that all pupils who completed the course arranged by the Regents and who passed the prescribed examinations should be granted a testimonial " which, when indorsed by any school commissioner, shall constitute a certificate of qualification and a license to teach in the common schools of his district for a period of one year from the date of such indorsement." [42]

In compliance with the law the Regents appointed an inspector, Dr A. B. Watkins, for teachers classes,[43] and added the following requirements: (1) Pupils admitted to the classes were required to pass the Regents preliminary examination, either before entering the course or before its close; (2) the number of pupils multiplied by the number of weeks of instruction should not exceed 250, but the number of weeks should not exceed thirteen; (3) the teachers class was to be organized separately, and to be instructed as a class at least one and one-half full hours each day; (4) the State would pay only for those members who had passed the entrance examination and the formal examination required at the close of the course; (5) it was necessary to notify the Regents of the organization of a class, and to make a detailed report within two weeks after the close of the course; (6) the curriculum was not changed, but was described in detail and much more emphasis was placed upon method of teaching.[44] It was objected by some principals that the admission standards established at this time were higher than the requirements for a teacher's certificate in many sections of the State, and that many pupils would be deprived of the benefit of the classes on that account.[45]

Not many changes were made in the organization and administration of teachers classes during the next seven years, at the end of which time they were transferred to the supervision of the Superintendent of Public Instruction.   Instruction in physiology and hygiene, with special reference to the effect of alcoholic drink upon the human system, was added to the curriculum of the teachers classes in 1885, because such subjects had been made a part of the

[41] Regents Rep't, 1882, p. xxiii, xxiv.
[42] Session Acts, 1882, chap. 318.
[43] Regents Rep't, 1883, p. xxii.
[44] Regents Rep't, 1883, p. 166–80.
[45] Regents Rep't, 1883, p. 403–16.

course of study in common schools.[46]   Beginning with the same year, each school commissioner was instructed to report, among other items, in what way he gave credit toward a license to teach for work done in teachers classes. The commissioners differed widely in their attitude toward those who held testimonials from the Regents. They were required to specify whether they indorsed the testimonials, if further examination was demanded of the candidate, if credit was given on the subjects pursued at the academies, or whether some other plan was adopted.[47]

It was the plan of certification in the law of 1882 that was a cause of a lack of harmony between the two administrative systems of the State, and led to the discontinuance of granting testimonials. An attempt was made to improve them by specifying the subjects the bearer had studied and the grades received.[48]   But when a uniform system of certifying teachers was adopted by the Superintendent, the testimonials were of no value and were discontinued.[49]

At a meeting of the Association of Academic Principals held at Syracuse 1888, the following resolution in regard to the instruction of teachers was adopted by a unanimous vote:

Resolved, That as the licensing of teachers has been placed in the hands of the Superintendent of Public Instruction ever since our school system was organized, and as it is desirable that the teachers classes should be part of a symmetrical system for the training of teachers, which system should include the normal schools, and be in consonance with the uniform examinations, we think that the management of the teachers classes should be transferred to the Department of Public Instruction.[50]

Superintendent Draper gave a number of reasons for approving the change as advocated by the principals,[51] and the Regents adopted the above resolution verbatim.[52]   As a result of these demands, the Legislature passed an act transferring the administration of teachers classes from the Regents to the Superintendent of Public Instruction.[53]

---

[46] Ibid., 1885, p. 20. Session Acts, 1884, chap. 30.
[47] Regents Rep't, 1885, p. 38.
[48] Ibid., 1886, p. 33, 34.
[49] Regents Rep't, 1889, p. 826.
[50] Sup't Rep't, 1889, p. 42.
[51] Ibid., p. 42, 43, 44, 45, 140, 141.
[52] Regents Rep't, 1890, p. 26.
[53] Session Acts, 1889, chap. 137. For an account of the teacher-training system in secondary schools of New York since 1889 see Gifford, W. J., The History of New York High Schools.

6

Results Accomplished, Second Period —

1849–1889

a Statistical

A somewhat detailed statement of the results of the first year's work in instructing teachers after the law of 1849 reestablished teachers classes in academies, will serve to indicate what was accomplished during the first part of the period. Reports were received from 42 of the 45 academies that had been appointed. The number of pupil-teachers instructed was 949, males 367, females 582. The males were from 16 to 21 years of age, the females from 15 to 23. All gave the required pledge except the pupils of one school where the principal overlooked the ordinance, but he vouched for the sincerity of the pupils and stated that at the time of the report all of them were either teaching or were students of his school. Additional teachers were engaged in 16 academies of the 42 reporting. The principal devoted extra time in nearly all in instructing the class. The term of instruction was continuous for 627 pupils, and otherwise for 289; one academy did not report this item. The irregularity in the term of instruction is shown in the fact that 17 academies taught 20 or more pupils for 4 months; 13 taught 20 or more pupils for 15 weeks and a smaller number for 16 weeks or longer; the remaining 12 schools were irregular in various ways; the term was too short, the number of pupils was too small, or the term was distributed in two years.[54]

---

[54] Senate Documents, 1851, v. 2, no. 58, p. 4, 5, 6, 7.

TABLE 31

Summary of the laws governing teacher-training in secondary schools from 1849 to 1889.

SESSION ACT OF	AMOUNT OF STATE AID GRANTED	MINIMUM REQUIREMENTS	PRESCRIBED COURSE OF STUDY	LIMITATIONS	OTHER FEATURES
1849, chap. 174	$250 to each academy appointed, or less if more than one in a county	Must teach 20 pupils for 4 months	Science of common school teaching	No county could receive more than $250	Passed for two years only; under administrative control of Regents
1851, chap. 536, sec. 4	$12.50 for each pupil instructed	Four months	No change	None	Under adminstrative control of Regents
1852, chap. 235	$10 for each pupil instructed	One-third of academic year	No change	None	No change
1853, chap. 402	$10 for each pupil instructed with a total of $18,000	One-third of academic year; pupils pledged to teach	Prescribed by Regents, including science of common school teaching	Not more than 25 pupils allowed to an academy	No change
1855, chap. 410	No change	No change	No change	Not more than 20 pupils allowed to an academy	No change
1864, chap. 556	Same as 1853 except $3000 might be used for instruction in physiology etc.	No change	No change except physiology and the laws of health were specified	No change	No change
1873, chap. 642, sec. 3	$15 for each pupil instructed; with a total of $30,000	Thirteen weeks	No change	Same rate for not less than 10 nor more than 20 weeks	No change
1877, chap. 425	$1, a week for each pupil instructed; with a total of $30,000	Ten weeks in one school term	Prescribed by the Regents, including science and practice of common school teaching	Not less than 10 nor more than 25 pupils allowed to an academy	No change
1882, chap. 318	No change	No change	No change	No change	Under administrative control of Regents and school commissioners; latter may grant license to teach to pupil-teachers

TABLE 32

Statistics of teachers classes in academies, including academic departments of union schools, from 1849 to 1889

YEAR[55]	ANNUAL ENROLMENT			NO. OF CLASSES REPORTING	COST TO THE STATE	SCHOOL POPULATION OF THE STATE[56]
	Male	Female	Total			
1850...................	367	582	949	42	$11 250	753 047
1851...................	337	663	1 000	46	11 356	1 100 613
1852...................	533	1 051	1 584	82	15 100	1 150 532
1853...................	508	1 062	1 570	85	15 520	1 186 709
1854...................	706	1 284	1 990	106	17 740	1 224 127
1855...................	590	1 213	1 803	87	17 850	[57]1 214 113
1856...................	524	1 153	1 677	110	15 284	1 214 771
1857...................	532	1 077	1 609	108	12 810	1 240 176
1858...................	601	1 096	1 697	90	14 160	[58]1 238 175
1859...................	711	1 093	1 804	96	15 738	1 272 486
1860...................	622	1 136	1 758	93	15 372	1 315 900
1861...................	595	1 117	1 712	93	16 740	1 348 167
1862...................	494	1 272	1 766	94	17 100	[59]1 322 823
1863...................	449	1 328	1 777	95	16 200	1 357 047
1864...................	363	1 323	1 686	93	16 346	1 307 822
1865...................	297	1 301	1 598	89	15 327	1 398 759
1866...................	363	1 122	1 485	86	14 510	1 364 675
1867...................	406	1 039	1 445	84	13 954	1 376 982
1868...................	463	1 026	1 489	89	13 955	1 464 669
1869...................	564	1 021	1 585	89	15 280	1 463 299
1870...................	503	991	1 494	87	14 502	1 480 761
1871...................	582	969	1 551	90	15 200	1 502 684
1872...................	592	1 002	1 594	88	15 333	1 521 953
1873...................	551	1 110	1 661	97	15 877	1 560 820
1874...................	614	1 400	2 014	92	29 338	1 596 846
1875...................	572	1 222	1 794	91	14 873	[60]1 583 064
1876...................	608	1 133	1 741	96	16 050	1 585 601
1877...................	811	1 433	2 244	102	24 592	1 586 234
1878...................	880	1 621	2 501	122	30 021	1 615 256
1879...................	863	1 551	2 213	115	17 107	1 628 727
1880...................	326	693	1 019	54	11 645	1 641 173
1881...................	128	193	321	18	3 669	1 662 122
1882...................	553	1 187	1 740	102	18 706	1 681 161
1883...................	433	1 178	1 611	95	12 999	1 685 100
1884...................	517	1 358	1 875	111	15 856	1 702 965
1885...................	711	1 635	2 348	143	20 571	1 721 126
1886...................	748	1 788	2 536	160	24 287	1 735 073
1887...................	?	?	2 972	213	35 524	1 763 115
1888...................	906	2 352	3 258	195	33 091	1 772 958
1889...................	883	2 624	3 507	212	31 820	1 803 667

Most of the significant fluctuations that occur in the figures given here may be explained by corresponding changes in the laws and ordinances governing teachers classes. The increase in attendance, number of classes and appropriations is fairly regular until 1860, when the number of males decreased rapidly from 711 to 297 in 1865;

[55] Only the last part of the academic year designated is written in this column; i. e. 1850 means the school year 1849–50.
[56] This includes the numbers of persons in the State between the ages of 4 and 21, except the first number, which is the number of persons between the ages of 5 and 16.
[57] Sup't Rep't, 1858, p. 6.
[58] Ibid., 1859, p. 5.
[59] Ibid., 1863, p. 8.
[60] Ibid.. 1876, p. 19.

then during the next six years it rose again to 582. It appears that the enlistment of young men in the army during the Civil War was the probable cause of the decline.[61] The fact that the number of females enrolled increased more than 200 from 1859 to 1865 leads to the same conclusion. However, the decrease of males from 711 to 622 between 1859 and 1860 could scarcely have been due to the approaching war.

The decided rise in attendance and funds from the State in 1874 is readily explained by generous payment for the instruction of teachers and by the mill tax. The repeal of those provisions the next year explains the decline in the figures. The effect of the law of 1877 is apparent in the numbers given for that year and the two following, and the failure of the revenue from the United States deposit fund brought the total enrolment down to 321 in two years time. The increased demands of the Regents in 1883 checked the number of classes and the enrolment for that year only.

The apparent decrease in the school population of the State for certain years, for example, 1875, is accounted for by the Superintendent. It was due to a poor system of collecting and reporting statistics. While the school population increased about 64 per cent, the number of pupils in teachers classes increased 350 per cent.

b Efficiency

Apart from the number of pupils enrolled as shown by statistics, there is a question of the real value of the teachers classes in supplying the common schools with better teachers, of the quality of instruction in elementary subjects and methods included in the course of study, and of general efficiency. The official reports and records contain evidence that indicates the effectiveness and excellence of the work of teacher-training. However, numerous expressions occur that suggest that the work was often formal and of little value; so the question of efficiency can not be answered categorically. It will be sufficient to call attention here to a number of criticisms both unfavorable and favorable, to afford a basis for an intelligent opinion on the question.

The Regents expressed their doubts of the wisdom of the teachers classes as organized in 1857, and suggested some radical changes.

---

[61] "And a patriotic impulse compels me to add, that of the one hundred and twenty-five young men of those who had been under my own tuition in the academy, in the ten years previous to 1864, who cheerfully gave themselves to their country's service in the late rebellion, sixty-seven of them had been good and tried members of the teachers class." Proceedings of University Convocation, 1868, p. 61, 62.

They say: "With few exceptions these have been taught with the other pupils of the academy, and no additional teacher has been employed for such instruction. In many of the academies some professional instruction has been given, while in others it does not appear that the instruction has, to any important extent, differed from that of the other pupils." [62]

The next year they mention the large number of academies and the small fee paid to each as causes of "very little specific instruction" having been given.[63] In commenting upon the improved condition of the classes some years later, the Regents state that in the past the teaching in them had often been "a matter of form, and with an apparent desire, in some instances, principally to secure the sum which the State agrees to pay." [64] The same thought is expressed more emphatically in another place: "Too often in the past has it been a just subject of reproach, that the payments made to the academies for the instruction of teachers classes, were only a species of gratuity, and that in many cases the service was merely a pretense." [65]

The Chancellor of the University in criticizing the teachers classes as they had been conducted previous to 1882 said: "We have felt, and no man has felt it more than I have, that during these forty years in which we have been applying the money of the State to teachers classes, the application has often been very improper, because the service performed was not good." [66]

But despite numerous disparaging expressions, an abundance of evidence pointing to the efficiency of the teacher-training efforts appears in the sources. When the results of the first year of the system adopted in 1849 were known, the literature committee of the Senate, judging from the following passage, thought the work had been successful: "In view of the great benefits which have arisen from the grant of money to such academies as might instruct in the science of common school teaching, during the years 1850 and 1851, provision (we recommend) be made by law for the continuance of such grant." [67]

In the Regents Reports of 1866 and 1867 the following occurs: "It is due to most of the academies to say that they have faithfully performed what the law and ordinances of the Regents have required

---

[62] Regents Rep't, 1857, p. 27, 28.
[63] Ibid., 1858, p. 17.
[64] Ibid., 1878, p. xii.
[65] Ibid., 1882, p. xxiii.
[66] Ibid., 1883, p. 416.
[67] Senate Documents, 1851, v. 2, no. 58, p. 12.

of them, and that the effect has been apparent in the improved character of teachers of common schools." [68]

Previous to that time the Regents said, the system of teachers classes " appears to present very prosperous results,"[69] and also stated that, " No change has been made during the past year in the prescribed course of study, and the Regents are gratified in the evidences which are before them of its more faithful prosecution, both on the part of teachers and pupils." [70]

In 1881 the Regents asserted that the teachers classes in academies were an effective and economical way of training teachers.[71]

The account that Principal Noah T. Clarke of Canandaigua has written of his personal experience for a period of thirty-one years in the teacher-training work of that academy, affords a close view of the character of instruction given in the teachers departments, or classes. He says:

Upon entering Canandaigua Academy, in April 1837, I found the teachers department in full operation. The " teachers class " numbered about *thirty* young men, and was mainly under the instruction of the principal, the late Mr Henry Howe. The time of the class was about half of it spent in the " teachers " course of study. That course consisted in studies and recitations of the common branches; a daily drill upon the best methods of teaching; lectures upon the theory of teaching, and also upon geology, natural and mental philosophy, physical geography and history, upon warming and ventilation, the laws of health, teachers associations, schoolhouses and blackboards, also upon the teacher's social habits and duties as a member of the community in which he might be placed.

For three summers, of twenty-two weeks each, I was permitted to enjoy the privileges of that class; and I am free to say that, although I had taught school before, yet I found the instruction of that course of incalculable value; and if I have ever been able to accomplish anything as an instructor of youth, I owe it, in no small degree, to the exercises of that teachers class. The members of that department were eagerly sought for the best class of winter schools, and at wages from 10 to 33⅓ per cent higher than the average of other teachers of the county.

This department was maintained under similar circumstances, and with but little interruption, until about 1848. In that year, the trustees of the academy spoke of the teachers department as follows: "A teachers class was first organized in this academy in 1830. Since that time nearly *five hundred young men* have entered this department." It is true that members of this department were not then, as now, required to pledge themselves

[68] Regents Rep't, 1866, p. 19; ibid., 1867, p. xxii.
[69] Ibid., 1853, p. 14.
[70] Ibid., 1860, p. 12; also repeated in the report of 1861.
[71] Ibid., 1881, p. xiv.

to teach common schools for any length of time; yet most, if not all of them, did engage in teaching more or less. Upon the resignation of Mr Howe, in 1849, my relation to the academy became more intimate, and since 1853, when I assumed charge of the institution, I have been entirely familiar with this department of instruction, as it has fallen mainly within my own sphere of duty. This department has since that time, as well as before, been a distinct organization. The class has always been under a course of special training, similar, as far as it goes, to that of the state normal school. This course has always consisted, first, of thorough reviews and drills in the elementary studies; second, of familiar lectures upon the theory of teaching and such other subjects as were pertinent to the teacher's work; third, of actual practice in teaching classes, under the eye of the instructor. . . . During the last eighteen years, nearly four hundred young men have been members of this department, making in all some nine hundred young men who, in one academy, by this most wise and judicious provision of the State, have been aided in their preparation for the teacher's work; and it is but simple justice and truth to say that the great majority of them took high positions among the teachers of our common schools, while not a few have proved themselves able and efficient instructors in our high schools and academies.[12]

School commissioners often expressed favorable opinions of the work of academies in training teachers. A few are repeated here as illustrations.

Our very best teachers are derived from the pupils instructed in the teachers classes in our academies, and I think the wisdom displayed by the Regents in their selection of schools to instruct such classes has been praiseworthy.[13]

The teachers classes in Cortlandville and Cincinnatus are rendering valuable aid in qualifying the teachers of the county.[14]

The teachers department of this institution, I am pleased to say, is under the control of Prof. Hoose, who has fulfilled the duties of his position to the entire satisfaction of parties interested. I am pleased to say the professor has sent out some of the best teachers; those who are an honor to the profession, and an honor to the institution that prepared them for their noble work.[15]

Similar expressions are found on pages 205, 230, 241, 328 and 377 of the twelfth annual report of the Superintendent of Public Instruction.

But adverse criticism of teachers departments by school commissioners was not lacking. The following two examples are typical:

In visiting the institution, I had some conversation with the principal in regard to teachers class. Mr Nichols said he thought such a class did not receive the benefit expected by the Regents of the University, and he did not care to have a teachers class in the academy.[16]

[12] Proceedings of the University Convocation, 1868, p. 60, 61.
[13] Sup't Rep't, 1866, p. 120.
[14] Ibid., p. 148.
[15] Ibid., p. 193.
[16] Ibid., p. 150.

I have taken some pains to compare the members of the teachers class with other teachers, and I confess I see no difference. I doubt the propriety of spending so large a portion of the public money for such purposes."[77]

No doubt the teachers classes were neither entirely deficient nor were they highly efficient. It is impossible to say accurately, judging by our present standards, just how successful they were, but the following statement is probably not far from the truth: " In a large number of institutions the work done has always been of the most faithful and intelligent kind. But in others, owing sometimes to a lack of skill on the part of the teachers, and sometimes to carelessness and unfaithfulness, the instruction was very imperfect." [78]

Summary

Near the close of the first quarter of the nineteenth century, about forty years after the academy system was established, the fact that the academies were training a large number of the teachers for the elementary schools was recognized by the leaders in educational affairs. It seems that the need for good teachers in the elementary schools, which the State had established in 1813, drew attention to the academies as the best agencies for meeting the new conditions. Thus the problem of teacher-training courses in secondary schools arose.

But as there was no precedent for such a plan of training teachers, a period of experimentation, learning by the trial and success method, ensued. Until the middle of the nineteenth century, an influential number of statesmen and educators thought that normal schools, similar to those of Prussia and other European countries, should be the exclusive means of preparing teachers for the elementary schools. However, a majority favored using the academies, in which the State had invested large sums, for that purpose. Although the latter plan was followed from 1827 until 1843, no well-established policy of administering the normal departments in academies prevailed. Prior to 1827 the teacher-training of academies received no legal recognition, and until 1834 remained unorganized and not directly supported by the State. The first plan adopted by the Regents was to limit the number of departments, and to provide a thorough academic and professional education for the prospective teachers. Since the influence of the system conducted upon that plan was not extensive enough, the number of normal departments was increased. The law passed in 1837 which placed the system under the Super-

---

[77] Ibid., p. 246.
[78] Regents Rept's, 1883, p. xxii.

intendent of Public Instruction was unfortunate. A year later the situation was confused by requiring all the academies that received $700 or more a year from the State to maintain teachers departments. In 1841 the number of academies that were especially appointed to instruct pupil-teachers and to receive appropriations for that purpose from the State, was increased from eight to sixteen. Two years later the whole system was abandoned by the State for six years.

The financial limitations were always a serious handicap to the success of the plan. With less than $5000 a year, about $6 for each pupil enrolled, for the work, the Regents and the State Superintendents vacillated between the alternatives of maintaining a few relatively strong normal departments, or a larger number of weaker ones. The trustees and the principals of the academies concerned could not plan their teachers classes with the assurance that the State would continue its support. These conditions of inadequate financial support and wavering administrative policy contributed to the growing dissatisfaction with the system. The unreasonable demands of many who expected that the pittance expended would give the State thousands of well-trained teachers, was an additional factor that led to dissatisfaction and the abandonment of the teacher departments in academies.

After the teacher-training system was reestablished in 1849 under the Regents, its improvement and growth were rapid. The dual administrative organization of public education whereby the Regents were in control of secondary schools and the State Superintendent was in charge of the elementary schools, for a number of years caused no serious difficulty. However, the friction between the two departments led in time to conditions that were unfavorable to the success of the teacher-training work, and at the request of both Regents and Superintendent the normal departments were transferred to the supervision of the State Superintendent in 1889. After this change very few academies continued their teachers classes, and within a few years such classes were conducted entirely by high schools. For this reason, an account of the teacher-training work in academies of the State might well close with this date, 1889.

Conclusions

The evidence brought out in the foregoing account of the teacher-training system in incorporated academies justifies the following conclusions:

1 In 1834 New York provided a definite system of academic and professional education for teachers in elementary schools, and was the first state in this country to provide a systematic preparation for that purpose.

2 The fact that the incorporated academies were used as a means of providing trained teachers for the elementary schools, strengthened the bond between those academies and the State, and was an important factor in their continuance as the principal secondary schools until the beginning of the third quarter of the nineteenth century.

3 Available statistical records show that many thousands of teachers for elementary schools, after 1850 about one-fourth of the number employed, were educated in the normal departments of academies. But the number of such teachers prepared by academies and not officially reported was even larger at certain periods than the number in the statistical report. Before 1849 the majority of the academies were not appointed to conduct teachers classes, and made no report of the number of their students who received instruction in pedagogy or who taught after they left the academy. It is probable that three-fourths of the elementary school teachers were prepared for their work in the secondary schools.

4 It is impossible to measure accurately the efficiency of the normal departments that were conducted in the academies. Typical contemporary expressions, some complimentary and some disparaging, are quoted above. Some of the latter may be accounted for by the fact that the whole academy system was under criticism, which might have extended to the teacher-training departments irrespective of their value. It is also significant that most of the adverse criticism came from officials of the elementary school system, who were probably prejudiced. Judging by the demand for the teachers trained in the normal departments and the higher salaries paid them by school directors, it is evident that they were superior to the other elementary teachers. On the whole, it seems that the academies sent out the best teachers available for the elementary schools.

CHAPTER VII

General Conclusions

For convenience, the general conclusions drawn from the preceding chapters may be grouped under three heads: (1) A statement of the more important historical facts; (2) an explanation of those facts in terms of certain related conditions, the causes corresponding to the facts mentioned; (3) the influence of the academy system upon later development of secondary education. The first of these three may be verified by reference to definite data; but the other two are to some extent, a matter of inference and less certain.

Conclusions Based upon a Summary of Historical Data and Facts

a The Academy Period

Academies were incorporated in greatest numbers in New York during the decade following 1835, and more were incorporated the first five years of that period than in any other five years. Although academies had reached their maximum rate of growth at that time, they had not yet developed to their full extent. The largest number of academies, excluding high schools, that reported to the Regents was reached about 1860, but the maximum attendance in academies occurred about 1855. It is evident that, judged by numbers, academies in the State of New York were at their height between 1855 and 1860. They were, however, the principal secondary schools of the State until 1875, when they were outnumbered by high schools, although the attendance in the academies was still greater than in the latter.

TABLE 33

A comparison of the number of academies incorporated at different periods in Massachusetts and New York

YEARS	MASSA-CHUSETTS	NEW YORK	YEARS	MASSA-CHUSETTS	NEW YORK
1780–85	5	0	1831–35	32	8
1786–90	1	4	1836–40	14	61
1791–95	7	11	1841–45	11	40
1796–1800	4	4	1846–50	10	29
1801–05	7	4	1851–55	14	47
1806–10	4	4	1856–60	5	23
1811–15	2	10	1861–65	4	15
1816–20	6	7	1866–70	6	15
1821–25	4	2	1871–75	5	7
1826–30	28	29	Totals	160	320

In Massachusetts, academies had ceased to dominate secondary education about the middle of the century,[1] a condition which did not occur until twenty-five years later in New York. It seems that the academy period in all states ended between those two dates. According to Dexter, the academy " from the time of the Revolution, until the middle of the nineteenth century was the undisputed leader in secondary education." [2] Brown says the academy was the dominant institution of secondary education for a century after the Revolution.[3]

b Educational Facilities Afforded by Academies

The opportunities for an advanced education provided by academies in New York is seen by a comparison of the number of academies and the number of children in the State of school age. Academies were numerous enough to provide secondary education for all who desired it, especially near the middle of the nineteenth century. However, a number of conditions that rendered academies less accessible than indicated by their numbers, prevailed. The small tuition fee was doubtless a barrier to many. Many large villages, and even some cities, were not provided with incorporated academies. This made it necessary for a large proportion of the pupils to live away from home while attending school.

The distribution of academies in urban and rural communities is illustrated by the situation in 1855. That year, 92 of the 155 academies reporting to the Regents were located in villages of less than 1000 population or in nonurban communities. About 15 of the other 63 were in cities of over 8000 inhabitants. Of the 13 cities in the State, 2 (Oswego and Syracuse) were without a Regents academy; and 101 incorporated villages of over 1000 population had no academy.[4] This relative isolation of academies limited their usefulness.

c Significance of Instruction Given in Academies

Academies served as preparatory schools for the greater number of those entering college, but this was a comparatively small part of the function of those schools. The proportion of those enrolled in academies who intended to enter college was always small, until near the close of the nineteenth century.

---

[1] Inglis, The Rise of the High School in Massachusetts, p. 150.
[2] Boone, Education in the United States, p. 90.
[3] Brown, The Making of Our Middle Schools, p. 228.
[4] Census for the State of New York for 1855, p. 1–15 and 18–23. Regents Rep't, 1856, p. 212–18.

The most important work of academies was the education of many thousands who depended upon the academy alone to prepare them for the duties of life. The records do not show the number of academy students who achieved success or distinction in life; but no doubt the greater number of the men and women who were prominent in the State during the past generation were educated wholly or in part in an academy. Until the middle of the nineteenth century, except the few who entered college, all who sought an education beyond the rudiments turned toward the academies.

The service of academies in educating teachers for common schools was undoubtedly of great importance. For a half century before the State had established a normal school, academies were supplying teachers with an academic education and for a part of that time with a professional training. Even after normal schools were in operation, academies continued to furnish the greater number of common school teachers.[5]

A body of professional secondary school teachers was also incidentally trained and developed by experience in the service of academies. The average number of teachers in an academy was less than three in 1827, but by 1883 had increased to about six. In 1830, the total number of teachers in Regents academies was 160, in 1840, 571, and in 1851, about 730.[6] In 1857, about 70 per cent of the academy teachers reported that they intended to make teaching a profession. From that time, the proportion of professional teachers increased, and in 1885 nearly all had adopted teaching as a permanent vocation. The academic training of those teachers can not be readily determined; the State required no definite preparation of them, but the records show that nearly two-thirds of the principals of academies were college graduates.[7]

d Innovations

A number of innovations in secondary education, most of which have already been mentioned, may be traced to academies. (1) The extension of the purpose of secondary schools to provide a general

---

[5] It was said in 1898, that since 1844 the teachers classes in academies "have ceased to occupy so prominent a part in the training of teachers." This seems to be a misconception. In the ten years from 1834 to 1844, 3389 pupil-teachers were instructed in such classes; while in the ten years from 1850 to 1860, 17,195 pupil-teachers were enrolled in teacher-training classes in academies. Measured by results achieved, academies have been many times more prominent in educating teachers; but they have not attracted so much attention in that work since 1844 as they did when the teacher-training classes were a novelty, and in this sense it is true that they have been less prominent. Cf. Hillis, A. P., "The Oswego Normal School," p. 8.
[6] Historical and Statistical Record of the University of the State of New York, p. 504.
[7] Ibid., p. 504, 576 ff.

and immediately practical education for those not intending to enter college, was an idea that first found extensive application in academies. (2) The introduction of much new subject matter into the curriculum, until nearly all subjects were offered, led to a more liberal and rational course of study than was found in Latin grammar schools. (3) The higher education of girls was not provided for in any schools preceding academies. Girls attended the latter schools even before the close of the eighteenth century.[8] The number of boys attending academies in the State of New York was somewhat greater than the number of girls until 1847, when there were 7007 boys and 7275 girls enrolled. Except for the four years beginning with 1857 and the year 1895, when there were a few more boys than girls, the girls remained in the majority until the close of the century. In 1900, there were 1280 more girls than boys enrolled in academies.[9] In view of these facts, it is surprising to find the statement, that " the academies had been for the most part for boys alone, while the public demanded equal secondary school privileges for boys and girls." [10] The records show that more girls than boys attended academies from 1842, when the numbers of boys and girls were first reported separately, to the close of the century. (4) Teacher-training classes. The professional training of teachers in secondary schools for elementary schools was first attempted on an extensive and systematic plan in the incorporated academies of the State of New York. This innovation was adopted by a number of states, and is at the present time more depended upon than ever before.

e Religious Instruction in Academies

Religious instruction was made a definite aim of practically all academies. One of the topics that received much emphasis by those in control of academies was the religious training of the pupils. Scarcely any prospectus or catalog of an academy failed to specify religious education as a part of the daily program. Bible reading, church attendance, attendance at the religious services of the school, and similar practices were often required.[11]

---

[8] These three features were probably characteristic of academies generally throughout the United States. Cf. Inglis, op. cit., p. 150. Graves, Frank Pierrepont, "A Student's History of Education," p. 414.

[9] Hough, op. cit., p. 503, 504; Education Dep't, Annual Rep't, 1914, p. 857.

[10] Education Dep't, Annual Rep't, 1905, p. 52.

[11] References on this point to a few catalogs of academies are inserted here; many more of a similar kind are available: Catalog of Mount Pleasant Academy, 1837, p. 8; Catalog of Irving Institute, 1840, p. 4; Catalog of Rhinebeck Academy, 1849, p. 14; Third Report of the Trustees of the Oneida Institute of Science and Industry, 1831, p. 6, 7.

Although religious instruction prevailed generally in academies, all sectarian teachings were excluded from every school in the University, and only a very few of them, until after 1890, were controlled by religious organizations.

Conditions that Contributed to the Results of the Academy System

a Organization: a Part of the University

The principal element of strength in the academy system of New York was its organization under the Regents of the University. This provided for the supervision and wise direction of the incorporated academies and gave them a legal status, prestige and other advantages.

Some of the ways in which the Regents strengthened the system were: (1) A high and continually advancing standard of scholarship was required of all schools in the University; (2) guarding against the establishment of transient and temporary schools, by demanding a liberal endowment fund and adequate property usually was effective; (3) the annual reports published and distributed kept the local authorities informed of the requirements of the Regents, and furnished a stimulus to good work by comparing the records of individual schools; (4) the state funds distributed annually relieved the financial condition of academies, and encouraged them to comply with the laws and ordinances; (5) visitation by appointed officers or committees, so far as it was practised, brought academies into closer relation with the Regents; (6) since the establishment of academies was voluntary, they were usually founded only in those communities where public sentiment was strong enough to insure loyal support.

b Slow Development of the Free School System

The slow development of the free school system favored the growth and continuation of schools supported by tuition. Academies of the old type could not thrive after rate bills were finally abolished. Had free public schools been realized in 1850, the transition from academies to public high schools would probably have occurred much earlier and more rapidly.

c Effects of Democracy

The growth of democratic sentiment in the last part of the eighteenth century is often assigned as a cause of the advent of academies. It seems that the further realization of the implications of the same principle was a fundamental cause of the transition from academies to high schools.   Equal educational opportunities for poor and rich were thought to be an essential part of democratic government, and the extension of this idea to secondary education meant a change in the system of secondary schools.   Further development of the same tendency that gave rise to academies led to their overthrow.

d Population of the State

New York is conspicuous among other states for the large number of academies established.   After the first part of the century, none of the other states approached her in this respect; and after 1841, more academies were established in New York than in all the other six states combined.[12]

That this condition was not due entirely to the superior system under which the New York system of academies was organized and maintained, is indicated by a consideration of the population of the several states.   From 1830 to 1890, the population of New York was about three times that of Massachusetts, and from about two-thirds to five-sixths that of all the other states combined.[13]   One would expect a greater number of schools in New York on account of the excess population.   But after making allowance for this factor, the comparison is still favorable to New York.

Influence of Academies on Later Development

Academies prepared the way for high schools.   Methods, curriculums, practices, organization and support of secondary education that prevail at the present time in high schools, had their beginnings in the academy system.   All the innovations mentioned above, coeducation, provision for practical life, a liberal curriculum, and the

---

[12] It is necessary to remember in this connection that the data are incomplete, and the relations might be changed by the complete figures for all the states.

For example, Kilpatrick in an unpublished study gives the following data for the state of Georgia:

Academies incorporated
1780–1789, 5 probable
1790–1799, 5 probable
1800–1809, 4 at least
1809–1819, 17 at least
1820–1829, 107* at least
1830–1839, 256* at least

[13] Census Rep'ts, Twelfth Census of the United States, Taken in the Year 1900, v. I, p. xxii, xxiii.

*Not all strictly academies.

training of teachers for elementary schools, which were first realized in academies, have been continued in some degree in high schools.

The support of advanced schools by taxation was the culmination of a number of steps toward that end. Public opinion had to be convinced of the value of advanced education, of the necessity of secondary schools, and of public support for such institutions. The principle that public wealth might be used to support advanced education was recognized by the Legislature in the eighteenth century, but its extensive application was a result of later growth. Generous voluntary support and local taxation were made customary by the academy system; and those practices helped to lead the public to the establishment of tax-supported high schools.

Conservative influences tended to continue academies long after conditions were favorable for high schools, and in that way to obstruct the growth of the latter. Had all state academies been abolished in 1850, free secondary education as it exists today might have been accomplished earlier. Inertia of custom and conservatism tend to preserve institutions that have lost their usefulness. The academy system after the middle of the nineteenth century was probably not an unqualified advantage to the educational interests of the State.

An attempt was made to establish normal schools in the State a quarter of a century before the first one was opened at Albany in 1844. As a majority had thought that academies afforded a sufficient means for training teachers, normals were delayed.[14]

The academy system was well adapted to the social, political and economic conditions of the times in which it thrived. It served the purpose for which it was established, and led to a more effective system.

---

[14] Cf. Graves, op. cit., p. 260.

BIBLIOGRAPHY

I Sources

(a) Documents and Contemporary Writings

Benedict, E. C. An address at the First Anniversary of the Free Academy of New York, New York, 1850.

Brooklyn. Annual report of the Superintendent of Schools 1857.

Griscom, John. Address at the Opening of the New York High School, New York 1825.

Lincoln, Charles Z. Messages from the Governors, Albany 1919. (Found also in the Journals of the Senate and the Assembly of the State of New York.)

New York (State). Documents of the Senate and the Assembly, Albany — 1830–1900.

New York (State). Journals of the Senate and the Assembly — Albany — 1784–1900.

New York (State). Session Acts, Albany, 1778–1900.

New York (State). Superintendent of Common Schools, Annual Reports. Albany, 1814–1854 —(Secretary of State ex-officio 1822–1854).

New York (State). Superintendent of Public Instruction, Annual Reports, Albany, 1855–1904.

New York (State). Education Department, Annual Reports, Albany, 1905–1914.

New York District School Journal (The.) Published by authority of the Legislature of the State of New York, Albany, 1840–1850.

New York Historial Society, Collection, Series I, Vol. V, New York, 1830.

O'Callaghan, Edmund Bailey. The Documentary History of the State of New York, Albany, 1849–1851.

Pratt, Daniel J. Annals of Public Education in the State of New York, Albany, 1869–1870–1873–1874–1876–1883 (In the Annual Reports of the Regents).

Rodenbeck, Adolph J. The Statutory Record of Unconsolidated Laws, Albany, 1911.

University of the State of New York. Annual Reports, Albany, 1788–1904. (Referred to as Regents' Reports.)

University of the State of New York. Regents' Instructions, Albany, 1834–1853.

University of the State of New York. Regents' (University) Manual, Albany, 1864–1888. (A continuation of Regents' Instructions).

University of the State of New York. Proceedings of the University Convocation. Albany, 1864 (After 1865, printed in the Regents' Reports).

University of the State of New York. Regents' Minutes, Albany, 1784–1900.

United States Commissioner of Education. Annual Report for 1903–1904 — Washington, 1905.

(b) Official Contemporary Literature of Individual Schools.

Albany Female Academy. Circular and Catalogues of the, Albany, 1843–1855.

Berkeley School (New York City.) Register for 1899–1900 — No place — No date.

Brooklyn Female Academy. Circular and Catalogue of the, New York, 1849.

Genesee Wesleyan Seminary. Catalogue of the Officers and Students of the, Rochester, 1840.

Irving Institute. Catalogue of, New York, 1840.

Mount Pleasant Academy. Annual Catalogue of the Officers and Students with an Exposition of Mount Pleasant Academy for the year 1836 — Mount Pleasant, 1837.

North Granville Ladies' Seminary. Fourth Annual Catalogue of the Officers, Instructors, Patrons, and Pupils, North Granville, 1859.

Oneida Institute of Science and Industry. Third Report of the Trustees of the, Utica, 1831.

Rhinebeck Academy. Catalogue of, Rhinebeck, 1849.

St. Thomas' Hall. Circular of, Flushing, L. I., 1841.

Van Doren's (Messers.) Collegiate Institute for Young Ladies, Brooklyn Heights, 1829.
NOTE:— The catalogs of Berkeley school and Oneida Institute of Science and Industry mentioned above are in the New York City Library, Fifth Avenue and 42d Street; all the others are in Bryson Library, Teachers College, Columbia University, New York City.

II. WRITINGS OTHER THAN SOURCES

Albany Academy. Celebration of the Semi-centennial Anniversary, Albany, 1863.
Boone, Richard G. Education in the United States, New York, 1893.
Broome, Edwin C. A Historical and Critical Discussion of College Admission Requirements, New York, 1903.
Brown, Elmer Ellsworth. The Making of our Middle Schools, New York, 1902.
Butler, Nicholas Murray. Monographs on Education in the United States, Vol. I, No. 4, (Secondary Education, by Elmer Ellsworth Brown), Albany, 1900.
The Celebration of the Centennial Anniversary of the Founding of the Albany Academy, Albany, 1914.
Clews, Elsie W. Educational Legislation and Administration of the Colonial Governments, New York, 1899.
Fairbanks, Mrs. A. W. Troy Female Seminary, New York, 1898.
Fitzpatrick, Edward A. The Educational Views and Influence of De Witt Clinton, New York, 1911.
Graves, Frank Pierrepont. A Student's History of Education, New York, 1915.
Hartwick Seminary, The Semi-centennial Anniversary, Albany, 1866.
Heydrick, B. A. Academies in the United States, 1907. (Manuscript in the Bryson Library, Teachers College, Columbia University, New York.)
Hough, Franklin B. Historical and Statistical Record of the University of the State of New York during the Century from 1784 to 1884, Albany, 1885.
Hough, Franklin B. History of St. Lawrence and Franklin Counties, Albany, 1853.
Inglis, Alexander James. The Rise of the High School in Massachusetts, New York, 1911.
Kemp, W. W. The Support of Schools in Colonial New York by the Society for the Propagation of the Gospel in Foreign Parts, New York, 1913.
Kilpatrick, William Heard. The Dutch School of the New Netherlands and Colonial New York, Washington, 1912.
Lowville Academy, Semi-centennial Anniversary.
Monroe, Paul. Cyclopedia of Education, New York, 1911–1913. Articles: Academy; Grammar School; New York, State of.
Monroe, Paul. Principles of Secondary Education, New York, 1914.
Sherwood, Sidney. University of the State of New York. History of Higher Education in the State of New York, Albany, 1893.
Strong, Thomas H. The History of the Flat Bush in Kings County, New York, 1842.
Wickersham, James Pyle. History of Education in Pennsylvania, Lancaster, Pa., 1886.

VITA

The author of this monograph, George Frederick Miller, was born near Farmington, Missouri, May 10, 1880. He attended a rural school from 1887 until 1896, and then attended Carleton College, Farmington, Missouri, until 1903. He attended Cape Girardeau, Missouri, State Normal School one year, 1904-05, and the University of Missouri part time from 1907 until 1912, when he received the B. S. degree from the latter institution. He taught rural schools in Missouri for three years, and in high schools in Missouri, Kentucky, and Illinois five years. He attended Teachers College, Columbia University two years, 1913–15.